WITCHCRAFT, SORCERY, RUMORS, AND GOSSIP

This book combines two classic topics in social anthropology in a new synthesis: the study of witchcraft and sorcery and the study of rumors and gossip. It does so in two ways. First, it shows how rumor and gossip are invariably important as catalysts for accusations of witchcraft and sorcery. Second, it demonstrates the role of rumor and gossip in the genesis of social and political violence, as in the case of both peasant rebellions and witch-hunts. Examples supporting the argument are drawn from Africa, Europe, India, Indonesia, Papua New Guinea, and Sri Lanka. They include discussions of witchcraft trials in England and Scotland in the seventeenth century, witch-hunts and vampire narratives in colonial and contemporary Africa, millenarian movements in New Guinea, the Indian Mutiny in nineteenth-century Uttar Pradesh, and rumors of construction sacrifice in Indonesia.

Pamela J. Stewart and Andrew Strathern are a husband and wife team and are both in the Department of Anthropology at the University of Pittsburgh. They have published many articles and books on their fieldwork in Papua New Guinea and Scotland. Their most recent coauthored books include *Minorities and Memories: Survivals and Extinctions in Scotland and Western Europe* (2001), *Remaking the World: Myth, Mining, and Ritual Change among the Duna of Papua New Guinea* (2002), and *Violence: Theory and Ethnography* (2002).

NEW DEPARTURES IN ANTHROPOLOGY

New Departures in Anthropology is a book series that focuses on emerging themes in social and cultural anthropology. With original perspectives and syntheses, authors introduce new areas of inquiry in anthropology, explore developments that cross disciplinary boundaries, and weigh in on current debates. Every book illustrates theoretical issues with ethnographic material drawn from current research or classic studies, as well as from literature, memoirs, and other genres of reportage. The aim of the series is to produce books that are accessible enough to be used by college students and instructors, but that also will stimulate, provoke, and inform anthropologists at all stages of their careers. Written clearly and concisely, books in the series are designed equally for advanced students and a broader audience of readers, inside and outside academic anthropology, who want to be brought up to date on the most exciting developments in the discipline.

Witchcraft, Sorcery, Rumors, and Gossip

PAMELA J. STEWART
ANDREW STRATHERN
University of Pittsburgh

CAMBRIDGE
UNIVERSITY PRESS

PUBLISHED BY THE PRESS SYNDICATE OF THE UNIVERSITY OF CAMBRIDGE
The Pitt Building, Trumpington Street, Cambridge, United Kingdom

CAMBRIDGE UNIVERSITY PRESS
The Edinburgh Building, Cambridge CB2 2RU, UK
40 West 20th Street, New York, NY 10011-4211, USA
477 Williamstown Road, Port Melbourne, VIC 3207, Australia
Ruiz de Alarcón 13, 28014 Madrid, Spain
Dock House, The Waterfront, Cape Town 8001, South Africa

http://www.cambridge.org

First published 2004

Printed in the United States of America

Typeface Minion 10.5/15 pt.   *System* LATEX 2ε [TB]

A catalog record for this book is available from the British Library.

Library of Congress Cataloging in Publication Data

Stewart, Pamela J.
Witchcraft, sorcery, rumors, and gossip / Pamela J. Stewart, Andrew Strathern.
    p.   cm. – (New departures in anthropology)
Includes bibliographical references (p.) and index.
ISBN 0-521-80868-5 – ISBN 0-521-00473-x (pb.)
    1. Witchcraft – Cross-cultural studies.   2. Gossip – Cross-cultural studies.   3. Social
conflict – Cross-cultural studies.   4. Violence – Cross-cultural studies.   I. Strathern,
Andrew.   II. Title.   III. Series.

GN475.5.S84   2004
133.4′3 – dc21   2003043949

ISBN 0 521 80868 5 hardback
ISBN 0 521 00473 x paperback

Contents

Foreword   *page* ix

1   Witchcraft and Sorcery: Modes of Analysis   1

2   Rumor and Gossip: An Overview   29

3   Africa   59

4   India   96

5   New Guinea   113

6   European and American Witchcraft   140

7   Rumors and Violence   168

8   Conclusions: Conflict and Cohesion   194

References   205

Index   217

Foreword

In this book we explore two intertwined themes: the study of witchcraft and sorcery and the analysis of rumor and gossip. While there is a considerable amount written on both themes, generally they have not been brought together systematically. It is illuminating to do so for several reasons. One is that gossip and rumors play an important part in the processes leading to accusations of "wrongdoing," which include witchcraft and sorcery accusations. Also, when witchcraft and sorcery ideas are not overtly at work, rumor and gossip may work as a covert form of witchcraft against persons. This leads to conflict, violence, and scapegoating in the same way as witchcraft accusations do. The two themes of our book are intrinsically, not casually, linked together. Both belong to the broader study of processes of conflict creation and resolution. In particular, they focus on the sources of tension in social relationships and the use of cultural themes and historical ideas in transforming these relationships. Witchcraft, sorcery, rumors, and gossip, which have been separate forms of stock in trade for anthropological descriptions, are in fact important general topics of social and historical analysis at large.

The sort of model of social action that we employ in our discussion of the topics is *processual*. We see witchcraft ideas not only as a set of cultural symbols expressing a mode of thought about the world, but also as deeply implicated in sequences of action. Such ideas both contribute meaning to action and draw their meanings from it. Witchcraft suspicions emerge into specific accusations in response to rising social and interpersonal tensions and are colored by broad historical circumstances. The same is true for rumor and gossip. They flourish in certain circumstances and in turn give further impetus to these circumstances. One can make linear representations of these processes over a period of time. But the processes may also be circular and recurrent. Fear of witches or sorcerers may reach a crescendo, only to die away later and then recur. The same is true of rumor generally. In all instances, patterns of communication between people over time and space are crucially involved. Suspicions, fears, resentments, and grievances enter collective discussion because of current conflicts and also shape and transform the conflicts themselves.

We pursue this general argument through a range of ethnographic contexts, providing some guidelines on the overall literature on our two themes and drawing on this literature to strengthen our approach to the topic. The ethnographic examples range across the world from Europe to the Pacific, through Africa and India, and belong to different time periods. We do not trace any history in detail. Our aim is to show common or overlapping patterns and processes that can be applied in many contexts. Using this method of presentation, peasant insurgencies in nineteenth-century colonial India will be seen to share certain vital processual elements with witch-hunts in Africa and community discussions on witchcraft and sorcery in New Guinea. In all these contexts, communication – by signs, actions, and words – is central (see Fig. 1).

There is a risk, in presenting materials of this sort, of overexoticizing the picture that is given of people's lives. In Africa, just as in England or in Papua New Guinea, people may spend most of their time going about the business of their lives without reference to ideas of witchcraft or sorcery. But in terms of conflict or tension, these ideas, or their contemporary replacements, may tend to emerge whenever people feel suspicious of one another and find untoward events hard to explain and cope with.

Here is the reason why we link witchcraft and sorcery with rumors and gossip. In all societies rumor and gossip tend to form networks of

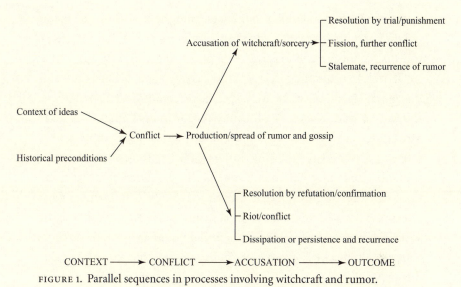

FIGURE 1. Parallel sequences in processes involving witchcraft and rumor.

communication in which fears and uncertainties emerge and challenges to existing power structures can be covertly made or overtly suppressed. Rumor and gossip form the substratum from which accusations of sorcery or witchcraft may be made, if such notions are culturally present or enter into people's life-worlds. Ideas about witchcraft and sorcery have often been pointed to by anthropologists and social historians as markers of social stress (notably by Marwick 1965). Our point is that rumors and gossip enter into the early stages of the development of stressful circumstances and so lead into later stages that may crystallize in accusations. Where centralized authorities hold power, these accusations may then lead to witchcraft trials or witch-hunts. Such trials have the special purpose of identifying the "evil wrongdoers" and not just punishing but purging them from society, in an attempt to remove "evil" or "pollution" and recreate "purity" (Douglas 1966). Contemporary accusations of abuse, especially against children, function in much the same way as witch trials did in Europe and North America in the seventeenth century.

Foreword

The theme that links all of our chapters together, then, is the theme of how conflict is generated and dealt with in social life, and the special role that confusion and uncertainty play in this process. Historically, in small-scale or community-level contexts, gossip about neighbors, always tinged with hostility arising from specific incidents of conflict and misfortune, or jealousy and resentment of the fortunes of others, has led to accusations of witchcraft and sorcery. Such local-level gossip has been influenced by more free-flowing rumors spreading from one community to another and reflecting wider historical changes. Witch trials represent the confluence of these local and interlocal events, culminating in acts of expurgation or scapegoating, usually directed against those who are socially weak or marginal. Often, the malign powers attributed to those who are socially weak can be interpreted as resulting from a fear that the weak will try to take revenge on the strong. Guilt mingles with outrage in these circumstances. While the witch or sorcerer is seen as the source of evil or wrongdoing, it is the accusers who can be seen as playing the aggressive role. In a more complex way, there is an interplay of aggressive acts between people that may polarize them and become transformed into acts of punishment or expulsion. The mobilization of public opinion is an important catalyst, and in this process rumor and gossip again are crucially effective. They may be called on by the powerful against the disempowered or vice-versa. They may also emerge in conflicts over power between equals. Leaked memoranda about governments or individual politicians act as a form of printed rumor or gossip, often leading to the "demonization" of those attacked and their resignation or removal from office, unless the rumor can be overwhelmingly refuted.

Rumor and gossip therefore form the common link between processes of conflict belonging to different places and historical periods. The materials in this book cover a wide geographical and historical range. We employ a selection of materials so as to summarize their main points that are relevant to the argument of this book. Our purpose in using the selected examples is to illustrate the pervasive and tenacious role of rumors and gossip in the production and outcomes of accusation that hit on fundamental, but often badly defined, arenas of morality and are classically enshrined in witch trials.

We emphasize the political context of our materials. It is this context that makes the topics we cover amenable to comparison and generalization. In the widest of terms, witchcraft and sorcery are seen as forms of special power, beyond that of ordinary people, that can be attributed to those who are either less or more successful than others. Wealth or poverty are themselves interpreted as signs of the effects of the actions of spirits. Those who are politically powerful may fear those they have subjugated and suspect or accuse them of using subversive counterpowers. Mutual fears of pollution operate between a colonial power, such as that of the British in India, and the Indians whom they ruled. In contemporary African contexts, as Peter Geschiere and others have shown (Geschiere 1997), postcolonial indigenous politicians fear the retributive witchcraft of jealous kin or constituents whom they have not assisted, while their constituents themselves may attribute the politicians' power and success to the use of magic and the support of spirits. In Papua New Guinea witchcraft accusations may reflect altering patterns of tension between women and men or between land-owners and incomers. In seventeenth-century Essex in England, some observers (e.g., Macfarlane 1970b) have argued, tensions centering on the obligations between neighbors produced patterns of local gossiping that could emerge into witch trials. Rhetorics associated with Christianity and its depiction of the world as divided between good and evil entered into both seventeenth-century discourse in Europe and the contemporary world of Africa and Papua New Guinea.

In the succeeding chapters of this book we pursue these themes at greater length. Our main purposes are to follow a processual and historical approach throughout, to highlight the importance of rumor and gossip, and to point to the dimensions of power that are involved in the cases we discuss.

Foreword

One caveat: it is not our aim to produce a new overall theory of witchcraft or of gossip and rumor. Our aim is more modest: to *relate* discussions of witchcraft and sorcery to the discussion of rumor and gossip and to show how the symbolism and practice of violence is tied in with both of these themes.

WITCHCRAFT, SORCERY, RUMORS, AND GOSSIP

∞

ONE

Witchcraft and Sorcery: Modes of Analysis

In this chapter we give a brief overview of some predominant ways in which anthropologists have analyzed the phenomena of witchcraft and sorcery. We then proceed to give a preliminary idea of the kinds of discussions of materials that have emerged from these orientations in ethnographic terms. Some of these materials we also discuss below in more detail. In particular we juxtapose here case histories from Africa and from Europe, to which we devote separate chapters subsequently. Our overall aim in looking at the materials here and throughout the book is to place in the foreground the virtues of an analytical approach that is processual and links microprocesses to larger historical themes. Our particular contribution to analysis is to highlight the intrinsically important roles played by gossip and rumor in the genesis of conflict.

Definitions and Perspectives

Anthropologists and social historians have approached the topics of witchcraft and sorcery in different ways. Before we discuss these, we need to take note of the definitional issues at stake. Do we conflate witchcraft and sorcery as forms of "mystical power," or do we attempt to make a clear distinction between them? In principle, as we note below, a distinction can be made between witchcraft as the expression of a malign power in a person's body and sorcery as the use of a magical craft or knowledge to harm or benefit others. Especially, what is labeled witchcraft is often seen as a consuming force. The witch eats the life power of the victim. But in fact, people's ways of putting ideas and practices together outrun any neat distinctions we may wish to make. Often what one writer translates as "sorcery" may look like "witchcraft" to another observer, depending on what features are emphasized. In Francophone Africa, *la sorcellerie* stands for what in English would be called "witchcraft." The original legislation in Europe against witchcraft also conflated the activities of ritual experts in charms, healers, practitioners of harm (*maleficium*) and protectors against these, prohibiting all of them as well as the activity of consulting them. All such actions were seen as outside the control of church or state and therefore potentially subversive and wrong.

In these circumstances it is not worthwhile to make and adhere to any rigid definitional distinctions. It is more important to recognize the complex and shifting boundaries of indigenous conceptualizations and how they change over time (cf. Mair 1969: 21 on the "nemesis of over-definition" of categories of analysis).

In British social anthropology, discussions about witchcraft have tended to take their departure point from the work of Evans-Pritchard on the Azande (Evans-Pritchard 1976 [1937]). Evans-Pritchard used the Azande people's own distinctions between what he translated as witchcraft and sorcery in his exposition of Zande beliefs. Analytically, his main purpose was to show how for the Azande ideas of witchcraft (his main focus) functioned as a means of explaining misfortunes that were difficult to explain in other ways. These ideas were then, he argued, harnessed to a way of settling suspicions between people. Once a person had been identified as exercising witchcraft against someone, their accuser could ask them to cool their witchcraft by blowing on a chicken's wing. In this way most suspicions could be dissipated. Evans-Pritchard's argument stressed the elements of the intellect and the moral imagination. Witchcraft for the Azande was a reasonable way of explaining things. It was not an irrational notion for them. Witchcraft also gave shape to people's moral worlds. Implicitly, a modified functionalist argument appears in Evans-Pritchard's account: witchcraft accusations were a means of expressing and discharging tensions between people within a particular social structure.

Mary Douglas (1970: xiv), however, points out that the main emphasis in Evans-Pritchard's book was on "the sociology of knowledge": that is, on how ambiguities and discrepancies in meanings could be tolerated because they were always dealt with in specific practical circumstances affecting individuals in their lives. In practice, it is important always to pay attention to how the working-out of ideas and accusations has an impact on people's accountability for their actions. In some instances, people may be severely punished, even put to death, for witchcraft. In others, as with the Azande, the emphasis is on the voluntary removal of the effects of witchcraft by a ritual of purgation. The collection of studies edited by Middleton and Winter (1963) on witchcraft and sorcery in East Africa shows the continuous working-out of functionalist ideas in Africanist ethnography of the time. A more recent collection by Watson and Ellen on Southeast Asia points out how studies in that part of the world have taken up a different set of problematics that fall within the sphere of medical anthropology (Watson and Ellen 1993; Ellen 1993: 20). Evans-Pritchard's legacy is reflected in multiple ways.

Evans-Pritchard's account therefore partakes of both "functionalist" and "intellectualist" tendencies in anthropological analysis, the first centering on social process and the maintenance of social order and the second on cognitive processes and the maintenance of mental order within a particular social structure. Clearly, the two can go together, although they need not do so. In British social anthropology generally, functionalist viewpoints prevailed until they became unfashionable with the demise of the idea of closed societies able to reproduce themselves over time. Africanist studies, coming to grips with historical change, tended to see witchcraft and sorcery accusations as reflections of the upheavals of community life brought on by labor migration, the movements of people, and epidemics. At a microlevel, accusations were related to tensions between people in ambiguous competitive relations such as contendants for office or workmates vying for promotion (Anderson 2002; Marwick 1965).

Victor Turner added to the functionalist paradigm his notion of the social drama in which conflicts exposed the weaknesses of lineage organization and caused fission in social groups (Turner 1996 [1957]). In Turner's view, witchcraft accusations were seen as the surface indicators of underlying conflicts over land and power. His processual models of social dramas remain valuable to this day, provided we recognize that resolutions of conflict may be open-ended.

The division between cognitive (intellectualist) and social (functional, processual) ways of approaching witchcraft remains significant. But in our view, these ways need to be brought together. Social processes feed off the moral imagination of people and their searches for explanations and order. The moral imagination reflects local structures of power, enshrined in class and ethnicity, for example. Michael Taussig, in his work on Bolivian tin mines, showed clearly how ideas about El Tio (literally, "Uncle," but also "the Devil") reflected a complex mix of indigenous ideas about the environment and introduced capitalist relations of production (Taussig 1980). El Tio functioned as an explanation for the wealth and poverty of people and of accidents that happened to them. Equally, ideas of El Tio reflected both acceptance of and resistance to the capitalist class structure. The same is true of witch beliefs around the world. A synthetic viewpoint is needed to understand them. Our argument here is that in the formation of the moral imagination and in the development of social processes, rumor and gossip play a vital part, one that has not always been adequately recognized by students of witchcraft and sorcery.

Equally, rumor and gossip tend to feed on and contribute to patterns of uncertainty in human communication that are intertwined with the probability of misunderstanding and conflict. Gossip becomes a way of trying to come to terms with, or negotiate, social situations in these circumstances, as Nigel Rapport (1996: 267) argues. Rapport refers to the work of John Haviland (1977) on gossip in Zinacantan, southeast Mexico, in this regard. Haviland's work showed how gossip enters pervasively into people's conversations, as much to damage people's reputations as to enhance them. "Talk is littered with failed careers, frustrated ambition, the pitiable and the laughable" (Haviland 1977: 111). Zinacantecans are clearly not unique in this regard. Discussions among academics at conferences or in departmental corridors are cases in point, especially in fraught and ambiguous times of conflicts such as those that accompany struggles over new appointments to faculty positions, where internal politics, rather than the basic merits of the candidate, play a major part in determining who will eventually be offered the job. Victor Turner's concept of the "social drama" applies to the in-fighting and gossip that takes place on these occasions as well as to the processes of fission in African villages.

Earlier theories of social change in places described as the Third World tended to assume that in the process of "modernization" witchcraft ideas would disappear as they supposedly did in Europe earlier. This was a superficial view, on two counts. First, people feed their own ideas into new circumstances. They do not simply abandon all ideas from the past, even if they say they are doing so. Witchcraft ideas in contemporary Africa have become a prominent way of conceptualizing, coping with, and criticizing the very "modernity" that was supposed to have done away with them. Second, at a deeper level, ideas that belong to the genre of witchcraft or sorcery reappear pervasively in modern "witch-hunts" and rumored explanations of untoward happenings in Europe as they do everywhere in the world. Contemporary anthropological studies come to grips with these points.

Much of the classic literature on witchcraft and sorcery, especially analyzed in processual terms, comes from colonial and postcolonial Africa and New Guinea. A longer tradition of writings deals with the historical experience of witchcraft trials in Europe, reexamined by contemporary historians and anthropologists. The basic ideas involved in all of these contexts are similar. Witchcraft is seen as a power belonging to persons through their bodies or spirits, giving them an ability to fly out of the body or to transform themselves into other creatures and to kill, harm, or inflict sickness on those whom they intend to weaken. Characteristically, the witch is seen as a kind of cannibal, eating the victim's life-force as a way of self-augmentation. Sorcerers also are seen as destroying a victim's life-force, not by directly consuming it but by inflicting sickness through magical means. These ideas can be conflated in various ways.

For instance, in the Pangia area of Papua New Guinea two types of sorcery were known in the 1960s. In one type, called *tomo*, the sorcerer was thought to slip lethal substances directly into people's food, causing them to become ill and die unless purgative medicine along with a spoken spell could be administered in time by a trained curer. In the other type, *nakenea*, someone with a grudge against the victim was said to pick up a part of their life-force held in a piece of clothing (such as a hair) or food remnant (an incompletely eaten piece of food) and to take or send this to an expert sorcerer living some distance away. The commissioned sorcerer was reported to have suspended the captured item over a pool of water and uttered spells over it, making the water rise up. If the item was covered by the rising water, the victim was said to have been marked for death. Another kind of Pangian magical expert, known as *kawei* or *kewanea*, was said to be able to send out from his own body red birds of paradise that could find and retrieve stolen items used to make the person ill. By bringing this item back, the victim was said to have his/her life-force restored, if this was done quickly enough after the sorcerer had performed the spells. The *kawei* could also use his familiars (the birds of paradise) to inflict sickness. All classes of experts in the use of magic required payments for their services in wealth items such as valuable shells. Knowledge of these experts and the putative actions of people in using their services or indirectly practicing sorcery was a matter of covert community comment and suspicion, maintained by the equivalent of gossip and rumor, since the supposed hostile magicians were never publicly accused or brought to trial. People were highly circumspect about leaving parts of meals or clothing behind after visiting another place, which might contain personal or group enemies. For example, they would crush chewed fragments of discarded sugarcane into puddles of rainwater whenever possible to "neutralize" their own life-force held in the remnants. People who picked up such remnants were said to do so with improvised tweezers made of twigs, to avoid mingling their own life-force with that of the victim, thereby avoiding the possibility of endangering themselves. People vigilantly watched one another for any signs that this form of "bio-terrorism" was being practiced, and they would spread gossip about any case they thought they had observed.

Claims and counterclaims about the activities of witches and sorcerers tend to exist in the background of community affairs in the societies where such ideas are held. They flourish in the shadows, fed by gossip and rumor, and emerge into public debate or accusations only in times of specific tension, most often following the actual sickness or death of someone in a prominent family. Notably, rumors follow the patterns of imputed jealousies, hostilities, and resentments that also keep mostly to the shadows or lurk in the background of social life, ready to reveal themselves in times of crisis. Or they swing into play at times of unusual or epidemic deaths that themselves cause panic and fear.

This point is well illustrated by Nutini and Roberts's extensive discussion of the idea of blood-sucking witches, or *tlahuepuchi*, among rural Tlaxcalans in Mexico (Nutini and Roberts 1993; discussed by Risjord 2000: 13–16). While Nutini was in the field on December 9, 1960, he was told that seven infants had died overnight, with bruises on their bodies indicating the work of the *tlahuepuchi*. This attribution of the deaths to witchcraft might be seen as a way of coping with an unusual and threatening disaster. The people also excluded other possible causes, such as accidents or illness, but they were socialized from childhood into accepting the idea of witchcraft, concomitantly with their Catholicism. Nutini and Roberts also suggest that possibly the children were inadvertently smothered in bed while heavily swaddled against the cold, and that the attribution of death by witchcraft might have alleviated a sense of guilt on the part of their mothers and the community at large.

Ideas of witchcraft and sorcery thus step in as forms of explanations for misfortunes in general, as Evans-Pritchard originally argued for the Azande people (Evans-Pritchard 1976 [1937]). The crucial point to note here is that such explanations are not appplied indiscriminately, still less "irrationally." They belong to local logics of explanation, and they are applied in cases that within such local logics call for special focus and attention. All deaths are likely to arouse emotions and a search for explanations, particularly if they are untoward and unexpected. The deaths of a number of infants all at the same time would be perceived by the Tlaxcalans as a threat to their reproductive future.

It is significant also to note here that forms of explanation are constituted in practice rather than as objects of theoretical thought. Inconsistencies do not matter, since people are concerned primarily with given cases and not with constructing a general cultural scheme of thought (Lambek 1993: 17, referring to Evans-Pritchard 1976 [1937]: 540–1). As Lambek further notes, explanations of misfortune "are not particular manifestations of closed, self-affirming systems of thought, but . . . they are rather provisional and contestable readings of events, moments in the life of narrative" (1993: 385). Nor does one such reading necessarily preclude another in the course of the search for causes and accountability. Given this open-ended character of discourse, it is evident why gossip and rumor are important, since they thrive on uncertainty and speculation.

Just as people may invoke witchcraft or sorcery as explanations for death and misfortune, so anthropologists have spent much effort in searching for explanations of witchcraft and sorcery ideas themselves. In the European context, one way of looking at these phenomena has been to see them as signs of pre-Christian forms of religious belief and practice, demonized through their incorporation into Christian theology in which they were seen as emanations of Satan (Ginzburg 1966).

Witch-hunts, persecutions, and trials have been seen as reflections of massive religious, political, and economic changes in early modern Europe, in which church authorities sought out heretics or people accused their neighbors who might be jealous of their wealth and to whom they themselves were unwilling to give charity (Macfarlane 1970a). In African studies, social anthropologists working first at the Rhodes-Livingstone Institute in Northern Rhodesia (Zambia) and later at Manchester University in England developed a mode of analysis of witchcraft cases that is of particular interest to us here: the processual approach, in which the focus is on community tensions and disputes that lead to crises in terms of accusations and attempts to resolve these. The crises may revolve around a sickness or death and may cause community fission. Victor Turner was a prominent exponent of this approach. He developed the term "social drama" to refer to sequences of this sort (Turner 1996 [1957]). Turner's work on conflict and ritual became widely known and influenced the field of ritual studies in general (Turner 1977). He saw witchcraft accusations as "social catalysts" that could precipitate unforeseen results.

African Cases

Turner's development of the processual approach emerged out of an earlier phase of thought that was influenced by functionalist explanations of social phenomena more so than today. He built on a set of analytical concepts developed by Max Gluckman, a South African anthropologist who was director of the Rhodes-Livingstone Institute in Zambia (at that time still called Northern Rhodesia). Gluckman characterized the small-scale African communities that he and others studied at the time as having "multiplex" relationships; that is, people were bound together in multiple roles. Gluckman argued that in such a context, conflicts that arose between people over one type of relationship (e.g., matrilineage members) could be resolved through appeal to other types of relationships within the wider community (e.g., Gluckman 1959). He also argued that in these kinds of community contexts, ritual was used to demarcate times when persons took up new roles that needed to be distinguished from other roles they had in the society. Gluckman presented a picture in which, by and large, conflicts were resolved and harmony restored. However, the African societies studied by anthropologists at that time were all undergoing long-standing processes of change. Young men were constantly drawn into labor migration. This drained the villages of their working capacity. Christian missions were at work everywhere, deploying new ideas and practices and destabilizing indigenous religious ideas, including notions of witchcraft and sorcery. These influences must have certainly made it harder to achieve harmonious resolution of conflicts.

Andrew Sanders uses African case materials from the Cewa people of Northern Rhodesia in his book on witchcraft (Sanders 1995). He discusses a case of a Christian village headman, Gombe, who trained as an evangelist, married a Christian woman, and became headman of his village when accusations of internal witchcraft caused some disgruntled members of the community to leave. As a headman, Gombe decided to take a second wife so as to better entertain guests. This act seriously antagonized his first wife and signaled his departure from the Christian practice of retaining only one wife (see also Mair 1969: 112 on this same case). Gombe and his second wife subsequently declared that they had found witchcraft substances in a "medicine horn" that was hidden in the first wife's hut. They took the first wife to court over this, causing her to be reprimanded. The Cewa said that "polygyny produces witchcraft," by which they meant that by the action of a man taking more than one wife, relationships between a husband and a first wife become strained. This can lead to notions that cowives bewitch one another. But Marwick argues that in marital disputes the couple can divorce, precluding recourse to witchcraft (Marwick 1965). Since the first wife in this case was Christian, it is possible that the solution of divorce was made less accessible because churches sometimes discourage divorce even under these difficult circumstances. The complicating presence of Christian doctrines could have led to an escalation in negative feelings here (Sanders 1995: 102–3). Sanders points out that Gombe's first wife was from his own father's matrilineage; that is, she was his patrilateral cross-cousin, and this for the Ceŵa "made divorce impossible" (ibid.). On two grounds, then, Gombe's actions set into play a conflict sequence.

Victor Turner's case histories from the Ndembu people show many similarities to Marwick's on the Ceŵa. Ndembu villages at the time of Turner's study in the 1950s were small groups centered on matrilineage segments, and village fission was common because of competition for the position of headman. Sanders, who also discusses the Ndembu case, significantly notes the influence of colonial change on patterns of competition. He says that village division became more frequent in the twentieth century "as men established farms and independent residences away from kinsmen in order to avoid claims on the income they derive from cash crops" (Sanders 1995: 123, citing Mair 1969: 130). Ambitious Ndembu men needed to keep women of their matrilineage with them and to found a matrilineage segment, but in time conflicts developed between a headman's sister's sons and his brothers, since the brothers expected to succeed to the headship (by adelphic succession) but the nephews were impatient and would try to preempt the situation by seceding with their own sisters, using accusations of witchcraft as a catalyst for fission. Rivals for the headman's position would consult diviners and seek to accuse each other of witchcraft. The colonial government, however, prohibited the use of diviners, making it harder to bring cases to resolution.

In a lengthy case history revolving around a man whom Turner himself employed as his cook, a man, Sandombu, was first suspected of killing his maternal uncle, the village headman, by witchcraft, and subsequently came into further conflict with a later claimant to the same position. Village gossip claimed that he had uttered threats that resulted in a villager's death, but there was gossip also against his rival. The wives of the succeeding headman declared it was the rival, Kasonda, who had bewitched the headman and made him ill, and that the fact that he was building a brick house was proof that he was scheming to obtain the headmanship for himself. Jealousy of the rival was increased by his having obtained the job of cook (which presumably brought in pay as well as prestige) for the anthropologist. The rival decided to found his own village, announcing that some would follow him and others would stay with Sandombu. Several other witchcraft accusations punctuated the narrative, and Turner pointed out that at least one of these was aimed at a widow who was from a different country, Angola, on the father's side of her family and was suspected of witchcraft because she was partly an outsider to the community (Sanders 1995: 127). Significantly, this same woman, Nyamuwang'a, was said to have become angry when a young woman who had later died had refused to give her some meat. This is an important detail, on two counts. First, it is a classic theme that witches themselves are thought to act out of resentment over the sharing of meat: the theme is found notably also in New Guinea. Second, as Ndembu matrilineages grew in size, it became less easy to satisfy their members in meat distributions, and witchcraft accusations were tied in with this process.

Further, we should note here that, as is also frequently found elsewhere, accusations centered on people *following a death*. They were post-hoc attempts to explain the death and pinpoint blame for it. Rumor and gossip particularly came into play on the occasions of death and sickness, bringing out veiled suspicions and animosities in the sequences that Turner called social dramas. Gossip may also center on people who are thought of as outsiders. Here, as in Max Gluckman's overall argument about gossip and scandal (see more on this in Chapter 2), gossip may be seen as picking on someone to *treat as* an outsider, thereby redrawing the boundaries of the community, but the immediate motive may have to do with local politics in circumstances where group cohesion is fragile. Rather than being a mark of a strong community, gossip may mark its weakness and may itself escalate conflict, weakening the community further.

From one viewpoint, the continual founding of new Ndembu villages may be seen as the phase of resolution in the social drama. But it is equally clear that this part of Africa generally was deeply affected by change and that large-scale historical events entered into villagers' worlds and produced their own twist on the foci of gossip. The theme of suspicion directed against people who succeed in building houses made of permanent materials turns up as a recurrent element in Peter Geschiere's discussion of witchcraft in Cameroon and tells us much about the correlation of hostilities with developing class structures and ideologies of consumption associated with money (Geschiere 1997). Luise White's extensive analysis of "vampire" narratives from parts of Africa also continually refers to this theme (White 2000). We consider these two studies more fully in a later chapter.

The African cases we briefly have looked at here testify clearly both to the long-ingrained status of ideas about witchcraft and to their intertwinement with processes of colonial change. It is notable that in the Ceŵa and Ndembu cases suspected witches could be taken to trial in a chief's court, which would be sanctioned by the colonial power (Britain). If convicted, they might simply be reprimanded, not put to death, in strong contrast to what we are accustomed to from the history of European witch trials of early modern times. We turn now to this context.

European Cases

Andrew Sanders, following work by the historian Keith Thomas (Thomas 1973), points out that on the European continent witch trials came to center on the idea of witchcraft as a heresy, involving a pact with the Devil. By contrast, he says, in England, where papal authority was more limited, specific acts of harm continued to be the focus, even though witches were also thought to obtain their power from the Devil. Even on the Continent itself, cases at the local level resembled the English pattern. When accusations reached the courts, however, the clergy and magistrates together emphasized their own theologically oriented concerns with the idea of Satanic "orgies" (Sanders 1995: 29). At the local level, among peasants themselves, witchcraft ideas and accusations in historical Europe are quite comparable to those from Africa.

Ideas regarding witchcraft in Europe were linked with notions about the use of magic, including potions and poisons, and so can be conflated partly with concepts of sorcery. These ideas go back both to Greek and Roman times and to the early notions of the pagan peoples of northern Europe. One persistent notion was that a "witch" could do good or harm. The same people might be healers or witches, and persons who claimed to be witch-finders might also be later accused of bewitching others, on the principle of "set a thief to catch a thief." The use of occult powers to harm others was called by the Latin term *maleficium*, but was not treated by the Catholic Church as heresy until the fourteenth century. Indeed, the Church at first derided the idea that witches had real occult powers, regarding them as simply deluded by the Devil. Prosecutions of witches had to be conducted privately, although an accused person might be subjected to an ordeal such as holding a red-hot iron in their hands (ibid.: 149).

The officialized incorporation of witch beliefs into Christian theology from the fourteenth century onward in continental Europe made of the witch a heretic, who was declared to deny his or her duty to God by giving himself or herself over to the Devil. Trials focused on the witches' putative attendance at meetings or sabbats where they worshiped the Devil. The Devil in turn was thought of as appearing to the witch at a time of distress and as promising occult powers in return for allegiance to him. In many instances the accused were females. The Devil was thought to mark the woman's body with his own baptismal mark, claiming her as his own. Witches were also said to anoint themselves with fat from murdered infants, enabling them to fly to sabbats, which were presided over by the Devil and marked by the *osculum infame*, the kissing of the Devil's anus (ibid.: 151), and a sexual orgy. Given such images, it is unsurprising that the punishment for witchcraft as heresy was burning to death, presumably thought of as followed by the soul's torments in Hell.

The witch had become the inversion of a true person, an anti-image of society rather than a maleficent but ordinary human with some magical powers. Witchcraft in this sense was "produced" by the Church hierarchy itself in the context of continuing struggles to assert its overall authority. Elements of pagan religion were incorporated into the theological picture of witchcraft and demonized as a part of this drive to essentialize and stereotype the phenomenon. Civil elites were concerned to carry out this project on the peasantry, while religious elites used it in struggles among themselves over Church reforms.

One group charged with Satan worship in this way was the Cathars, who were influential in Europe from the tenth to the fourteenth century. The Catholic authorities charged them with "cannibalism, infanticide, and holding sexual orgies" (ibid.: 153). The Cathars in southern France were also known as Albigensians, and their continued survival caused the Catholic Pope Gregory IX to establish the Inquisition in 1232. The Cathars held that the world, including the Catholic Church, was inherently evil and to be avoided, thus maintaining an oppositional theology of their own. One family of Albigensians is said to have made its way to Ayrshire in Scotland at the end of the twelfth century. These were the Howies, who many generations later in the seventeenth century figured as staunch Covenanters, opposed to the Church of Rome (Carslaw in Howie 1870 [1775]: ix). Others persecuted by the Pope were the Waldensians, whose sect was founded by Peter Waldo in 1173. Both the Cathars and the Waldensians were branded as witches by the Catholic Church. Their ideas fed into those of the Lollards, or "Murmurers," followers of John Wyclif who also opposed the authority of the Pope and argued that the Bible should be available to all in their own vernaculars. Lollards also made their way to Ayrshire and persisted there through the sixteenth century (see Davies 1999: 454; Howie 1870 [1775]: 9). All these groups were forerunners of the massive Protestant Reformation of the sixteenth century, including the Calvinism that fed into the creation of the Presbyterian Church of Scotland. Such a narrative shows us that social movements and institutions grow by defining themselves in dialectical opposition to others, and that what is stigmatized at one time as heresy may emerge later elsewhere as a new orthodoxy with a legacy of historical animosity against its original persecutors. The Catholic Church clearly created the character of "diabolical witchcraft" as an anti-image of itself, applied the term to some of its rivals, and subsequently fed this image back into popular conceptions of *maleficium*. At the same time, most of the elements that were systematized in the Church's theology also had existed in an informal way in earlier popular conceptions (see also Bailey 2003).

In the history of European witchcraft it is easy to forget this particular aspect of history because of the overwhelming emphasis on witchcraft trials, mostly directed against certain peasant women who were often perceived, as Sanders argues, as outsiders or deviants. These trials themselves also reflected another dimension of the wars of religion in Europe, in this case the war on the remaining fragments of pre-Christian European religious ideas. In both contexts the Church and civil hierarchies in effect defined the "enemies" whom they wished to punish by labeling them as being in league with the Devil. By declaring rival sects to be heretical, the Church gave itself the power to persecute them and to strengthen its own political power. In the case of witchcraft trials, we have to see these rather as ritual dramas whose purposes included the intimidation of certain individuals in local communities and the confirmation of people's allegiance to orthodox religious authority. The drama consisted of the age-old process of identifying evil, driving it out, and recreating order: misfortune is followed by counteraction and the restoration of society. In practice, what is striking in all accounts of this process is the way or ways in which local suspicions and accusations led into more dramatic and severe forms of counteraction emanating from the state and its religious authorities. And the starting point for suspicions is invariably some misfortune that is attributed to witchcraft or sorcery, followed by an accumulation of such suspicions. A severe illness or a death may then crystallize these suspicions into an accusation. Quite typically, a sick person may make a

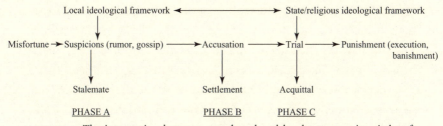

FIGURE 2. The intersection between state-based and local processes in witchcraft trials.

deathbed accusation that sets the relatives into a direct effort to bring the accused person to trial. We summarize these processes in Figure 2.

This figure repeats the basic structure of processes given above in Figure 1. Phase A leads to phase C only if suspicions develop into a specific accusation. In phase A, events belong to a local community context. Phase A does not necessarily lead to phase B, which represents the intersection between levels involved. It is necessary to recognize that local and state ideological frameworks are at work both separately and together. This is signaled by the double-headed arrow linking these two frameworks horizontally, while vertical arrows show their separate impingements in phases A and C. The two-way connection at the ideological level records the fact that state codifications affect local ideas and attitudes, but local ideas also feed into the state or religious apparatus. The local framework is therefore already an amalgam of earlier ideas and Christian codifications, but it may not articulate these codifications very clearly. Nevertheless, it provides the catalyst that can move processes into phase C, in which the state or Church authorities impose their own definitions and methods, moving toward the clear stigmatizing and punishment of a single individual named as a witch or sorcerer. Inchoate suspicion is transformed into scapegoating.

It is also striking in case histories how events themselves become translated into suspicions. Sanders argues that such suspicions generally fell on families perceived as both poor and abnormal. Such families were vulnerable to suspicion presumably because they might be thought to resent others. Sanders quotes a case from 1612 in Pendle Forest, Lancashire, England, in which the daughter in one such family, Alizon Device, "met a pedlar, John Law of Halifax. She asked him for some pins, and became angry when he refused. Almost immediately, he suffered a stroke.... When he recovered his speech he accused Alizon of bewitching him.... She confessed to bewitching him and begged his pardon. The father accepted her pardon," but his son laid a complaint before the local magistrate (Sanders 1995: 35).

Here, phase A in Figure 2 proceeded to phase B, but the event might have ended in a settlement if the peddler's son had not decided to take the case further. Perhaps he wished to preempt any further incidents. The initial occurrence that triggered the whole sequence is significant. The girl made a minor request, was refused, and became angry. Fear of her anger lay behind the wish to punish her, as well as the thought that she herself could punish others. The process involved here is classically diagnostic of ideas prevalent in societies organized around the principle of the gift (Mauss 1967 [1925]). Gifts are predicated on an idea of goodwill; a refusal to give therefore denies this idea and creates ill will, which in turn leads to a fear of retribution. In some New Guinea societies, the frustrated desire of a person who has been denied something is pictured in the idea that they may swallow their saliva, and this action itself is held to act as a kind of automatic sorcery or witchcraft, causing sickness to those against whom the person's frustration is directed. While it is not entirely clear from this case of Alizon Device and the peddler whether she asked him for some pins without an offer of immediate payment (i.e., as a "gift"), the logic of the case suggests that this was so.

After the peddler's son took the case to the magistrate, events became more complex. Alizon said she had a black dog as her familiar, and that her old grandmother had initiated her into witchcraft. The grandmother had had an altercation with a miller who refused to pay for some work Alizon's mother Elizabeth had done for him, and the miller's daughter had fallen ill and died. Alizon further accused another old woman of the community of killing her father, James Device, for failing to make a yearly payment (gift) of meal to her, which he had been accustomed to give her in order to avert her witchcraft powers, and she added a roster of further accusations. In turn, the grandmother confessed to her own witchcraft, and said that her familiar was the Devil in the form of a dog, called Tibb, who killed others for her in return for her soul, and the other old woman, called Chattox, made a similar confession, with a recitation of deaths she had caused, and claimed that the grandmother of Alizon Device had first taught her to be a witch. Gradually the whole families of those accused were brought into the net of confession and accusation. Twelve witches were found guilty and ten were condemned to death and hanged. Kinsfolk both confessed to their own acts and testified against each other, and some said the Devil had broken his bargain with them.

We meet here the classic phenomenon of confessions by witches and their mutual accusations against one another. Perhaps we may see these as attempts by accused persons to deflect blame or obtain pardons for themselves. The year 1612 places the Pendle witch trials in the reign of King James VI and I of Scotland and England, who himself had published a treatise on demonology in 1597, drawing on ideas that were current at the time (Summers 1972 [1930]: xxii). At this time the Anglican Church in England, created in the reign of Henry VIII, maintained the basic theology of the Catholic Church but did not accept the absolute authority of the Pope. Witchcraft as the work of the Devil remained a strong part of both popular ideas and Church orthodoxy. Peasant people, including those accused of witchcraft, would be partially indoctrinated with these ideas and may have used them to claim certain powers for themselves as a means of redressing their poverty or securing payments in the ways the Pendle case history indicates. If their reputations were not brought to the attention of the authorities, matters might be balanced out at a local level. But once the opportunity of bringing an accusation to court was taken by the relatives of a victim, the fate of the accused was likely to be sealed whether they self-confessed or not. A long "prehistory" of rumor and gossip must have preceded the phase of accusation, requiring only a shift in context to produce an investigation and trial. Rumor and gossip therefore belong largely to phase A in Figure 2, but no doubt would continue to feed into phases B and C and would contribute further to historical memories of cases, leading to new cases over time, tied to local circuits of relationships.

It is notable in the Pendle case that the accusation was brought to a civil magistrate, not to the church. The English parliament had made statutes against witchcraft in 1542 during the reign of Henry VIII, in 1563 while Elizabeth I was Queen, and in 1604 during the reign of James VI and I. The Scottish parliament made its own statute in 1563. Witchcraft was therefore repeatedly defined as a crime during the time of the Tudor and Stuart dynasties (Levack 1987: 80; Macfarlane 1970: 82). It is possible that this definition of witchcraft as a crime punishable by a magistrate's court made the process of making accusations easier or more accessible to ordinary people. This would have increased the likelihood of gossip crystallizing into a trial.

Levack makes several observations on this transition from ecclesiastical to secular courts relating to witchcraft. In some cases, the laws allowed the courts to try people simply for entertaining spirits, seen as evil, or for making a pact with the Devil. The Catholic Inquisitions had been weakened by the Protestant Reformation, making it easier for secular courts to take over the prosecution of witches. The ecclesiastical courts had begun to return to "the traditional penitential and admonitory functions" (Levack 1987: 81) that they had originally employed. The secular courts, however, were concerned with public order and did not hesitate to impose harsh sanctions. They also publicized their actions in doing so. Levack notes that in Scotland, "large-scale witch-hunts did not begin until after the Scottish parliament defined witchcraft as a secular crime in 1563" (ibid.). In these hunts for witches the clergy remained active as the auxiliaries of secular authorities, perhaps putting pressure on them to persecute suspects and preaching from the pulpit against witchcraft. For their part, secular authorities punished witchcraft as heresy, ordering witches to be burnt, perhaps so that they "would not return from the dead by means of sorcery" (p. 83). This point reveals that the authorities were themselves affected by popular beliefs and fears. The courts that were given powers to deal with witches were local rather than central courts of the state, and they showed more zeal in prosecuting cases than central authorities did (p. 85). This was because they had a more immediate fear of the witches they tried and were more affected by popular feelings, including gossip and rumor.

In Scotland cases could be heard by local ad hoc courts, staffed by local landowners and magistrates, and execution rates were much higher when these officials heard cases than when judges in the central justiciary courts did (91 percent of 100 cases recorded in the local courts, as opposed to 55 percent of 197 cases heard in the central courts; p. 88). These local practices may have been intensified by the fact that in 1590 King James VI had taken a leading role in "one of the largest witch-hunts in Scotland history" (p. 89). State building in general involved, Levack says, "an attack upon traditional communal arrangements" (p. 89), but at local levels this "attack" was itself deeply influenced by popular pressures.

If we refer again to the Pendle case discussed above, we can see that if the women involved had been able to call on the judicial structure to settle their grievances, their stereotyping as witches might not have occurred so readily. But once the process of stigmatizing has begun, it is difficult if not impossible to stop, not because of legal definitions but because of local gossip mills that are themselves part of "communal arrangements."

Alan Macfarlane has made a long-term study of witchcraft accusations in the county of Essex, England, between 1560 and 1680. He found records of 545 people accused of witchcraft in this period, of whom seventy-four were recorded as executed at the Essex Assizes. Out of 426 villages in Essex at the time, 227 were connected with witchcraft prosecutions. The village of Hatfield Peverel, with a population of 500, had fifteen suspected witches over a twenty-five-year period. Macfarlane estimates that about a quarter of those suspected were never formally accused. He notes that behind a given accusation there could exist a complex web of related suspicions (Macfarlane 1970b: 84). The web was highly gendered. Of 270 suspected witches, 247 were women. Women were also said to be more likely to be bewitched. Almost all cases involved neighbors (p. 87). A witch that was unable to bewitch someone because of their "godly" life might be said to bewitch his or her children or animals instead (p. 90).

Noting that quarrels and suspicions tended to precede rather than simply follow an accident or other misfortune, Macfarlane quotes the English clergyman George Gifford, writing in 1587, who laid out precisely the kind of events and complaints involved: a woman quarrels with her neighbor, who then suffers a misfortune. The matter is repeated, and she becomes known as a witch. People are careful not to offend her, but if anyone falls sick they are asked whether they have done anything to make her angry. Some small incident can usually be recalled, and people say they saw a weasel running from her yard to that of a neighbor who is now sick, this being seen as her familiar. So she is apprehended and taken to prison (p. 91). The typical reasons for quarrels and bad feelings cited by Macfarlane from Essex strongly resemble those from Pendle in Lancashire in 1612: the refusal of work, the denial of a gift or a payment. "Witchcraft was seen as a reply to un-neighbourly behaviour" (p. 92).

Macfarlane further points out that the Christian response to requests from the poor should theoretically have been to grant them relief by alms (p. 93); yet Christians were also adjured not to give indiscriminate charity for fear of witches, and not to accept gifts of food from suspected witches since these could be the vehicle of witchcraft (p. 94). Suspects could hardly escape the stigma of suspicion in such a double-bind situation. Macfarlane argues in general that those who accused others of bewitching them were people who were trying to free themselves from the restraints of communal obligations. This might explain why they turned outward to the authorities rather than back into the community itself to settle their disputes, in effect being rewarded for what might appear to be their own reneging on obligations of charity (see, e.g., the detailed lists in Macfarlane 1970a: 173). The witch's complaint against her neighbor could have been seen as a quest for legitimate "justice"; instead, it was labeled as an act of illegitimate "revenge" or negative reciprocity. "When a woman refused a neighbor some milk on the excuse that she had not got enough to suckle for her own calf, the calf was soon destroyed by witchcraft" (Macfarlane 1970a: 174). The assumption made was that the person refused a favor would strike back in revenge. Apparently these "communities" did not have in them adequate informal or formal means of *redressing* the grievances of those who later became accused of bewitching others, as we have already noted above. Rumor and gossip in such a context are less a means of resolving disputes than a method of exacerbating tensions between people that can lead to the persecution of particular individuals perceived as being weak.

Macfarlane's statistical materials come from Essex and he cautions against generalizing them to the whole of England. Levack also notes that while witchcraft accusations were certainly in part a product of tensions resulting from social changes, "such accusations could occur in a relatively static as well as in a rapidly changing world" (Levack 1987: 119). This seems correct, since communities never function in total harmony, individuals always have grievances, which they cannot necessarily settle, and others are always ready to gossip against them. Whether a specific product of historical change or not, however, the basic schema of a denial of a favor or a payment followed by the expectation of revenge by witchcraft is a durable feature of both "relatively static" circumstances and ones involving rapid change, especially in urban conditions. Also, epidemics of sickness caused by the plague led to accusations and prosecutions of plague spreaders, "persons who had allegedly succeeded in distilling the essence of the plague in the form of an unguent, which they then used to infect various parts of towns" (ibid.: 122). A similar situation arose with the search in 2001 in the United States of America for those who contaminated the postal system by sending through it envelopes tainted with anthrax spores. Rumors spread about the extent of the dispersal of contaminated envelopes and new rumors developed that other types of contagious materials were also being transmitted through the postal system. Anthrax-tainted envelopes did make some recipients of the envelopes and some postal handlers ill, and a few deaths also ensued. The parallels here lie in the ways that fears, whether based in fantasy or experience, can produce similar types of responses. In this context, the "terrorists" who carried out the acts were labeled as "evil"; this term is the historical successor to the early modern claim in Europe that plague spreaders were worshipers of the Devil, acting collectively, so that they became indistinguishable from witches. Urban residents, not knowing their neighbors, might also readily suspect them of witchcraft, Levack suggests (p. 123). In both rural and urban contexts rumors would be the means, swift or slow, whereby suspicions were generated and issued later in panics, accusations, and trials. In the towns and cities, Levack notes, these rumors could also fasten on male magicians who were said to have used sorcery to advance their political status. Accusations and trials of these men blended in with witchcraft trials.

Macfarlane's figures for the predominance of accusations against women are largely replicated in a much larger sample from different parts of Europe, including Scotland where between 1560 and 1727, some 242 men were recorded as accused, in comparison with 1,491 women, making an 86 percent incidence of accusations against women (Levack 1987: 124, including also Macfarlane's Essex data). Levack considers some reasons for this gender imbalance. First, he quotes the *Malleus maleficarum* ("The Hammer of the Witches"), a handbook published in 1486 by the Dominicans Jacob Sprenger and Heinrich Kraemer (Institoris) as a manual for witch-hunters (Sanders 1995: 167). Besides listing definitional aspects of witchcraft, these two authors firmly placed witchcraft primarily

on women, declaring that women were intellectually inferior and subject to greater sexual passion, making them more susceptible to Satanic
influences. They linked witchcraft itself to carnal lust, saying that this
was insatiable in some women. Clerics in particular seized on this claim,
in line with Biblical images of the Devil tempting Eve in the Garden of
Eden, thus conveniently ignoring the Biblical narrative of Adam's compli-
ance in the events. Sprenger and Institoris were active in south Germany,
opposing the idea that witchcraft was not prevalent there, and their publication was followed by an increase in witchcraft trials. Lyndal Roper
has extensively examined gender relations in sixteenth-century Germany,
providing a background for the misogyny of the *Malleus maleficarum*
(Roper 1994). (Incidentally, Macfarlane notes in passing that although
the Essex witches were predominantly women, there does not "seem to
have been any marked sexual element in Essex witchcraft" (1970b: 84),
and there was only one case of overlap between cases of sexual misbehavior and a suspected witch. Germany may have had some particular
sexual fantasies of its own kind about women.) Roper argues that the
onset of the Reformation and the dominance of the Lutheran Church in
Germany brought with it a resurgent form of patriarchalism emphasizing
the power of male household heads, and that this trend took place also
in Catholic areas, along with declining employment opportunities for
women (Roper 1994: 39). Among Catholic orders, this trend was accompanied by the rise of Marian all-male brotherhoods fixed on an ideal of
womanhood separated from the realm of sexuality (ibid.). Marriage for
the laity was set up as a sacred principle of society, conceived of in terms
of the authority of the husband-father (p. 40).

The blame for sexual misbehavior was shifted onto prostitutes and
by extension onto "wanton" women in general (p. 41). (Again, these
images of women conveniently ignored the fact that the customers of
the prostitutes were men, often married men seeking sexual pleasure.) In
this light, all women were instructed that marriage was the proper state
of being for women. According to the Protestants, all sexual activities

outside marriage were considered sinful. Male Protestant clergy were both sexual beings and considered to be the upholders of household morality. In Protestant fantasy, Catholic monks and nuns became, instead of exemplars of celibacy, like whores of the Devil (p. 43), and the Catholic Church became in Luther's terminology like an anus in which people had been trapped prior to the Reformation (p. 44; cultural themes again appear prominent here). Roper considers that this stress on patriarchy did not bring with it the sort of security of power that it projected. Rather, she suggests, it may have reflected unresolved anxieties and tensions that continue to exist in the sphere of sexual relations today (p. 48).

In Augsburg, Germany, in the seventeenth century, witchcraft accusations were typically made by recent mothers against elderly maids who were caring for their infants. Their narratives were fashioned, Roper says, in circles of gossip through which they exorcized their feelings of guilt and projected these on the witch as a scapegoat. As a caregiver and feeder, the maid was an obvious target for suspicions of poisoning (p. 207) and could be seen as a kind of "evil mother" (p. 211). The birth mother, in turn, would be responsible to the household patriarch for the welfare of her children. The maid here stands in an analogous position to a midwife, who held powers of healing but who might also be seen as malevolent (Forbes 1966; Levack 1987: 127).

Roper refers her explanatory discussions to the realm of the psyche and its historical changes, stressing, as we have seen, the arena of sexual anxieties. Levack generalizes this theme of anxiety further, arguing that the epoch of the great witch hunts in Europe, from 1450 to 1750, was in general a period of great turbulence, in which there was a strong tendency to project the causes of social turmoil on witches as a way to maintain a semblance of equilibrium at times of stress (Levack, p. 141). Further, people were made greatly conscious "of their need to attain salvation" (p. 142). Moral transgressions and lapses caused anxiety, and the act of prosecuting persons seen as "intrinsically evil" (ibid.) relieved these anxieties somewhat. We might comment on how remarkable it is that anxieties were resolved by accusing precisely those who themselves had felt wronged in the first place, at least in the case of the Essex witch trials and those from Pendle forest in Lancashire. Understanding the place of the "gossip circle" is crucial to seeing how this could happen, and Roper's reference to such circles among women in Augsburg points in the same direction. The accuser is the aggressor from this viewpoint, but projects that aggression onto the person accused. Alternatively, accusations may signify fantasized ways of reflecting exploitative or unequal relationships, as shown below by "vampire" stories from Africa.

Conclusion

In this chapter we have given some extended illustrations of the kinds of themes outlined in our Foreword, for example, by discussing cases anthropologists have described from Africa and from Essex in England. Throughout these examples we have sought to bring out three things. The first is that witchcraft accusations have to be seen *historically*, that is, as products of wide-scale changes running through people's lives. The second is that they must be seen *processually*, that is, as sets of events that involve complex interactions between individuals constituting microhistories of their own. And the third is that in these historical and processual events the predominant patterns crucially involve the *emergence of gossip and rumor* between people as steps to the crystallization of suspicion into accusation.

In substantive terms we have drawn here successively on examples from Papua New Guinea, Africa, England, and Scotland to show how the idiom of witchcraft or sorcery is used in all cases as a persuasive way of explaining sickness or death, relating these to the patterns of jealousy and distrust between people. It is always some misfortune that triggers accusations. Whether someone is a witch or not does not matter until people cast around for explanations of misfortune. When they have suffered some setback, people at once begin to generate or to tap into the mills of gossip. Sickness (physical or economic) in particular may set these mills rolling in the absence of other convincing explanations of it, or even in spite of them. The same human envies and jealousies feed into gossip generally and witchcraft accusations in particular. In the next chapter we look more closely at anthropological discussions of gossip and rumor as such.

∞

TWO

Rumor and Gossip: An Overview

In the preceding chapter we have pointed out the crucial significance of rumor and gossip in community contexts that lead to accusations of witchcraft. It is a part of our overall argument that even when particular notions of witchcraft or sorcery are not involved, rumor and gossip themselves may act as a kind of witchcraft, projecting guilt on others in ways that may cause them harm: for example, to lose their jobs, to be physically attacked, or to be socially shamed. Because rumor and gossip work covertly, outside formal mechanisms for social control, they cannot easily be checked on or verified by explicit means. They can nevertheless produce results in themselves regardless of verification, as all political "spin" artists and propagandists know. Asked why a false rumor of wrongdoing by an opponent should be disseminated, the propagandist may advise his client that this will force the opponent publicly to deny the rumor, which may only increase people's suspicions that it is in some way accurate. Legal rules of libel and slander are developed to control the escalation of such attacks, just as rules are put in place to punish those found guilty of threatening hoaxes. Journalists may be threatened with lawsuits for defamation following their repetition of stories against public personalities, such as Dominick Dunne's story about the politician Gary Condit (see the *New York Times*, January 28, 2003, p. B1).

The point that words as such can be used as effective combat devices, or that careless words may produce real disasters, is neither trivial nor self-evident, although it is well known to be true in human experience. For words to be harmful, even lethal, in this way, they have to be spoken in contexts of ideology that are congenial to them. It is therefore the ideological and historical context rather than the words themselves that ultimately produces the effects. But this context is itself the product of repeated conversations and memories from the past, sedimented into patterns of presupposition and interpretive thought that are employed to understand all events in the world, not just matters of gossip. Moreover, in all societies there are everyday ways of evaluating evidence, and not all stories are accepted as simply true. A great deal depends on who is telling the stories and what their perceived motive for spreading gossip actually is, that is, their own self-advancement, revenge, hatred, jealousy, and so on. An emotional component enters in. At times of fear or threat, for example, actions otherwise considered innocent may be viewed with suspicion. Outside the context of sickness and death, the appearance of a weasel crossing from one backyard to another might not be seen as a sign of witchcraft. In times of crisis, the citizens of a state are often urged to be "on the alert" more than usual. This means that they may also inappropriately read more meaning into events than would otherwise be warranted, as well as perhaps successfully detecting sources of true danger. In such a context rumors may act in two ways: either to spread undue alarm or to help people survive.

These two possibilities correspond to what we may call the *interpretive ambiguity* of rumor and gossip. Analysts have tended to stress either positive or negative "functions" of these two activities. But there is always the possibility of both positive and negative results, and sometimes these may be mutually implicated: a "positive" result for some people may be "negative" for others.

The functionalist interpretation of rumors and gossip, stressing the idea that they reinforce community "norms" over time, is famously associated with the work of the anthropologist Max Gluckman (1963). Gluckman began his discussion of this theme by quoting the earlier observation of Paul Radin that "tribal peoples" (for which we can read "people") were inveterate gossips, who were concerned to denigrate each others' skills as narrators or possessors of ritual knowledge (a description that would seem to apply very well to academics). Gluckman went on to discuss Melville Herskovits's work among the members of a religious sect called the Shouters in Trinidad. The members of the sect were fond of gossiping about the events surrounding the prosecution and jailing of fellow Shouters by the government. In their gossip they mixed blame of certain individuals with sympathy for those jailed, embroidering the narrative so as to weave a story that repeated the theme of grievance against discrimination. Generally, the more wealthy members of other denominations were accused of leading the police to a proscribed meeting of the Shouters. Gluckman further cites Herskovits's study of songs sung by participants in working bees in Haiti, noting that in these songs people obliquely criticized their neighbors for inhospitality, meanness, sexual improprieties, or the use of hostile magic (sorcery). The leader of such a song group became feared, presumably because the songs were effective in shaming those criticized.

Gluckman gives all these examples in pursuit of his general analysis that gossip helps to maintain the unity and the morality of the groups involved in it. A closer look at these examples, without seeking more details than he himself gives, might lead us to reconsider his overall conclusion. In the first example, drawn from Radin (and possibly inspired by materials on the Kwakiutl people or another Native American group, the Winnebago, with whom Radin worked), there is no evidence produced at all that gossip actually unified the group. It seems rather simply to have expressed competition, even if it was fairly friendly. We might imagine that it was a kind of back-handed way of expressing an in-group identity, but this hardly equates with unity in the sense of solidarity.

The second example, on the Shouters, more clearly shows the throwing of blame onto the members of outside churches, and so the internal gossip can indeed be seen as a way of promoting group unity: the target of the gossip is outside the group, in contrast to the first example, and this makes its function quite different. In the third example, we see a pattern of veiled in-group criticism through which a song leader might gain personal prestige. We can understand how these songs would produce shame in individuals and that because of their coded form only in-group members would understand them. So we might say that the songs were a way of criticizing or warning insiders without involving outside authorities. If such warnings resulted in the modification of behavior, group unity might indeed be strengthened. But what is left out of this picture is whether the implications of the songs were justified or not. If not, they might simply have been ways for individuals to stir up trouble with others, causing disunity rather than unity. As a coded form of gossip, they protected themselves against counteraccusations of slander, and yet from the cover of their coding they could inflict harm on a target. Herskovits himself quoted an informant as saying that the song leader was a journalist and a Judas. With his eye already fixed on his functionalist conclusion, Gluckman does not dwell on the ambivalent meanings of these designations.

Gluckman also appears to draw on his own experience when he writes "that every single day, and for a large part of each day, most of us are engaged in gossiping" (1963: 308). He does not restrict this generalization to his own reference group of academics, but perhaps it does reflect best the small-scale in-group networks of social anthropologists in Britain at the time (and perhaps still today), in which there were a few recognized professors and heads of major departments and many others struggling to enter or to rise in the ranks with only a few positions available. In such a context in-group gossip might certainly be expected to flourish, but it might be seen more as playing into the hands of the powerful few than as assisting the claims of the many aspirants for job security. According to Gluckman himself, gossip circles maintain group unity, control "aspiring individuals," and "make possible the selection of leaders without embarrassment" (p. 308). But such circles are not in themselves composed of individuals who are mutually equal. Gossip can be manipulated by the powerful against others. It can also be used against the powerful and can bring embarrassment into the selection of leaders rather than removing it from such a selection. Slanderous gossip can be used as a means of getting rid of a rival or of inducing an incumbent to vacate a position and giving it to a favorite of one's own to whom reciprocity is due. Once again, Gluckman himself provides a clue. He notes that old-hand academic practitioners "have only to hint in technical argument at some personal fact about the person who advanced the theory discussed" (p. 309) to make their juniors feel ignorant and uncomfortable. Obviously, only the powerful can do this with impunity, and the junior is usually not in a position to check the "personal fact" at stake. Gluckman's proposition that "the more exclusive the group, the greater will be the amount of gossip in it" has to be understood in a hierarchical sense: in an exclusive group, those who are of high status will seek to exercise control over others by gossip with their equals, while their subordinates will seek to undermine the power of their superiors by equivalent forms of gossip. It is still possible that in segmentary terms such a group may unite in denying gossiping rights about its members to outsiders. But this does not stop them from destructive internal gossip or the occasional betrayal of "secrets" to others in tactical pursuit of their own ends.

A further example Gluckman uses is that of the Makah Indians near Vancouver Island in British Columbia, Canada, studied by Elizabeth Colson (Colson 1953). These people had suffered severe effects of social change. They were greatly reduced in numbers by introduced diseases. The American Indian Service had prohibited them from following their local customs, at least until 1932 when policies changed. They were able to gain a living from fishing and working for lumber companies. They were exposed to the influences of cinema and radio and many were converts to Christianity. They mingled in church services with non–Native Americans. Colson noted how these Makah were given certain privileges such as exemption from taxes by the government and that they themselves sought to keep their numbers low. At the same time people tried to keep their own relatives on the tribal roll while keeping the descendants of others off it.

Colson noted how the Makah were torn by internal dissension and struggles and used gossip and scandal about one another "to keep one another in their proper place" (Gluckman 1963: 310) or, we may suggest, simply to do one another down and advance their own interests (cf. Haviland 1977 on the Zinacantecan patterns of gossip). Much of the denigration between people had to do with their own traditional social structure with its division of people into chiefs, commoners, and slaves and its system of competition for rank achieved through potlatch feasts in which large amounts of foodstuffs and wealth goods were given away to rivals. The Makah practices belonged to the same cultural complex that was characteristic of the Kwakiutl people. Boasting over rivals was a part of potlatch competitions. In the confused circumstances of historical change among the Makah when Colson studied them, this set of circumstances led to endless claims that others were not of chiefly but of slave descent or were addicted to the use of sorcery, a low-status practice. "Everyone is likely to accuse others of being sorcerers and to be accused in turn" (Gluckman 1963: 310).

The Makah were caught in a kind of historical and cultural bind. While all disputed the proper status of others, they still felt obliged to help distant kin, so that it was difficult for them to rise in the social class system of the non–Native Americans. On the other hand they themselves relentlessly pulled down by scandal anyone among them who tried to attain to political leadership. Colson, and Gluckman following her, attempted to pick out from this pattern of small-group conflict and tension some positive functions of the gossiping process. Colson argued that the gossip represented a reassertion of Makah values and that skill in gossiping itself was among these values (ibid.: 311). Gluckman's reformulation of this process is that "scandalizing is one of the principal means by which the group's separateness is expressed" (p. 312). The evidence, however, might just as well be used to assert that scandal was a prime means whereby the group was continually torn apart and made less effective, either in asserting a Makah identity or in entering into the wider class system. What kept the Makah Makah was partially the advantages they enjoyed in the state system, while what kept them weak within that same system was the historical set of disadvantages imposed on them coupled with their own practices of in-group bickering. It took the confidence of a powerful professor such as Max Gluckman to turn such a narrative into a functionalist scheme of "maintaining values." He himself notes that the contemporary pattern appeared to be one of insistent egalitarianism, a pattern that was quite out of tune with the supposed traditional patterns of hierarchy. And in apparent recognition of the flip side of his own argument at the end of his discussion, he admits that when he is gossiping about others, he thinks of this as performing a social duty, but when he hears that others are gossiping "viciously" about himself, he is "rightfully filled with righteous indignation" (p. 315), a view that many persons hold.

An early critic of Gluckman's views was Robert Paine. Paine saw gossip as "a genre of informal communication" and also "a device intended to forward and protect individual interests" (Paine 1967: 278). Paine mentions also that the imputed role of gossip in social control "is near to that which has been recognized for wizardry [witchcraft]" (ibid.). He points out that such hypotheses tend to depend on an idea that information is shared sufficiently for people to make judgments: an idea that we have already seen is negated by evidence, since gossipers do not have equal power and knowledge, and those gossiped about are at the disadvantage of not even knowing exactly what it is that is being said about them. If they do by chance get to know this, they may be able to confront the gossipers and refute their words, thereby turning the tables.

Thus, the gossiper is seen as a malicious storyteller rather than a purveyor of valued information and thereby loses the advantage he or she hoped to gain. In other words, malicious and inaccurate gossip often depends for its effects precisely on its untested and untestable character.

Gluckman's hypothesis tended implicitly to depend on the idea that gossip was factual. Paine points out in this context that the Makah communicated not information about one another but speculative scandal designed to discredit others in the eyes of officials. Paine suggests that the maintenance of values might be seen as a "latent function" of Makah scandal, but we have seen that this is also problematic. Colson's own idea that values would disappear unless supported by back-biting seems to beg the question further. Why could they not have been supported by the cultural shows that some Makah leaders wanted to stage but that were always sabotaged and sandbagged by the gossip of their jealous rivals?

Paine attacks Gluckman's argument "because it makes the community the centre of attention instead of the individual." This causes Gluckman "to attribute to gossipers the 'unity' of their community as their paramount value" (p. 280), but Paine suggests that gossipers have rival interests and they gossip to forward those interests, and that they avoid face-to-face accusations from fear not so much that their community might fall apart but that their claims might be refuted and their aims thwarted. Paine takes the case of the Sarakatsani shepherds of northern Greece, studied by Campbell (1964), among whom families struggled for prestige and competed for status by invoking moral claims for themselves and against others. Their concern was with morality, but not with communal unity. They cast moral doubts on other families in order to raise their own status (p. 281). Exactly the same argument would seem to apply to the Makah case (p. 282). Paine goes on to point out that what we call groups are sometimes "a coterie of rival interest-based quasi-groups" (following Mayer 1963); hence gossip within them is likely to be competitive and hostile. Academic departments are again a good example of this phenomenon, especially so when less productive academics become jealous of their peers' scholarly works.

Paine recognizes that gossip is a catalyst to social process, whether it avoids conflict or exacerbates it. He also notes that gossipers gossip to obtain information from one another as well as to plant thoughts or narratives in others' ears. They tell their listeners information that will be valued when they themselves want valued information in return. (The information may not be correct, but it does not have to be correct to be of value or use; indeed, the opposite may be the case so long as the information is never passed to unsympathetic hearers who might expose it or retell it back to the person who is its object.) So the gossiper is involved in a series of more or less calculated prestations or gifts with others, and gossip "can be a powerful social instrument" for those who learn to manage and direct it (p. 283; see also Rosnow 1974). Coincidentally, it might support social values. Indeed, to be effective it may have to be presented as doing so. But this is not its main aim, which is to secure results the gossiper seeks by participation in the network of storytelling.

Table 1 summarizes the differences at issue between Gluckman and Paine on rumor and gossip.

Paine's brief discussion effectively pointed to a whole field of analysis Gluckman had ignored or swept past even when the evidence he cited called out for it. The kinds of information that academics and others seek

TABLE 1. The Views of Max Gluckman and Robert Paine on Gossip

	Basic proposition	Expansion of proposition	Examples used (selection)
Gluckman (1963)	Gossip contributes to the unity of the group	Gossip (1) reinforces norms (2) controls individual conduct (3) facilitates choices of leaders	Shouters Haitian villagers Makah Indians
Paine (1967)	Gossip is conducted by individuals seeking to forward their own interests	Gossip (1) denigrates others (2) seeks to advance the status of the gossiper (3) is in general a catalyst of social process	Makah Indians Sarakatsani

and exchange at meetings, conferences, and seminars and in the context of job searches are often related to people's own interests, and informal gossip can indeed be a useful way to find out "what is really going on" at a publishing house, a department, or in the work of a colleague that may impinge on a person's own interests. The kind of emphasis placed on a round of telephone calls in the context of a job search indicates that gossip may come into play as a kind of check on what is "on paper," yet that gossip too may be unreliable hearsay. Nevertheless, people may accept it because they are skeptical of formal evaluations that are often made accessible to candidates themselves, or whose contents, it is feared, may be "leaked."

Gossip in these cases is the search for "the 'truth' behind the 'truth.'" It can also be invasive and destructive. Depending on its motive, it can function exactly like an accusation of witchcraft. The same can be said of other forms of communication that circulate in contexts that are secret, in terms of either the identity of the author of a document or its content, or both. Evaluations of manuscripts submitted for publication are a case in point. A skilled and experienced writer of such an evaluation may know just what is minimally necessary to damn a manuscript or a proposal without having to demonstrate a point at length. Phrases such as "The manuscript is not ready for publication in its present form" might simply imply that the manuscript could be improved by some revisions that the authors are well equipped to undertake. But the ambiguous phrasing and open-ended evaluation could be sufficient grounds for a press to torpedo a project if it is disinclined to take it in any case. The exact choice of phrasing used by a person to transmit information is akin to the rhetorical turns of oral gossip and makes a dramatic difference in the final results and treatment of the person commented on, depending on how the "information" is received and translated into action.

A useful distinction can be made here between gossip, rumor, and scandal. Gossip takes place mutually among people in networks or groups. Rumor is unsubstantiated information, true or untrue, that passes by word of mouth, often in wider networks than gossip. Scandal is news that is unambiguously deleterious to those it is directed against, whereas gossip and rumor need not be so (although they often are). Gossip may proceed into circuits of rumor, and rumor may get into gossip networks. Scandal may penetrate both and also become more publicly and overtly known or referred to. Gossip may be the term used more frequently for local forms of the types of discourse that we discuss here, while rumor is perhaps used more frequently for the extension of this process into wider areas.

The mills of rumor and gossip may also find their way into long-lasting networks or group contexts where they result in the storage of information that can lie unused for years but is a resource that can be pulled out in subsequent contexts of change and conflict. Transmitted inertly for many years, like a slow-acting virus, a rumor may form part of an informal "dossier" about a person, until it is pulled out as a weapon against that person in some context of competitive interests. The fact that it has been in existence for many years may itself be taken as a sign of authenticity, even if it is based on a chance remark years before that may have been only partially connected with reality. The potentially long-lasting power to damage its object is therefore an important latent characteristic of rumor. A formal example of a similar phenomenon may be found in government secret files, such as those kept by the Stasi in Communist East Germany. The question of what to do with such "information" since the fall of the East German government and the reunification of Germany has subsequently proved difficult to deal with. These files represent a kind of sorcery practiced by citizens against one another and by the Stasi against all of the East German citizenry. Similar issues arise in relation to all "secret intelligence" work, the justification for which has to be "security" (such as "the unity of the group") but which also depends for its efficacy on how accurate the information is if it is to be used to apprehend actual criminals rather than to persecute innocent persons. The Stasi files may not have needed to depend on "truth" in this way.

Anthropologists have generally followed Gluckman's lead in concentrating on community-based gossip and stressing its more positive social functions. Christopher Boehm, for example, in his account of blood revenge and feuds among the Montenegrins, notes that in this honor- and shame-dominated society bad opinions of people entered into local gossip mills, and that "information that begins by being exchanged confidentially between people who are very close is passed along as a 'secret' until eventually it falls into the hands of individuals who have little sense of obligation to keep it quiet" (Boehm 1984: 82). The subject of the gossip might not know about it until a public accusation took place. Gossip involved much speculation and inference about motivations and actions. The imputed personal record of a person and even the moral standing of his or her parents was brought into account.

Under these circumstances there was a very real fear of gossip, which could dissuade people from wrongdoing or might make them elaborately try to avoid detection, Boehm says (p. 83). He calls gossip a kind of "courtroom" and concludes that "gossip functions as a system through which the group's idea of what should be morally acceptable or unacceptable is continuously rehashed and refreshed" (p. 84). At the same time, he notes that most people themselves felt that gossip "was a rather insidious instrument of morality." An imperfect one also, we must add, because it could easily be fabricated or distorted. In passing, Boehm notes that people also gossiped to praise others, hence it could have some positive concomitants. It is this kind of detail that is often missing from accounts, and it is curious that Boehm chooses to include it almost as an afterthought. But surely tribe-wide positive fame and reputation must also have been communicated orally by rumor and repetition.

Studies by social psychologists have tended to concentrate less on gossip and its putative "functions" and more on the characteristics of rumor as a mode of communication. Gordon Allport and Leo Postman published their study on the psychology of rumor in 1947, shortly after World War II. Their research was closely related to the problems of the U.S.

government with rumor control and public fears during the war itself, starting with rumors surrounding the Japanese attack on Pearl Harbor and public distrust of news put out by the administration. They noted (1947: 2) that "rumor travels when events have importance in the lives of individuals and when the news received about them is either lacking or subjectively ambiguous." This kind of context for rumor is quite different from that which starts with the putative wrongdoings of individuals in communities. In both contexts, emotions are involved, but in the context Allport and Postman deal with large-scale events have already impinged on people's lives, causing them to speculate further about their meanings, scale, and implications. In the gossip and rumor mills of small communities rumors may rather be attempts to guess at events that may not have occurred at all. Similar rumors may gather around large-scale events themselves, especially by way of exaggeration or narratives of secret contributing causes of them. Allport and Postman specify the categories of "bogy" rumors and "wish" rumors in this context. They cite also (p. 10) "hate" or "wedge-driving" rumors, for example, about categories of people allegedly evading the military draft in wartime, and provide a table of 1,000 rumors reported in the United States in the summer of 1942, in conjunction with the entry of the United States into the Pacific war. And they discuss the methods adopted by government to erect defenses against rumors that might undermine confidence in the project of war. Implicit in this applied focus is the notion that rumor is not only unverified but also perhaps unverifiable or in large part simply inaccurate.

In abstract terms Allport and Postman proposed (pp. 33–4) a formula to the effect that "the amount of rumor in circulation will vary with the importance of the subject to the individuals concerned times the ambiguity of the evidence pertaining to the issue." Aside from the problem of quantifying the variables involved here, this formula does catch the two issues of importance and ambiguity and points out that both are at stake in the production and transmission of rumor. The authors recognize also that a more general human tendency is at work, the inclination to find meaning in one's environment (p. 37). Rumors often work as explanatory devices, filling in the interpretive gaps around "facts" or "reports" and making narratives that fit with people's fears and presuppositions, their emotional conditions in general.

The other main part of Allport and Postman's work on rumors was experimental. By setting up chains of transmission of information between people they showed that accounts were subject to three processes as they were relayed from person to person: *leveling*, that is, "the tendency of accounts to become shorter, more concise, and more easily grasped" (Allport and Postman 1947, as summarized by Shibutani 1966: 5); *sharpening*, that is, selective retention and reporting (this seems to go with leveling); and *assimilation*, "the tendency of reports to become more coherent and more consistent with the presuppositions and interests of the subjects" (Shibutani, ibid.). In fact, all three of these processes seem to depend on the relative homogeneity of a rumor network and its ideological formation. In cases where a rumor passes through several such networks, its transformations are likely to be more complex than these propositions suggest. The general implication made by Allport and Postman is not only that rumors deviate farther from "the truth" as they travel farther, but that in doing so they become more, rather than less, standardized forms of narratives. The phase or process of *assimilation* seems to correspond with gossip, and gossip may in turn be transformed over time into the category of "urban legend."

Allport and Postman suggest that legend in general "may be regarded as a solidified rumor," which "ceases to change as it is transmitted from generation to generation." Realizing that legend and myth are akin and that they encapsulate values, they recognize that both rumors and legends convey evaluations of others and are *appraisive* of the world, not just informative of it (1947: 167). They suggest that, presumably for this reason, "rumors and legends saturate our social relationships" (p. 169) and represent a "fusion of passions and antipathies" (p. 173), particularly in the spheres of ethnicity, sexuality, and politics. Allport and Postman also introduce the idea of "rumor publics," constituencies of people who are susceptible to particular narratives and who may be actively engaged and interested in passing on and discussing rumors (p. 182). Finally, they make a point to which we also return below, that "no riot ever occurs without rumors to incite, accompany, and intensify the violence" (p. 193).

Tamotsu Shibutani added a number of sociological observations to the work of Allport and Postman, as well as investigating in considerable depth World War II–related rumors, usefully seen from both American and Japanese perspectives. Shibutani does not start from any proposition that rumor is unverified, unreliable, or false. He characterizes rumor as "improvised news" and stresses that it is in "constant construction" (1966: 9) and that transformations in its content are not just distortions but a part of the process of arriving at a consensus (p. 16). He suggests that "it might be regarded as a form of problem-solving" (p. 17), and that "the reality to be studied, then, is not distortion in serial transmission but the social interaction of people caught in inadequately defined situations. To act intelligently such persons seek news, and rumor is essentially a type of news" (p. 17). Shibutani thus takes his approach from political sociology and treats rumor more as a form of rational action than as an expression or projection of emotions. Clearly, it can in fact be either or both of these two things.

Shibutani's parallel with news is helpful. It indicates that the news printed in newspapers or broadcast is not necessarily objectively true but also consists of opinions and assumptions guided by values. In central-ized societies, he says, institutional channels control the dissemination of information, and people seek auxiliary channels to supplement these, perhaps transgressing officially claimed prerogatives. Rumor can there-fore be subversive in its intent or its results. Shibutani illustrates the place of rumor in the production of violence with reference to rumors about brigands and noblemen's plots that circulated from 1789 to 1793 in pre-Revolutionary France (case 46, p. 103). He also neatly exemplifies the personal equation in processes of rumor making from a study of a rural Canadian community made by Leonard Doob in 1941.

In this community Doob found a rumor that a stranger who was renting a cabin was a German spy. The four most active persons in spreading this rumor were, first, "a woman who had wanted to rent her cabin to the stranger and had been turned down"; second, "a man who had originally defended the stranger and had gotten into trouble for it"; third, "a man with a long-standing feud with the family supplying dairy products to the stranger"; and, finally, "a person reputed to be suspicious of everyone" (p. 121). We may add that the stranger presumably lacked a stable support group in the community and so was particularly vulnerable to accusations. He stood, in other words, potentially in the role of the witch. The case history illustrates exactly processes of scapegoating or blaming that can occur, provided the wider context is conducive to them, whether or not a specific misfortune or disaster has happened in a community.

The anecdote from Doob is paralleled on a much wider scale by rumors that circulated about the 160,000 Japanese persons who were in Hawai'i at the time of the attack on Pearl Harbor. One rumor declared that they had poisoned the local water supply, another that Japanese plantation workers had cut canes pointing to Pearl Harbor in Oahu to guide Japanese planes, and another that Japanese residents had waved women's kimonos in greeting to the Japanese pilots (p. 132). Here the accused have an ambiguous identity, converted into the outsider category by declaring them to have been treacherous. Such treachery is the stereotypical mark of the witch in at least one Papua New Guinea society, that of the Wahgi people (O'Hanlon 1989).

Jean-Noël Kapferer's study of rumor picks up from Shibutani's observation that rumor is, intrinsically, not a deviation from the "truth" but an effort to arrive at a consensus of opinion about what is the truth. The context involved, Shibutani wrote, is one in which "demand for news is positively associated with intensity of collective excitement" (1966: 164). Rumor expands to meet the demand. Kapferer writes (1990: 3) that "rumors do not take off from the truth but rather seek out the truth." This search takes place outside authorized or official channels and also outside formal verification, so that rumors can easily be transgressive. People appeal to authority or the media as sources for the truth, thus delegating verification, but rumor impinges on this process. This is one of the reasons why government authorities in particular often are concerned to control or negate rumors that might cause public unrest, panic, or dissatisfaction. Rumor hotlines are set up for this purpose. During the anthrax scare after the September 11 disaster of 2001 in which highjackers destroyed the World Trade Center in New York by flying commercial airlines directly into it, killing themselves, the airline passengers, and thousands of workers in the center itself, numerous false messages regarding the presence of anthrax in government buildings were circulated, and in Pittsburgh, for example, a government rumor hotline was quickly established to deal with the emotional and cognitive problems experienced by people. The primary purpose of the hotline was to act as an oracle, declaring rumors to be true or false. This exercise went on concomitantly with the realization that anthrax spores were actually being discovered in various government buildings in Washington, D.C., and in media offices in New York City and in Florida State, and that it was difficult to uncover the trail of "sorcery" by which they were being disseminated. The actual spread of the spores therefore took place at the same time as the spread of false stories about them, increasing people's anxieties and confusions.

A particular website from snopes.com (http://www.snopes2.com/rumors/rumors/htm) printed a whole series of rumors regarding both the airplane highjackings and the spread of anthrax spores, coding the rumors in four ways with a circle next to each one. A green circle indicated true statements, red was for statements that were false, yellow for statements of "undetermined or ambiguous veracity," and gray for "legends of indeterminate origin." An example of a rumor marked as true was that "in the days just prior to the terrorist attacks, the stocks of United and

American Airlines [whose planes were in the crashes] were shorted by parties unknown." This came directly from newspaper reports, but might also have been passed on by word of mouth. An example of an untrue rumor was that "CNN used old footage to fake images of Palestinians dancing in the street after the terrorist attack on the U.S.A." The footage was widely seen and commented on, indicating, perhaps painfully, to Americans how others might feel happy because of the disaster, linking it to America's support for Israel. Finally, an example of a gray-coded "urban legend" was that "images of the World Trade Center fire reveal the face of Satan." This snippet was matched by a graphic visual of two photographs in which demonic facial images might be discerned in the smoke patterns. The Internet source cites an unattributed passage from a putative commentator suggesting that the photos "depict Satan being awakened from his hiding place in the World Trade Center" – rather than, perhaps, the horror of the attack itself.

The classification of this rumor as an urban legend reminds us that such legends are not just innocuous circulating stories. Like rumors and gossip generally, they grow from a highly charged and oppositional ideological context. Kapferer argues (p. 14) that "a rumor constitutes a relation to authority," often an oppositional relationship because it may oppose official disclaimers. More broadly again, rumors and gossip may simply represent opposition and dislike among groups or categories of people in the society at large, particularly categories seen in class or ethnic terms and based on ideas of exclusion or inclusion. The genesis of a rumor depends on scarcity of information about an event or putative event and the anxiety that flows from such uncertainty or scarcity.

The "explanation" of the "image" of Satan in the World Trade Center fire is of a piece with a rumor that Kapferer foregrounds regarding the large business firm Procter and Gamble. Without specifying the source of this rumor in exact terms, Kapferer notes that it emanated from a pastor or pastors belonging to a fundamentalist Christian sect in the Bible Belt of western Mississippi in the southern part of the United States (p. 21). The rumor stated that "the company's emblem – a human face contemplating myriads of stars – was said to hide within it a great many Satanic signs," in particular the number 666, the mark of the Beast from the Book of Revelation. "Procter and Gamble was rumored to have made a pact with the Devil in order to increase sales, and was sending 10 percent of its profits to a satanic sect" (Kapferer, p. ix). The rumor spread rapidly and Procter and Gamble was overwhelmed with telephone calls about it. After a long struggle against the rumor, the firm removed its logo from its products, and the rumor eventually calmed down.

This was a rumor akin to a circulating urban legend that drew on a long history of religious ideas about apocalyptic signs in millennial Christian traditions, ideas that have spread widely throughout the world with the spread of charismatic and fundamentalist versions of Christianity itself, including to places such as New Guinea (Stewart and Strathern 1997, 2000b). The citation from the Internet source quoted above about the Devil's image in the smoke of the World Trade Center fire went on to say: "Usury according to the Bible is Satan's method of enslaving the world under his priesthood, the accountants and bankers of the world. . . . All this will usher in 666, which is an economic mark of commerce according to the Book of Revelation (Ch 13, 17)."

The story about Procter and Gamble carried an extra edge to it because of its twist regarding the number 666, but it also belongs to a number of other pejorative rumors about commercial firms and their operations, for example, the rumor about a snake hidden in a K-mart store that bites a child, or about bits of mice found in Coca-Cola, or about women captured and sold into the white slave trade after being pricked by a needle in the dressing room of a clothing store. Such stories can also be attached to injurious ethnic innuendoes about store owners engaged in these trades or others, for example, rat bones putatively found in Chinese, Turkish, or Greek restaurants in Europe. These are rumors directed against outsiders or "others" in the same way as are accusations against witches or sorcerers. They may tap into deep fears of contamination or conspiracy. And they must surely gain some of their power from the fact that hostile attacks of a truly sorcerous kind are made, as with the anthrax spores sent in the mail or by other means in the United States in fall and winter of 2001. Rumors may feed on or emerge from fantasy and emotional states, but they gain plausibility through their connection with real-world events of one sort or another. Finally, Kapferer points out "that there is no such thing as politics without rumor" (p. 215), especially at the time of elections. And rumors can be effective political tools by focusing attention on an issue even if the specific claim made in the rumor turns out to be false.

Patricia Turner's (1993) study of urban rumors and legends amply confirms Kapferer's observations, and makes it clear that such stories can function as a part of political resistance toward dominant groups. Her focus is on African American stories in the United States. The first one, like ones we have cited above, is an attack on a particular firm. The stories tend to be accusations of deliberate genocide, reflecting a pervasive idea of demographic competition over reproduction and sexuality. Turner gives examples of these early on, such as (p. 2) the one that says that "Church's [fast food chicken franchise] is owned by the Ku Klux Klan, and they put something in it to make black men sterile." The rumor plays on various fears. The Church's franchise was focused on southern locations with large African American populations, and this was interpreted as a kind of infiltration or contamination. Fast food is seen as an African American preference by some and the idea that the Klan, a white supremacist organization, might seek to profit from this invokes the notion of conspiracy. The notion that in addition the food was polluted or poisoned corresponds exactly to the category of food sorcery we find in other parts of the world. And the added notion that this sorcery would make "black men sterile" (Turner, loc. cit.), rather than affecting black people whether men or women, seems to reflect a further layer of anxieties, centered on ideas of sexual competition. A whole complex of historically derived notions is therefore bundled together in this rumor.

The rumor complex, like that against Procter and Gamble, can itself be seen as a kind of weapon in a set of historical conflicts within the larger society. Undoubtedly, it damaged the firm. In classic form the accusation of hostile sorcery is itself an expression of enduring hostility against the person or organization accused. And, equally, the presumably false rumor springs from a history of conflict and domination dating back to the struggles over slavery and the American Civil War.

Another rumor that Turner cites as having been told to her is "that U.S. scientists created AIDS in a laboratory . . . and they needed to test the virus, so they go to Africa, as they [Africans] are expendable, introduce the disease, and then are unable to control its spread to Europeans and Americans" (ibid.). This rumor springs from the historical experience that governments have sometimes been seriously accused of using citizens or others as "guinea pigs" for medical experiments. The rumor also stands in opposition to the possible impression that because AIDS became known as a condition in humans early on in Africa, somehow the African populations themselves might be thought of as responsible for its genesis or spread. It removes this undesirable attribution and places it back, conspiracy-wise, on "U.S. scientists." The rumor is somewhat akin to another one that Turner notes, which states that "the production and mass distribution of drugs is an attempt by the white man to keep blacks who are striving to better themselves from making it in the world" (ibid.). Responsibility is again laid outside of the group and placed on the "other" within the overall system.

A version of another rumor targets Reebok, a company that makes sports shoes, and states that "all of the money they make off of those shoes goes to support whites in South Africa" (ibid.). This claim is similar to a part of the claim against Church's restaurants: that the company makes money from sales to black people and the profits support white people. It thus reflects a wider perception of exploitative relations in the business sector at large. Turner notes that Reebok shoes are not made in South

Africa and that the company in fact since 1985 had taken a lead in declining to market its shoes there because of opposition to apartheid (pp. 129–30). She suggests that Reebok's success may have caused it to be a target of these malicious rumors (p. 131), and she notes that some young people ceased to wear Reebok shoes out of shame and fear they would be criticized, so the rumor did hurt the company's sales. Violence might be shown to people wearing "unpopular" or stigmatized clothes, she says (p. 133).

Earlier in her discussion she also notes that the African American parents of young children and adolescents may "have ambivalent and sometimes downright hostile attitudes about the expenses incurred by their fashion-conscious children" (p. 129). This suggests that such parents may have possibly gone along with the rumor in order to dissuade their children from desiring the expensive Reebok shoes. The reverse could also happen: young people, believing the rumor, might tell their elders not to wear the shoes so as to make a stand against apartheid. Turner does not suggest any further reasons for the rumor other than that "the folk will rely on their sense of black history to construct motifs consistent with past experience but applicable to the issues at hand" (p. 136). The rumor about Reebok could have produced damage, on the principle we have noted earlier that even an accurate denial may simply draw more attention to the accusation and make people see it as the smoke that signals fire. Further, the general effects of the rumor are clear: it must worsen interethnic relations at large. People draw on history to interpret the present and by doing so they inadvertently or purposely create the future.

Turner devotes a chapter to the theme of cannibalism, noting that in Africa, reciprocal rumors grew up between Europeans and Africans portraying each other as cannibals. She notes that such narratives reflect the fact that "group conflict can foster anxiety about the motives of others regarding the bodies of an entire group" (p. 23). We can certainly remark here that this proposition is in line with Mary Douglas's famous argument that the body acts as a symbol for social relations, and that anxiety about the breaching of bodily surfaces reflects group feelings of vulnerability (Douglas 1966). Turner also quotes in this connection William Arens's well-known argument that accusations of cannibalism are generally made against categories of "the other" (neighboring language groups, for example, in the past in places such as New Guinea; Turner, p. 24, citing Arens 1979). Her own explanation of such rumors among Europeans is that they helped to justify the exploitation of Africans, who were seen as "primitive cannibals." Interestingly, the same explanation has sometimes been given for the legend in Ayrshire of Sawny Bean, a recluse who lived in a cave on the coast and was reputed to eat people. Some commentators have suggested the legend arose as anti-Scots propaganda put about by the English. Turner's take on why Africans saw Europeans as cannibals seems less specific. Presumably, it would be that in this case "cannibalism" becomes a symbol for rapacious exploitation itself rather than the justification for such exploitation. This would indicate that the meanings given to cannibalism on either side would be divergent.

It would be interesting to know the reaction of either side to knowing the stereotype projected on it by the other. But we rarely get two sides of the picture in rumor research or in discussions of witchcraft and sorcery. The imputed witch is not usually the one interviewed. It is of interest to note that Turner quotes Arens's observation that in Tanzania he met "Africans who believed that whites sojourning in Africa were in need of or desired Africans' blood or body parts," and this rumor continued by stating that African victims were taken to hospitals by fire engines where their jugular veins were slit and their blood extracted for this purpose (Turner, p. 22, citing Arens 1979: 12). This passage gives us the kernel of Luise White's extensive work on this theme, signaled in the title of her book, *Speaking with Vampires* (2000). White argues that studies of such rumors or legends can be an important way of accessing history, and Turner would no doubt agree with this proposition.

The reason why rumor and gossip are so critically important in many historical processes is that their appeal to people's predilections and sensibilities itself provides the grounds of their verification in people's minds. Put simply, people tend to believe what they want to believe, and if you call someone a witch enough times they become a witch in the eyes of society. In an elegant survey of materials that draws on many historical examples from Europe and compares these with the work of Gluckman, Colson, Malinowski, and others, Hans-Joachim Neubauer tells the story of the Harvard professor, Hugo Münsterberg, who carried out some experimental work in Idaho on an accused murderer named Harry Orchard. Münsterberg attempted by various techniques to test the phenomenon of false memories and illusions. Newspaper reporters heard of his work and reported that he had used three machines that could detect lies. The scientist denied this elaborately but without success. The rumor stuck. "The dreamed-up machine designed to force truth out of criminals had, in fact, forced truth out of the picture; hearsay was mightier than the witness" (Neubauer 1999: 155).

This anecdote testifies to the way in which rumors, including those about witchcraft, can take hold of people's imaginations and displace reality, becoming a reality of their own making. If the Harvard scientist was unable to dispel a rumor about his own technical work, how much less can a supposed witch successfully deny accusations made against him or her? The "witch" is already stigmatized and peripheral and unlikely to be listened to, or if listened to, is likely to be misunderstood. Given this, the "confessions of witches" may perhaps be read as wearied and confused acts of surrender to the forces surrounding those accused, including the force of rumor. Similar considerations may apply to the confessions of people accused of crimes, including crimes of violence, helping to explain why such persons may falsely incriminate themselves or even come to believe the accusations against them.

Neubauer's book is full of interesting examples from European contexts, and it begins with an appealing survey of ancient Greek and Latin notions of *pheme* and *fama*. He quotes the striking passage from the Greek poet and farmer Hesiod of Boeotia, who composed his works around 700 B.C.E.: "Avoid the wretched talk of mortals, for talk is evil, lightweight, and very easy to lift, but painful to carry, and hard to put aside. No talk that many people make perishes completely. Talk herself is a kind of goddess" (Hesiod, *Works and Days*, lines 760–5; we have used here the translation by Tandy and Neale (1996), rather than the one cited by Neubauer, p. 17). Hesiod's passage reveals well the ambivalence of his attitude to "talk." "The wretched talk of mortals" is clearly gossip, which can be very harmful to people. Hesiod's poem is full of advice to his brother Perses, who out of bad luck or mismanagement had lost his farm through debt. Possibly Perses had listened to a neighbor's mischievous bad information or advice, or perhaps he had been damned by local gossips and so lost credit. Hesiod warns that it is easy to begin saying something or lending an ear to gossip and rumor, but very hard to deal with its consequences. This is also because once a rumor is started, it is hard to quell it. It becomes immortal. Finally, Hesiod shifts his position, and in a twist says that "talk" in this sense is a deity.

The twist expresses well the power of rumor and gossip, later depicted vividly also in the work of Virgil in his epic the *Aeneid*, writing on the *fama* (rumor, news, or reputation) that passed into the public realm after the wandering Trojan hero Aeneas and the Carthaginian queen Dido first made love (Neubauer, p. 37). *Fama* may be good or bad. In either case, its chief characteristic is its multiplicity. Virgil's account, later to be echoed by many others, catches this feature, and also gives *fama* a mythological origin.

> Now in no time at all
> Through all the African cities Rumor goes –
> Nimble as quicksilver among evils. Rumor
> Thrives on motion, stronger for the running,
> Lowly at first through fear, then rearing high
> She treads the land and hides her head in cloud.
> (Virgil, *Aeneid*, lines 173–7; trans.
> by Robert Fitzgerald, 1990: 101–2)

Virgil goes on to say that *fama* (rumor) was borne by Earth, who was angry with the gods, as a sister to the Titans Coeus and Enceladus, making her swift on foot and wing, but also monstrous and deformed.

> Pinioned, with
> An eye beneath for every body feather,
> And, strange to say, as many tongues and buzzing
> Mouths as eyes, as many pricked-up ears,
> By night she flies between the earth and heaven
> Shrieking through darkness, and she never turns
> Her eyelids down to sleep.
>
> (lines 181–5)

The multiplicity here lies in the profusion of eyes lurking behind her feathers, matched in numbers by tongues, mouths, and ears. Notable here is that the rumor is not untrue, although it may have been elaborated on. Truth and falsehood may multiply out of human curiosity or even a desire for entertainment (see Lienhardt 1975).

The personification of "talk," or even its deification in Hesiod's phrase, is a vivid reminder of the power of talk generally in social life, including its dangerousness (Brenneis and Myers 1984). Raymond Firth, in his study of rumor on Tikopia island in the Solomons, noted that the term he translated as "rumor" in fact meant simply "word" or "talk," and that it covered all news. He also noted the prevalence of rumors on this small Pacific island of 1,200 people, and the interest of chiefs in particular about happenings in parts of the island other than their own. Firth and his assistant, James Spillius, recorded seventy rumors over a period of about twenty-eight months in two field trips of 1928–9 and 1952 (Firth 1967: 148). This interest in news and a certain scrupulousness about whether the news is reliable or not is highly characteristic of Pacific cultures in general. Far from Tikopia, in the highlands of Papua New Guinea, this theme turns up in regard to colonial contexts and relations between Australian government patrol officers and the local people. These patrol officers were empowered to hear local disputes and to keep records of all social trends and movements in their areas. They interacted with the people using Tok Pisin, a lingua franca with an English-language vocabulary base. When disputes were brought to them, the litigants would often begin their statements with "ol i tok," meaning "people are saying." The patrol officers often found it hard to get at the truth of such talk so as to settle cases, as indeed the people themselves did. (This was in the 1960s, well prior to Papua New Guinea becoming an independent nation in 1975.) They adopted the phrase "ol i" and made it into a singular substantive, "Orly," expressing their feeling of being confronted with a collectivity of rumors. "Orly isn't keen on the road project," they would say. The people became their talk, and their talk was made into a single person. In the same way, talk also makes out of the multiplicities of a given person the stereotypes of the witch.

Conclusion

Our purpose in this chapter has been to show the multiple social contexts in which rumor and gossip exercise influence. We have examined at some length the debate between Gluckman and Paine in order to trace the transition in anthropology from early functionalist ideas stressing group unity to later analyses that concentrate either on the individual as such or on networks of competitive relationships marked by tension, distrust, and ambiguity. It is in these relationships that ideas of witchcraft or sorcery easily arise and flourish. To bring these points home to our academic readers, we point out that hidden processes in academic life often correspond closely to veiled accusations of sorcery or to acts of witchcraft and sorcery. Words uttered or written on paper can destroy a person's or a project's integrity, while ostensibly operating as a part of a confidential review process. "Damning with faint praise" is equivalent to denying a person or project an identity as a group member. An insistence on an "analytical perspective" may also function as a demand for a particular kind of analysis as opposed to some other viewpoint. In circumstances of tension, such as the struggles over faculty appointments that we have remarked on earlier, this parallel with sorcery may become even more clear. For example, an unsigned letter containing accusations or imputations of wrongdoing on the part of others may be sent to a departmental chairperson or even a dean. The anonymity of the writer gives the person the character of a sorcerer, whose harmful actions are openly seen but who hides from taking responsibility for them. Sorcery killings also may lack a definite "signature" of those responsible for them. The sorcerer kills or attempts to kill, but seeks to evade retaliation or rebuttal. A further layer of evasion of responsibility is generated when the immediate "sorcerer" is acting under duress as the agent of a more manipulative but hidden sponsor.

The work of anthropologists such as John Campbell (1964), Juliet du Boulay (1974), and John Haviland (1977) illustrates clearly how people use gossip to argue about status and to create particular views of the world around them. Rumor and gossip, like talk in general, are constitutive of, rather than simply reflect, social realities. Campbell's study points out the intimate connections among the Sarakatsani people of northern Greece among senses of self-regard, honor, identity, shame, gossip, ridicule, and laughter. Taking the community as his point of reference and arguing largely in functionalist terms, he stresses how gossip implicitly upholds values. His account makes it clear that gossip is competitive and largely destructive. "Gossip never ceases and it seizes on the pettiest of details and circumstances," he notes (1964: 314). He sees gossip and self-regard as mutually reinforcing. His analysis closely mirrors Gluckman's general theory of gossip. But his data also hint at how gossip can be used to destroy the reputations of others and how the laughter it generates is invariably malicious (cf. Just 2000: 159–60). His point of reference is men, thereby following Sarakatsani male ideology. But gossip probably is important among Sarakatsani women also. Du Boulay's study indicates clearly that in Ambéli in Greece gossip in fact was "an activity indulged in pre-eminently by women" (1974: 204), often with no particular purpose but as a form of entertainment. Ambéli women were, nevertheless, "highly sensitive to the dangers of interested parties meeting and talking" whenever their own concerns and reputations were at stake (p. 206). And gossip was given a somewhat negative cast. The villagers recognized that it contributed to the further fragmentation of "an already dwindling community" (p. 209). Du Boulay points out here that we cannot say that gossip is simply constructive or destructive, since "it is in the nature of gossip not to be completely one thing or the other" (p. 212). Haviland (1977: 172) notes that gossip requires skill and that it "dwells on precisely the issues that concern" people most: "the familiar world of neighbors and kin, dissected into relevant bits and marked more often as petty successes or mishaps than as, say, triumphs, tragedies, or revelations." It is this same world of talk, mundane as it is, that forms the basis for the more dramatic worlds of the witch-hunts of Europe and Africa. A detailed case study from the Bocage area in Western France illustrates the ramifications of talk and its intersections with other actions in the context of witchcraft accusations that often center on the division of land and property (Favret-Saada 1977). Unusual ways of speaking, touching, or looking are all interpreted as signs of witchcraft activity, and Favret-Saada frequently cites verbatim conversations in which the fear of witches regularly enters, intruding into everyday life. The title of her book draws attention to the power of talk: *Deadly Words*.

The perspectives of anthropologists themselves can well be complemented by taking into account the work of social psychologists. Here we have traced a movement from the work of Allport and Postman, which was concerned to study how rumors deviate from "the truth," to later viewpoints such as those of Shibutani and Jean-Noel Kapferer, which look on rumor as a search for information and an attempt at problem solving. From these analyses also we can see clearly how this search is shaped by people's emotional proclivities and social relationships, in particular, their views of themselves and others in the world.

Patricia Turner's work usefully highlights the genesis of rumor as a tool of social criticism and a weapon against perceived domination. Here rumor takes the form of imputing aggression, such as poisoning activities, against others, or even suggesting a Taussig-like association between capitalism and the Devil (Taussig 1980). Urban legend thus enters the sphere of traditions about Satanic pacts, which also belong to European witchcraft and subsequently have entered into Africa. The transformation of ideas of witchcraft in Africa is our next topic.

THREE

〜

Africa

We have already seen in Chapter 1 how in terms of local-level cases of witchcraft accusations we can find similarities between colonial Africa and historical Europe of the seventeenth century. And in Chapter 2 we mentioned how William Arens had uncovered the theme of African suspicions that Europeans were using their colonial subordinates to obtain the blood of Africans, a notion akin to that of cannibalism. Arens has extensively documented the fantasies of cannibalism imputed to "others" in many historical contexts, including those marked by colonialism. He concludes by comparing what he calls the "man-eating myth" to the fantasy of the witches' sabbath that led, through the imaginings of intellectuals, to witch-hunts in Europe (Arens 1979: 178). (The parallel does not, of course, disprove the existence of cannibalism.)

African ideas about witchcraft mutated from their local-level contexts into ones much more influenced by colonial, and later postcolonial, relations at large, just as, in continental Europe, the idea of linking witchcraft with the Devil was promoted by the authorities of church and state. Presumably, these mutations, representing the impingement of state relations on local levels of society, were already to some degree at work from earlier times, and local-level processes have also continued, intertwined with state relations, as Geschiere's (1997) work particularly shows for Africa. State-based social change was already affecting the cases studied in the 1940s and 1950s by anthropologists such as Max Marwick and

Victor Turner. Nevertheless, the shift to a preoccupation with rumors of predatory relations between Europeans as a whole and Africans represents a significant transformation of notions and of foci of anxiety, just as the link made between witchcraft and the Devil in a sense threw witchcraft onto a larger canvas of power relations and greatly increased the stigmatization of the witch. Both processes reveal widening gaps in society. The African context shows the rift between class-based groups intersecting with ethnicity and leading to suspicions of the dominated against the dominant; the Europe example shows the opposite, the rise of an elite and their use of witchcraft as a theme against those weaker than themselves.

In this chapter we look at the "new" African context, while not forgetting its background in earlier notions and "witch-hunts" of the past, which could also, in response to rumors, pass from one local area to another. It is indeed striking that the contemporary cycles of rumors tend to fit into a picture of expanded and extended relationships signaled by the term "globalization," and that they all tend to depict the equivalent of government or business "conspiracies" against the people, themes that we also have seen to be strikingly pervasive in the urban legends or rumors collected by Patricia Turner in the African American context (Turner 1993). This is hardly surprising, given that the African and African American contexts are historically linked.

Witch Finding among the Bemba: Mirrors and Medicines

Many of the themes that can be considered forerunners of the rumors about witchcraft and exploitation today are found in the older literature on witch-hunts of colonial times. Audrey Richards (1935) wrote about a witch-finding movement among the Bemba people of N.E. Rhodesia (Zambia) that swept through her area of study in 1934. The witch finders were called Bamucapi. Richards notes that they were young men who were dressed in European clothing and went around in ones or twos accompanied by paid local assistants (p. 448). They had a "founding myth" that the originator of their movement was called Kamwende from Nyasaland (Malawi), an area that had entered into "modernization" before the Bemba. Kamwende was said to have received a revelation of his powers in the grave, from which he had risen after two days, partially disabled but with knowledge of the anti-witchcraft *mucapi* medicine. If his followers failed to find all of the witches or sorcerers in a village, they said he would later come, beating his drum, and compel all witches to follow him to the graveyard where they would be revealed.

When the witch-finders arrived in a village, they would, in colonial style, have all the men and women line up before the headman, as for an inspection. They were told to pass by the witch-finder, who caught their image ("spirit") in a small mirror and was said to be able to tell at once whether they were guilty of witchcraft. Those selected were told to yield up their "horns of medicine," and these were then collected at a cross-roads outside the village for everyone to inspect. Each person was told to drink the *mucapi* liquid, a name related to the term *kucapa*, for "washing clothes," and they were then declared free of witchcraft. Anyone who drank the medicine but afterward returned to the ways of witchcraft would die a grisly death and so self-destruct. As a sideline the witch-finders also sold minor protective charms and medicines sewn in small cloth bags (p. 449). By far the most expensive one was "a charm for winning the favour of the local Government officials" (ibid.); it was said that few could afford to pay for it.

Richards examined a heap of 139 horns and charms and found that, according to her interpretation of them, 125 were in fact containers of protective magic. Public opinion, however – for which we may read rumor and gossip – had made of many of these objects the irrefutable signs of the actions of witches and sorcerers. The whole ritual process instituted by the witch-finders therefore acted both as a kind of stimulus to public imagination and as a form of therapy to remove the fear of witchcraft heightened in the campaign against it. It also offered a way out for those found guilty to return to society after being "washed" by the *mucapi* medicine. The blending of governmental style social procedures with mission-style cultural themes is also striking. The movement claimed the support of the administration but was openly hostile to the Christian missionaries, who instructed their adherents not to participate in the rituals. Like the Christian churches themselves, the witch-finders claimed the power to fight "evil," the anti-image of society represented by the sorcerer or witch. They did not challenge the indigenous structure of ideas and practices in which misfortunes were mostly attributed to people's own wrongdoings and were seen as punishment by ancestral spirits, with the permission of the High-God Lesa (p. 456) and the approval of the chiefs. The *nganga*, ritual experts, could determine the causes of disasters and prescribe confession followed by laborious rituals of atonement. But the activities of witches were seen as impervious to this system of justice, and people tried to guard against their powers by purchasing magic charms from the *nganga* themselves. Chiefs in the precolonial past had administered the poison ordeal to those accused of witchcraft, but they were no longer permitted to do so, nor could witches be charged in the colonial courts. Into this gap stepped the witch-finders, taking on themselves the mantle of the *nganga* but operating in the new world of colonial space, outside the powers of chiefs and traditional diviners, as new cultural bricoleurs and entrepreneurs. The people at large regarded their activities as having the blessing of the British colonial power. Richards herself points to the fact that the movement was a part of the commoditization process induced by wage labor and the use of money. To gain security, people were willing to pay for a service that blended old and new elements together in a potent package.

Zombies in the Transvaal

Isak Niehaus, in a detailed study of witch-hunting in the Transvaal, South Africa, from 1930 to 1991, provides a very useful expansion of the discussion of change by Richards (Niehaus 1993; see also Niehaus et al. 2001). The earlier colonial phase outlined by Niehaus corresponds to Richards's account. "Until 1956 Green Valley [the fieldwork site] was characterized by a high degree of agricultural self-sufficiency, networks of reciprocal co-operation between domestic units, and by stable chiefships. In this context witchcraft was seen as a threat to the whole community" (Niehaus 1993, p. 504).

The chiefs, aided by diviners (*mungoma*), were the ones who identified and punished witches. Although crops had sometimes been destroyed by drought and worms, neighbors helped one another with their work. But in 1948 the area had also received hundreds of families displaced from white-owned farms onto trust lands, reducing the size of farm lots for existing residents; this was followed in 1960 by a so-called betterment scheme that formally reallocated land and reduced holdings of stock. Chiefly rule was weakened in the succeeding years, and by the mid-1980s the power of chiefs was supplanted by that of cross-community youth groups. The chiefs lost their association with witch-hunting and also their control over agricultural activities. They were supplanted by magistrates and white agricultural officers. Parents found it more difficult to socialize and control the younger generation. Neighbors became very suspicious of one another.

Suspicions and accusation fastened on persons with odd patterns of behavior (p. 512). The *mungoma* diviners were still consulted and they would point to such persons as the witches. Youths then burnt down the houses of the accused or drove them out. Because government officials would not prosecute suspected witches, the local people thought they in fact protected them, and this increased people's collective fears. Youth groups stepped in aggressively to accuse and punish witches by whipping them with rawhide thongs. Many of these youths were educated but unemployed at a time of crisis in the South African economy (p. 514). They declared that witches kept baboons as familiars or that they had captured people and kept them as *tokolose* (zombies) to work for them.

The youths sometimes worked with *mungoma* diviners, bringing suspects to them to be tested. At times, they themselves engaged in overt violence and were arrested by the police. Those accused were often, in classic fashion, relatives who had had quarrels with persons who subsequently died. A mixture of accusations might be made against witches. "They were accused of keeping familiars, sending a *tokolose* to rape young women, killing their relatives . . . and burying a human brain under the gate of [the chief's house] to stupefy him" (p. 521). Other accusations were that they desecrated tombstones, poisoned their neighbors, or made their in-laws sterile. African National Congress party officials were involved in protecting those accused from crowds and tried to hold rituals of confession and abjuration to calm the feelings against them. Diviners also were called in to authenticate the identification of the witches and to make them confess. Most of the accused were people who were socially peripheral and not very powerful and might be seen as deviant.

Niehaus reports at the beginning of his study cases where many "convicted" witches were reportedly killed by stoning, burning, or "necklacing" (killing with a tire set on fire around the neck), sometimes by youth groups fighting against political opponents and including "collaborators" along with "witches" as their targets. These examples, which differ from those Niehaus details at the end of the study, show the lengths to which witchcraft accusations could be joined with politics to produce collective violence in parts of South Africa.

Putting together the papers by Richards and Niehaus, in Table 2 we outline different phases of witchcraft accusations in African colonial and postcoloinal history. We may suggest that the role of rumor and gossip escalates through historical time as we move from phase 1 to phase 3 in Table 2. In phase 1, gossip may cause someone to be accused in the chief's court, but the matter ends there and the witch can be ritually rehabilitated. In phase 2 the process becomes more loose and open-ended and much gossip surrounds the witch-finders themselves as well as the "evidence" they publicly assemble for comment. In phase 3 the whole process is

TABLE 2. Historical Phases in Witchcraft Accusations in Southern Africa (from Niehaus 1993 and Richards 1935), 1930s–1990s

Phase 1	
Witches accused in chief's court Identified by diviners	Punishment by ritual atonement
Phase 2	
Witches identified by witch-finders who acted as diviners; powers of chief in decline	Those found guilty drink "medicine" and are putatively "cleansed"
Phase 3	
Community disintegration; rise of political parties	Punishment/retaliation for supposed offenses by killing
Witches pursued by youth groups and mobs	Diviners may attempt to impose ritual solutions as in Phases 1 and 2
Final identification by diviners	Courts may prosecute witch killers for murder

more volatile again: gossip and rumor escalate and may result in mob killings, even though authorities subsequently prosecute the killers. As the chiefs' control and group cohesion decline, gossip and rumor, with their potential for violence, increase in intensity and scope.

Both Richards and Niehaus report a medley of cultural notions about witches that came into play. We suggest that because Christian missions were ubiquitous in colonial Africa, missionary pronouncements and tracts must have fed into a developing hybrid set of ideas that could be transmitted in particular by trans-local witch-hunts. In particular, Christian notions derived from the historical European context that stressed the diabolical associations of witchcraft could have contributed to the collective demonization of witches that we see in phase 3 in Table 2. It is worthwhile to recall here that in his classic study of witchcraft among the Azande of the Sudan, Evans-Pritchard noted that when a person was accused of witchcraft he was typically expected to take some water in his mouth and blow it out on the wing of a chicken presented to him by a messenger. The chicken was one that had been sacrificed to an oracle that produced the accused's name. Having blown out the water, the accused would say that he was unaware that his witchcraft had been active and would ask it to be cool inside him. This would ease the situation and the person whose sickness occasioned the oracular divination was said to have gotten better (Evans-Pritchard 1976 [1937]: 42). Evans-Pritchard noted further that "the position of a witch is in no way analogous to that of a criminal in our society" (p. 54). While these citations do not tell the whole story about Zande ideas or Zande history, they do bring forcefully to attention the point that witchcraft powers were not always everywhere considered diabolically evil and worthy of being punished by death. More congenial solutions were sometimes prevalent.

In the "modern" context, however (phase 3 of Table 2), different processes come to the fore. Niehaus stresses that "witches" might be mildly deviant and in particular might be vulnerable people. Youth groups tended to target people of their parental generation, who in a sense became scapegoats on whom blame for numerous deaths and misfortunes was loaded. This, then, is one pattern. However, another dominant pattern is the dislike and jealousy of the new political elites and people who have become rich through business. If the successful are also younger than those similar to them would have been in former times, this also may lead them to accuse older and less successful people of attacking them out of jealousy. We also saw in Niehaus's work the theme of the *tokolose*, the zombie who acts as a slave worker for the witch who has brought him back to life by necromancy. This clearly reflects a fantasized image of the capitalist labor system mixed with precapitalist images of slavery. If such imaginations surround those who get rich faster than others, the implication is that the successful, themselves, may also be seen as witches. Those who are successful fear the jealousy of those less fortunate than themselves, while the latter think that only by witchcraft and magic could the rich and powerful have attained their position. Witchcraft fears work in a two-way shuttle, keeping suspicion between people at a high level. Rumor and gossip fill in the blanks in people's knowledge of what "the others" do.

Witchcraft, Money, and Social Reproduction: The Ngoni and Other Cases

Misty Bastian (1993), in a study of contemporary ideas among the Igbo people of Onitsha in Nigeria, points out cogently how suspicions of witchcraft open up between urban- and rural-based members of a given lineage, categories that may correspond to rich and poor in a monetary sense. The prime image of the witch also centers on the notion of an immoral or amoral selfishness or greed. This idea may cut two ways. Rural people may see the urban elites as selfish, while urban people may feel indignant that they are denied the identity of properly belonging to the rural areas from which they have migrated into the town. As we see it, this seems to indicate that either side may suspect the other of making witchcraft to their advantage.

Mark Auslander has studied further dimensions of witchcraft in Eastern Zambia (Auslander 1993). His findings can be compared directly with those of Richards and Niehaus on witch-finding movements. The movements he observed took place in 1988–9, and in them young male witch-finders accused senior men and women of blocking the fertility of their juniors. The witch-finders beat severely those they accused and incised their skin with cuts into which they pressed "anti-witchcraft" medicines. Such rituals appear to have been the violent counterparts of those Richards observed among the Bemba in 1934, but directed against senior people and focused on fertility. The senior people were said to have sent dangerous witchcraft horns through the sky, penetrating the houses of those they targeted and rendering them impotent. Such a form of symbolism clearly indicates tension between the generations, a sense of reproduction gone wrong, with fertility linked to social harmony and sterility linked to conflict. Patterns of thought of this kind underlie rituals in many parts of the world. The example of the Duna people in Papua New Guinea springs immediately to mind (Stewart and Strathern 2002a). An acknowledgment of intergenerational conflict therefore at once resonates symbolically with fears regarding sexuality and reproduction.

In another regard there is a close parallel between Auslander's materials on the Ngoni people and societies of the Papua New Guinea Highlands. Auslander notes that in a social system characterized by obligations of giving and sharing, there is always the fear of those who are left out in any given event. Those who are excluded and are defined as at the margins of social interaction are liable to be thought of as witches or sorcerers. Ngoni representations of this idea focus on the image of the witch as an old woman who greedily eats alone in her house. The notions of the "excluded other" and the "greedy hoarder" appear to come together in this image. Apparently poor and marginal people may be fantasized as being secretly rich in money and maize corn because of their hidden nightly activities.

Ngoni witchcraft could as well be described as sorcery, for the witch is said to collect the *chisambe*, or life force, of people, present in footprints, hair, or soil they have urinated on, and to mix such residues with "medicines" taken from the organs of dead people. The witch addresses the mixture, explaining how the intended victim has done harm and denied reciprocity, for example, by refusing to share soap. Sometimes the medicine is thought to be in the witchcraft horn that the witch projects through the sky. Such a horn may be said to be purchased with a cow, in a kind of anti-image of the symbolism of bridewealth payments. The horn stands for the denial of the achievement of reproductive status, resulting in the confinement of young men to clientage roles. It represents the supposed jealousy of the old for the young and their supposed incessant demands, as well as the fear that their power must itself have been gained by witchcraft. Female witches are imaged as turning themselves into lionesses who pitilessly attack their prey. The imagery partly derives from Ngoni history in which the incoming Ngoni males married local Cewa and Nsenga wives, leaving a sense that women have a special relationship with the landscape. But younger women also suspect the malevolence of older women, such as a classificatory mother-in-law (wife of husband's father).

By contrast, the older people themselves fear the junior generation, seeing them as caught up in cash cropping and as willing to sell cows for cash, destroying proper social hierarchy. Young men desire autonomy and resent their elders' reluctance to sell cattle for cash in order to fund, for example, transport businesses that link rural to urban areas. Roads are a focus for both ambition and anxiety. Young men like to experience the freedom to travel on them, but they fear the passage of AIDs and the movement of women who elude their control.

A classic avoidance of ostentation goes with the fear of witchcraft. Chemical fertilizers, greatly valued because of their power to produce crops but also feared as a kind of "poison," are kept in secret; gifts of oil or soap are made discreetly; also, adulterous affairs, if discovered, are felt to arouse the vengeful witchcraft of betrayed spouses. People buy "medicines" to protect themselves and hire *ng'anga* to conduct divinations and identify witches. Identified witches are sometimes expelled and migrate to "witch villages." At deaths "proper" Christian burial is held to protect the corpse from consumption by witches, and fine displays of mourning songs and dances are thought to soothe the anger of the living and the dead and ward off jealous witchcraft. Witches themselves are thought to gather in cemeteries to unearth the dead and engage in liberal sexual practices.

In the past, male elders were buried in a central cattle barn in the settlement, and groves of trees that grew in the sites of abandoned barns were thought to be the home of the ancestral shades. Christian missions from the end of the nineteenth century altered this pattern, creating a separation between settlement and graveyard. Cemeteries became places that people would not ordinarily enter. At the same time all neighbors are required to attend a funeral if they are within earshot of the funeral drums.

Funerals express community, but witches are said to enter cemeteries at night, apart from funeral occasions, and use them to express their anti-communal values. Funeral rituals expressly guard against the incursion of witches by the burning of fires. They also seal off the dead from the village rather than, as before, reincorporating them into it. Women have a special responsibility for wailing over the corpse and settling it in the cemetery. Witches, in turn, are said to subvert the proper effects of the funeral and thus the relations between living and dead kin. For example, they are supposed to steal the body parts of the dead, especially the genitals. Orators at funerals work hard to cool hard feelings and so to reduce the likelihood of such attacks on the grave by witches.

The evidence here suggests that Christian practices have themselves contributed not to the abolition of witch beliefs but to their transformation. Christian graveyards, separated from the community of the living, have become places where witches are imagined to gather. Communication with the dead themselves has been disrupted. This in itself could lead to intergenerational tensions among the living. Graveyards have become secret, taboo places, the kind of places around which rumor and gossip can accrete.

While Ngoni elders fear the "poison" of the junior generation, expressed in the notion of dangerous chemical fertilizer, Auslander documents an actual accusation by a young male witch-finder against a senior woman, accusing her of blocking the wombs of younger women. The witch-finder's henchmen violently searched her house and that of other senior women, beat them, and rubbed anti-witchcraft medicines into incisions in their skin. The witch-finder proclaimed that now witchcraft would be eliminated and people could "make money" safely (Auslander 1993:167). Here the pathways of fertility and exchange were linked together and the elders were accused of blocking them. The womb stood for all the capacities for reproduction seen as secretly closed off by the elders.

The generalized image of fertility as "flow" is reminiscent of Christopher Taylor's analysis of Tutsi ideology in Rwanda (Taylor 1992,

1999). Such an image is also an image of power, and Auslander indicates that the witch-finders' aim during their campaign in 1987–8 was to overturn the power of their seniors and appropriate it for themselves (p. 179). Auslander followed an itinerant witch-finder called Doctor Moses through eleven witch-finding rituals in one district (Chipata) during 1988. This man was clearly an entrepreneur who was adept at capturing people's imaginations. He was affiliated with the Zionist version of Christianity, in which bodily rituals are emphasized. Zionist prophets are highly mobile and are condemned by priests of mainstream churches for engaging in Satanic practices. In turn, they declare that Church ministers themselves covertly practice witchcraft. Witch-finding is thus embroiled in disputes between churches. It is also a business. Young males helped to collect considerable "donations" as fees for Doctor Moses (p. 176).

At the same time, the witch-finders in 1988 targeted senior people who, they said, were profiting from stealing maize and turning people into slave laborers as zombies. They were also, they said, stopping wealth from coming into the communities. The witch-finders lined up people in the village, with the old people at one end and the children at the other. (This action is directly comparable to that described by Audrey Richards in the 1930s among the Bemba.) They used medicines said to have been obtained from "Europeans" to restore vitality to people's bodies. They employed mirrors said to operate like televisions or computers and also to take people's "temperature." Their actions mimicked those of colonial health patrols to eliminate yaws and syphilis. They washed people's feet in an action similar to cattle-dipping, a procedure used to remove infection from cattle as they move across pastures. And they offered protection to bodies by rubbing medicines into cuts in the skin.

Doctor Moses declared that he was doing God's work, and that God would heal people of witchcraft; he further declared that the biblical figure of Moses had revealed this work to him in dreams. And he wore a white, clinical-style, robe marked with red crosses, making multiple evocations of the state, biomedicine, international agencies, and God, all in one. He staged in the middle of the village a kind of authoritative "roadblock" through which "patients" passed, as he "straightened out" the crooked pathways of witchcraft (p. 184). He himself exhibited his powers to track down the erratic movements of witches by racing up and down and behaving in an unpredictable way as the Spirit of Moses supposedly took him. He brought the high-speed world of the road, the tarmac, to the village (ibid.). But he concentrated his attentions on the villagers' own houses, purporting to discover the secret horns they harbored in the houses and breaking them open to do so, with particular emphasis on their enclosing roofs that were held to conceal secret powers. The mirror that he used was spoken of as magical, like an x-ray, or like the pieces of mirrors sometimes embedded in figurines to see witches and the land of the dead. His mirror was seen as a "modern" device used to overcome the "ancient" power of the medicine horn and to constitute young males as a political force. Gradually, chiefs and senior men allied themselves with the witch-finders and partially regained powers for themselves (p. 186).

Auslander's account vividly portrays how the witch-finding movement's progress across the countryside was preceded by a wave of rumor, bringing with it a mass of jumbled information. By the time the movement actually reached a place, the rumor wave had already washed over it and saturated it with its own particles. While witch-finders declared that they were there to "cleanse" the communities of pollution by witchcraft, it is clear that they set up a force field of propaganda that itself might be seen as redirecting people's perceptions of "reality."

Another feature of these materials is how closely they parallel the account by Richards of the 1934 Bamucapi movement among the Bemba. Traditions of witch-finding must have accreted in Zambia and have swirled backward and forward over time, creating a kind of semantic network of associations that could quickly be funneled and channeled into a particular stream of rumor once a new movement began.

A very general theme that underlies studies of witchcraft and modernity is the effect of monetization on the conditions under which such rumors circulate. We almost invariably learn that monetization creates an expanded market both in lethal forms of witchcraft or sorcery and in charms against it. We also learn that monetization exacerbates people's frustrations and desires by placing many commodities theoretically in accessibility but in practice making them unattainable: the basic circumstance of capitalist consumerism. This theme firmly links together the historical experiences of people in Africa and Papua New Guinea (see for example the studies in Akin and Robbins 1999, and for an earlier cross-cultural overview, Parry and Bloch 1989; also numerous pertinent studies in Moore and Sanders 2001b).

Monetization perhaps also tends to increase the range of differences of wealth between people in village communities because of their different life opportunities. And it may enable people to withdraw from or deny the kinds of "leveling" obligations of reciprocity and redistribution entailed by the norms of village life. Or if they try to maintain such obligations, they soon find that they cannot meet their ends and that others are still unsatisfied. A pervasive aura and fear of jealousy is thus set up.

Pamela Schmoll's study of soul-eaters among Hausa speakers in Niger well exemplifies these processes. Soul-eaters are held to have special stones in their stomach, and when these move their desire is activated. Soul-eaters are said to transform themselves into uncanny versions of animals and to startle people so that their souls jump out of their bodies and can be snapped up (Schmoll 1993: 201). The soul-eater may store the soul and later cut its throat, roast it, and eat it. The soul-eater is motivated by jealousy of those who are prosperous and have good luck. The victims suffer total debilitation as their life is drained from them. In short the soul-eater is a classic form of the cannibalistic witch.

The propensities to eat souls can, it is thought, be inherited from either father's semen or mother's milk (Schmoll, p. 204). But nowadays, Schmoll was told, such powers can be purchased with money. A soul-eater vomits up a male and female stone and the purchaser swallows these. They reproduce in the person's stomach and the person becomes a soul-eater. Buyers are said to be motivated by greed and jealousy of others whom they wish to harm. Once they have the power, they cannot control it. Instead, it controls them. (Highly comparable ideas regarding *kum* stones are found in the Mount Hagen area of Papua New Guinea; see Strathern 1982; Stewart and Strathern 1999a.)

It is in the stomach that jealousy as well as happiness or unhappiness are said to reside. Emotions in general have to be controlled. The head is supposed to rule the stomach, and children are socialized to control the expression of, for example, hunger. "Eating" is a general term for gratification of desire, but also suffering. It can refer to sexual intercourse as well as consumption of food, and also to the effects of pain. Soul-eaters are said to express desire by licking at the souls of victims. The mouth is also thought of as the source of dangerous talk that can travel out and harm people (see Weiner 1984 and Strathern and Stewart 1999b for Pacific parallels).

Treatment of sickness caused by soul-eating is thought to depend on catching the soul-eater and naming him, then making him jump naked over the victim, thus releasing the captured soul: a procedure not easy to accomplish since an accusation against the soul-eater may land the accuser in court charged with false rumor. People take preventive "medicine" to protect themselves. Possession of the soul-eating stones is thought to be dangerous: the stones demand to be satisfied and act as though they will kill their owner, causing him pain and driving him to seek victims.

Schmoll interprets these materials as reflecting the monetarization of relationships that has taken place among these Hausa people, seeing soul-eating as "a framework for a sophisticated and nuanced commentary on the problem of uncontrolled desire for power and wealth and the use of immoral means to achieve them" (p. 205). The concept of "eating" draws on fundamental bodily processes and uses these to stand for social processes of exploitation that "have been profoundly affected by colonialism and capitalism" (p. 206). The same image is used by Hagen people in

Papua New Guinea when they describe outsiders as coming and "eating" their land (*tininga möi nonomen*). The idea that soul-eaters particularly target children, the future of the society, is in accordance with the idea that cannibalism is seen as threatening society itself.

Schmoll's analysis is not imported into her data just as a corollary of a particular theoretical approach. It echoes what the people themselves said to her, since they blame the French for having incited new desires for goods, and the jealousies and greed that go with these. The commoditization of soul-eating (p. 212) is both an example of social change and a major perceived multiplier of it. If people can buy these powers, many more people, it is thought, must have them, thus increasing people's fears. Supplementary thoughts are added, for instance, that men nowadays travel more widely and marry beautiful young girls from other places without knowing that they are soul-eaters, so bringing the practice into their own families. We heard similar notions expressed about incautious acts of marriage nowadays among the Duna people in Papua New Guinea. Those most caught up in the pressures of "modernity" brought about by education, travel, and urban salaries see themselves as most sharply threatened by the "epidemic" of soul-eating. Interestingly, Schmoll suggests in passing (p. 214) that "the increasing appeal of Islam is perhaps, in fact, born of this conflict." The suggestion she makes appears to be that Islam may be held to provide a counterideology to the ideology of capitalism and/or perhaps a religious form of protective power against soul-eaters. Given the spread of Islam in the north of Africa, this might be a productive idea to pursue.

What seems to be involved in the forms of condensed symbols that people make is a kind of search for identification or certainty, a way to pinpoint the causes of a feeling of malaise or confusion. Rumor plays its part here in its guise of a "search for the truth," as Jean-Noël Kapferer (1990) suggested (see Chapter 2). In their introduction to the volume in which Auslander's and Schmoll's chapters appear, Jean and John Comaroff argue that what contemporary rituals such as witch-finding illustrate is "less about giving voice to shared values than about opening fields of argument" (1993: xxiii). If this is so, we perhaps should nevertheless note that contemporary rituals and ideas represent a search for closure on, and solutions to, the pressingly fragmented problems of existence that people experience. Expressing social complexities in terms of body imagery is a way of trying to cope with those complexities and to develop some defenses against them. As the Comaroffs themselves note, bodies are thus made to speak powerfully about social problems and ultimate values. Indeed, we should not regard contemporary witchcraft notions as simply metaphors or ways of referring to social processes. Since they are grounded in the body and the emotions, they directly recognize that it is people's bodily energies and their mental faculties that are used up or "consumed" in the stresses of life. The Comaroffs also point out that it is not by chance that ideas of witchcraft are quite often attached to women, since women sometimes gain more economic freedom in circumstances of change. Here, however, we meet again the bifurcated character of witchcraft suspicions. Some are directed against persons newly empowered, often those of a younger generation. But suspicions are often also aimed at older persons, who may appear to be jealous of or threatened by the activities of the young. Witches, both female and male, thus "are modernity's prototypical malcontents," and they "embody all the contradictions of the experience of modernity itself" (p. xxix). Since accusations of witchcraft represent projections of aggression, we would have also to say that the accusers of putative witches share in the "malcontent" to which the Comaroffs refer.

Witchcraft and Modernity in Cameroon

The connections between modernity and witchcraft have been pursued in depth by Peter Geschiere (1997). Geschiere's work focuses on southern and western Cameroon in Africa. He traces two contradictory themes: the idea that people accumulate power and wealth through witchcraft, and the notion that the fear of witchcraft levels inequalities between people by motivating people to share their resources. In the first idea, the implication is that witchcraft powers increase inequality; in the second, it is that fear of such powers that acts to decrease inequality. Of course, these two implications can perfectly well be seen as counterbalancing forms of interpretation held by people.

Significantly, Geschiere stresses that the contexts in which such contemporary notions flourish are ones in which secrecy is prevalent. Powerful politicians tend to keep their activities and deliberations secret, reinforcing the popular impression that they have magical or witchcraft powers. Newspapers and radio programs contribute to such impressions by reporting spectacular stories about witchcraft among the elite (Geschiere 1997: 2). The media draw on urban rumors or legends as their sources and multiply their circulation. Modern technological items are often cited as intertwined with witchcraft ideas, for example, in references to a witch's x-ray eyes or claims that people are forced as zombies to "drive planes" at night. Geschiere reports the anecdote of a woman in which she declared to her Baptist church minister that she drove a plane at night, bringing in food to her own people, adding that "all planes are in the world of witchcraft and when the white man gets it from the black man he then interprets it into real life" (p. 3).

The basic idea here again shows a remarkable parallel with "cargo" notions in New Guinea, which involved a basic belief in the power of magic and a notion that the wealth possessed by outsiders originally came from the ancestors of the New Guineans themselves, thus reversing the relationship of superiority between outsiders and insiders.

Geschiere stresses the intensity with which rumors of this kind circulate and mutate, especially in the more wealthy urban sectors of society (p. 3). State authorities suspect villagers of subverting plans for development, thus reiterating the colonial notion that villagers' conservative customs stand in the way of modernization, but attributing agency and emotions of jealousy to the villagers rather than viewing them as passive resisters.

In one case when a deposed dictator in Cameroon was brought to trial, his sorcerer "openly threatened the judges with his occult powers" (p. 7). Geschiere comments that "as soon as a new political space is opened, it is overrun by rumors about the use of sorcery and witchcraft" (ibid.).

The basic concept of magical power involved here among the Maka people whom Geschiere studied is called *djambe*, which he translates as "occult force," noting that the Maka now gloss this in French as *sorcellerie*. *Djambe* is a generalized power that can be used both to benefit and to harm people, and it is exercised by the *nganga*, ritual specialists who act as healers, witch-finders, and also manipulators of witchcraft power, according to their reputation. *Nganga* are said to work on behalf of politicians, so that their intervention, even in democratic regimes, appears "to remove power from the people" (p. 9), thereby making people take witchcraft the more seriously. Michael Rowlands and Jean-Pierre Garnier (1988) drew attention in this context to the complex and ambivalent concomitants of witchcraft and power in the Cameroon state.

Geschiere brings out a number of general points. One is that ideas of witchcraft play an ambiguous or double role in society. Villagers see witchcraft as a tool used by elites to gain their own ends, while the elites see it "as a weapon of the weak against the state" (p. 10). Occult force can be seen as both reinforcing and undermining power. A second point Geschiere makes is that there is a connection between witchcraft and the kinship relations that hold within the household. Jealousy and aggression are held to exist not just between classes or political opponents but between members of the same household.

Among the Maka the *djambe* was sometimes said to be like a gray mouse living in a person's stomach or "a small ferocious beast with mean teeth" (p. 38). The possessor of such a *djambe* is said to have an insatiable drive to take part in nocturnal cannibalistic feasts with other witches and has to sacrifice his or her parents to the witches in doing so. The witch's double can also go out and attack others, but it too can be ambushed and killed unless aid is sought from a healer with greater powers. Witches who cannot or will not hand over their kin to be eaten have to sacrifice themselves instead to pay their cannibal debts. These dilemmas of witchcraft power, according to Geschiere, seem "to express the fundamental doubts of the Maka with respect to power as such" (p. 43). Power, in fact, appears to be seen as the product of battles between opposing occult forces. The Maka household itself can easily be understood as subject to various structural tensions. In one case Geschiere discusses tensions between the cowives of a man that led to suspicions that one of them had "handed over" another wife to the witches out of hatred and jealousy. When the accused wife herself became sick, this was at first seen as confirmation of her guilt, but when she died her brothers in turn accused the husband of being the one who had given his wives over to the witches, and they refused to give up her body to be buried in the husband's compound, provoking a brawl. Later the husband accused another woman who had come to live in his household. The incidence of sickness and death in households thus automatically generates accusations of witchcraft within it (p. 46). Anderson (2002) further stresses the importance of conflicts within kinship networks in Murambinda, Zimbabwe, as a source of accusations of witchcraft, pointing out the significance of mobility and translocal relations in weakening kin solidarities. Anderson's approach returns us to the earlier sociological analyses by writers such as Marwick (1965). Strikingly, Anderson links witchcraft accusations to the spread of AIDS and also quotes a Murambinda saying that ties witchcraft to gossip: "we bewitch each other, we gossip about each other, that makes us kill each other, that's why we are poor!" (2002: 425).

A system of this kind is relatively impervious to any falsification, as Evans-Pritchard (1976 [1937]) long ago observed. But it is not just a system for providing explanations of misfortune. It itself generates conflict between people or brings to a head conflicts that exist already. In their daily lives the Maka coexist with fears of witchcraft among their own kin, which makes it more likely that they would also project such ideas onto the broader political scene. With the village notables and elders, who hold their positions partly through kinship and partly through their own abilities, suspicions may develop against them that their *djambe* powers, which enable them to overcome opposition in debates, have become overdeveloped, causing them to kill others (p. 94). Society cannot function without the power of *djambe*, but this power can also lead to wrongdoing. Geschiere refers here to the "constant tension between an egalitarian ideology and highly inegalitarian practices" (p. 97).

In the case of the new educated Maka elites who are city-based, this tension is further exacerbated. These elites are liable to be accused of neglecting their own village kin, and they are expected to obtain benefits for their kin at home. The perceived sanction involved is witchcraft. When one politician became ill, villagers gossiped that witches had put a mixture of herbs and saliva on the pathway behind his house, and his own magic had not been strong enough to protect him against this. The reason his magic failed, they said, was that his own kin must have broken its powers, possibly his jealous cousins who had recently been refused access to a banquet the politician had sponsored. Geschiere notes that "it was almost impossible to deduce from the flows of rumors who the true instigators of the attack might have been" (p. 111). Several candidates' names were mentioned. So no actual accusations emerged.

The rumors worked, however, to sustain people's feelings against the politician and to reinforce the "leveling" effect of witchcraft ideas against the accumulation of wealth by political figures. *Djambe* thus becomes an element of popular political action. And on the other hand the rich are said to use their wealth to buy powerful magic to protect themselves, using their urban connections to do so. The rich themselves may contribute to such ideas, in order to make others less likely to attack them. Geschiere points out that in authoritarian states, villagers are largely shut out of politics, so they create rumors about events such as a fatal car accident that they declare to have been the result of the witchcraft of political rivals. In this way they effect a reentry into political processes (p. 123). Again, similar processes occur in Papua New Guinea today in which car accidents that result in deaths of politicians become the focus of accusations of sorcery that can result in major confrontations and disruptions of community life, erupting further into national politics. It is important to note that it is the rumors themselves, attached to other rumors regarding jealousies among people, which are responsible for causing such disruptions. The idiom of witchcraft provides the necessary driving force in people's minds to turn rumors into actions.

Speaking with Vampires

This is the title of Luise White's book on "rumor and history in colonial Africa" (White 2000). As we have seen, witchcraft ideas typically assert that the witch is a cannibal who consumes the life-force of victims, and accusations of witchcraft arise from incidents of sickness and death. Such accusations feed on a much wider spectrum of rumors and notions that circulate in urban and rural contexts. White's work concentrates on this world of rumor in colonial contexts of the kind that preceded the postcolonial politics discussed by Geschiere. In colonial times, rumors tended to fix on allegations that the European colonialists used indigenous minions to collect blood from Africans, which they then consumed to augment their own life-force. Europeans in this image were therefore seen as similar to vampires. The clusters of rumors that formed around this theme fall under the category of urban legends. A central feature in these legends is that firemen in Nairobi, who traveled in red trucks, were ordered by their superiors to catch victims and bring them to fire stations where they were suspended over pits and drained of their blood. This practice was called *mumiani*. In its emphasis on the terrifying image of draining blood from people as if they were carcasses of meat, the legend resembles the images of assault sorcery that we find in Australia and New Guinea (see Stewart and Strathern 1998a).

The idea that Europeans are cannibals also finds its parallels in New Guinea, along with the idea that they are not humans but spirits. White recognizes that these elements of the story form a "transnational genre" in Africa, and the elements take on particular local meanings (White 2000: 9). They also show transpositions from Europe to Africa. White cites a Swahili-French dictionary from Zanzibar published in 1941 in which *mumiani* is defined as a "mummy" (i.e., a body drained of blood) "and a medicine Africans believed was made from dried blood. Jews . . . were in charge of getting the blood from people" (p. 11). The term for "firemen" in Swahili is *wazimamoto*, but it was applied in Uganda before actual fire services were instituted and given to surveyors and health department personnel in charge of yellow fever control, and it carried the connotation of blood-extractor or vampire (p. 14). In an expansion of the rumor it was said that prostitutes dug pits in their toilets in which to trap customers and give them to the *wazimamoto*. Sometimes police stations were also said to have such pits, cleverly hidden (p. 17).

White recognizes that these rumors had their origins partly in witchcraft ideas and partly in other currents of historical transition, but she sees them as "a fairly obvious metaphor for state-sponsored extractions" (p. 18). This is probably true, but Geschiere's study shows us the parallel, contemporary significance of witchcraft beliefs that are also ways of talking about inequality and extraction, and not only ways of talking about events but also ways of influencing them. The studies by Niehaus, Auslander, and Schmoll all argue that the redeployment of witchcraft accusations and their intensification in modern times is a spin-off from the pressures of monetarization coupled with social dislocation of people. The contexts from colonial times that White describes are likely to have contained comparable elements, since she stresses that the *wazimamoto* were supposed to do their work primarily to get money. Informants said that the work was a kind of secret service, sponsored by the government and well paid (p. 29). In other words, it was associated with the impersonal, bureaucratic, and hierarchical forms of power of colonial times. Vampires were "seen to be internationalized, professionalized, supervised, and commodifying" (ibid.). The image of the vampire also "straddles the connection between medicine and violence" and between indigenous ideas of the supernatural and introduced kinds of scientific technology such as those dealing with public health and hospital procedures of taking blood donations (ibid.). Vampire rumors purported to unmask the true malevolent intent behind colonial public services. (We note there that White uses the term "vampire" broadly; neither Europeans nor their supposed minions were thought directly to suck blood or other bodily fluids, hence the emphasis on the professionalized image of the *wazimamoto*, as vampires in uniform.)

While the specific dynamics of vampire stories represent a special twist on witchcraft beliefs, the functions of rumor are the same in all of these cases. White points out, for example, that people "construct and repeat stories that carry the values and meanings that most forcibly get their points across" (p. 30). Stories help people understand incomprehensible events, such as the disappearance of people. Continuous talk makes a story "true." "Hearsay is a kind of fact when people believe it" (p. 34). Rumors therefore resolve the confusions that result from experience. People were puzzled by the institutions of police and firemen and interpreted these as a new kind of secret society in which blood-sucking practices were the focus of secrecy. Rumors of this kind were ambiguous sources of "news," we might say, following the usage of Shibutani (1966). They are, as White puts it, poised between an explanation and an assertion. Gossip and rumor "occupy the interstices of respectability" (p. 62), giving us particular access to local concerns. White also recognizes, following Gluckman's original formulation, that gossiping creates intimacy, as well as disclosing "the boundaries of attack and subversion" (p. 63). Here again we may compare gossip directly to assault sorcery. It is a form of assault on people's reputations just as sorcery attacks their bodies. A kind of verbal sorcery that accuses others of bodily sorcery is thus likely to carry a powerful charge.

White's book is replete with detailed examples. We take just a few points here. One point she makes (p. 81) is that the specific Europeans who were mentioned in rumors as vampires were ones who were actually quite close to Africans and knew aspects of African culture. This seems like an important observation, and one that modifies her argument regarding the "professionalization" of vampires and their removal from indigenous contexts of witchcraft. Europeans who were relatively close to Africans were in colonial times likely to have been looked at ambiguously and ambivalently by both their fellow-colonialists and Africans. Africans' perceptions of them might be compared to the reactions Papua New Guinea people had to plain-clothes police personnel. In an ingenious, if probably unintended twist, they interpreted the term "plain clothes" as "*pren-kros*" in the lingua franca Tok Pisin, the vocabulary of which is largely based on English. These police, they said, behaved as "friends" (*pren*) but underneath they were out to incriminate people: they were "cross" (*kros*). A profound distrust of apparently mediating categories of people is shown here.

As to why police and firemen were generally targeted by the rumors, the same considerations probably apply. Police and firemen might be interpreted as the friends or protectors of the people, but they could also be seen as enemies who infiltrated under a guise of goodwill. Symbolism and serendipity came into play. The red color of fire engines was reminiscent of blood. The police and fire departments were often the only ones that had vehicles and could carry blood donors to hospitals. The yellow fever departments had to use the fire brigade's vehicles. People feared the Europeans' vehicles and their ability to transport people away (p. 133). The police and firemen had to be ready for service at night, when witches are about, so this increased fear of them. Malaria control trucks in Tanganyika (Tanzania) in the 1950s were also said to carry people whose blood would be drained (an exaggerated version perhaps of the fact that blood samples were taken for identifying malaria parasites).

Cars themselves were said to have special straps (seat-belts?) that restrained victims and seats that could drain blood as people sat on them. Hospitals were said to sell corpses to criminals who filled them with gold and used them to smuggle it into the Congo: if challenged, the drivers said they were taking sick relatives for treatment across the border. Africans were said to be captured, turned into pigs, and canned as meat on Sabena aircraft. The use of curtains to veil the windows of vehicles and aircraft contributed to the ease with which such stories about the interior spaces of "extractive power" were constructed (pp. 128–36). Anthropologists were not immune from such rumors, and they clearly fell into the category of Europeans who were relatively close to Africans. White cites a story about John Middleton, who studied the Lugbara in Northern Uganda. He had a bright red van closed at the back, and people said he used to steal and eat babies, using their blood to touch up its paintwork. Middleton had a mechanic install rear windows so that people could look inside the vehicle, and the rumor was dispelled (p. 136).

Similar confused rumors surrounded missionaries, and these were sometimes fed by accusations among rival missionary groups themselves. White reports that the Watchtower people accused the Catholics of cannibalism. Fat priests and ones with long beards particularly came under suspicion (p. 182). The locale here was Northern Rhodesia and the Catholics were the French-speaking White Fathers, so named because of robes they wore. In one rumor they were said to mark their victims with the sign of the cross, causing them later to rush to a parked truck where they would be drained of their blood or turned into meat (p. 183). The message of the Eucharist was interpreted by some as a form of cannibalism; if Europeans ate their revered deity, there was certainly nothing to stop them from eating Africans (p. 190). Conflict after 1935 between Protestant churches and the Catholics probably produced or exacerbated rumors of this kind, and there was surely some carry-over from European history. White does not stress the idea that European missionaries, and Europeans generally, probably made a contribution to the gossip mills as well as being their object. But we may plausibly surmise that rumor was as much a political tool for the expatriates as for the indigenous people.

Blood was not the only focus of Africans' fears. They also feared that Europeans took people's internal organs to cure European diseases, and the illness of a European was accordingly enough to cause a panic (p. 195). It caused not only panic, we suggest, but also hostility against Europeans generally. While White sees the rumors as reflective of the perceived extractive activities of the colonialists, it seems evident that these stories were capable of being used as political tools by those who told them and could have played a part in generating anti-colonial movements. At the least, they clearly reveal hostility in addition to fear. The theme of organ stealing, however, relates to the globalized circulation of such stories that has caught the attention of anthropologists. The postcolonial world in Africa also continues to produce vampire rumors. Two newspaper reports from the *New York Times* detail a new wave of such suspicions in Malawi. Vampires are said to carry syringes and to draw blood from victims they have drugged with sleeping gas. Men patrol at night carrying axes and clubs to combat these marauders. Three priests and the governor of Blantyre were physically attacked after being accused of harboring vampires. And the rumors claim that the country's government colludes with vampires to obtain blood in return for food (*New York Times*, December 29, 2002, and January 14, 2003).

Organ-Stealing as a Globalized Witchcraft Theme

The idea that witches steal people's organs and use them for curative medicines is not new but a part of the traditional repertoire of notions about the powers of the body and powers over the body, in Africa and elsewhere. However, rumors about international traffic in stolen organs, as well as documented discussions of illicit trade in them and studies of organ donation in legal contexts have become a major arena of comment and debate.

Nancy Scheper-Hughes came across organ-stealing rumors in the shantytown Alto do Cruzeiro in Northeast Brazil (Scheper-Hughes

1996: 3). The people she worked with there told stories of American and Japanese agents driving around in large blue and yellow vans searching for stray youngsters in poor neighborhoods. The agents were said to snatch children, remove various organs such as heart, lungs, liver, kidney, and eyes, and then dump their bodies. The detail about the vans is highly reminiscent of the vampire stories from Africa reviewed above. Afraid of the stories, parents kept small children locked in at home while they themselves were out working. Scheper-Hughes refers to the work of White and Niehaus on Africa as a part of a globalized genre of such stories. In stories from Italy, for example, a black ambulance is featured as the kidnap vehicle. Scheper-Hughes links the stories to shadowy practices of international adoption and to actual traffic in organs from poor to rich countries. She suggests connections with rumors of Satanic child abuse in the United States and Britain (La Fontaine 1994, 1998) and with notions circulating in New Age circles in which the body is seen as vulnerable to threats from anarchy and assault ("terrorism" would be the contemporary term). And she mentions that the rumors constitute a genre of urban legends. But her specific interest is to show how these rumors relate to the lived, daily bodily experiences of people, in which they encounter hospitals, morgues, and cemetery sites for the poor. She found that poor people's bodies are "mishandled, disrespected, and abused in mundane medical encounters" (p. 5). The bodies of their dead are sometimes mixed up or lost and are claimed by the state if they died in hospital: hence the people fear hospitalization. They also fear that their organs will be cut out and used. Doctors "over-medicate the poor with useless or contra-indicated drugs . . . and perform unnecessary surgery and amputations for otherwise treatable conditions" (p. 6). Patients are left scarred and disabled. This treatment of the poor goes on while the wealthy indulge in the "most sophisticated forms of clinical medicine, body sculpting and plastic surgery" (ibid.). Only the rich can afford to buy body parts they need, and the poor fear that the organs removed from them go to the rich. The rumor thus exactly reproduces the form of cargo rumors in New

Guinea, witchcraft and technology rumors in Africa, and *mumiani* rumors in particular. In a zero-sum view of the world, the rich are pictured as gaining not only their wealth but their health, procured in body parts, from the poor. The poor in turn are pictured, as in classic Marxist theory, as having only their bodies as a resource: "labor power" transmuted into "body parts" in a latter-day medical update. (See also the further critical discussion in Scheper-Hughes 2000.)

Scheper-Hughes notes that poor Brazilians do sell their body parts, or offer to do so, in spite of denials by Brazilian transplant surgeons that such a covert trade exists (p. 7). One poor man suggested that if he could sell an eye or a kidney he could invest the money in the stock market and so never have to work again. The idea of a trade in "spare" body parts goes further along with the putative trade in "spare" children for international adoption.

Scheper-Hughes notes that abduction stories tend to occur in societies that have experienced dictatorship, military regimes, police states, and "dirty" internal wars in which people do regularly disappear. This is certainly a vital observation and ought to apply in principle to at least some of the contexts discussed by Luise White for colonial Africa. Certainly in postcolonial African contexts such scenarios have been frequent, including in the countries from which White drew her stories from colonial times, such as Uganda and the Congo. In Brazil itself, Scheper-Hughes asserts that paramilitary death squads have been known to operate in shantytowns, and in cities generally unwanted street children are murdered (p. 8). Rumors of abduction and the stealing of body parts thus serve to alert the poor to the "states of emergency" in which they live (p. 9). Their fears were probably increased by the Brazilian Senate's decision to establish a norm of "presumed consent" to organ donation. The step from such a presumption to killing someone in order to "harvest" their organs is not so great, as news reports of the harvesting of the organs of executed criminals in the People's Republic of China might suggest.

Scheper-Hughes's discussion of organ-stealing rumors makes significant points. First, she relates the rumors to actual conditions of life among the poor, in which bodies are maltreated in medical settings. Second, she remarks on the social class background to the rumors, in which the poor fear that the rich prey on them. And third, she notes that people's fears also rest on the ambiguity of rules and laws regarding organ donation at death generally, here extending her analysis to "developed" countries such as the United States. Her major perspective is one that is applicable across the board: witchcraft ideas and urban legends are not simply metaphors that express ideas of exploitation and trickery; rather, they grow out of people's bodily experiences in daily life – and in their regular encounters with death.

Occult Economies

The Comaroffs, who instituted the study of "modernity and its malcontents" in Africa with their 1993 edited book, have more recently returned to the wide range of themes we have been exploring here. They refer to the present as the Age of Futilitarianism (1999: 279) and speak of pyramid schemes that put the "con" in economics (p. 281), pointing to the trickeries and frustrations of "modernity" in which many become rich but more stay poor. They highlight the return of ideas of the Devil and senses of "an epidemic of mystical evil" (p. 282). And they bring together, in text and footnotes, a great many examples from around the world, suggesting that the underlying determination of these rests with "millennial capitalism," an era of volatile swings in fortunes that generates frustrations among the young and impels them to accuse and in some cases kill the old, whom they see as blocking their own advancement.

Their argument provides an interesting blend of description and explanation, including data on witch-finding and witch-killings of the kind that we have earlier quoted from Auslander's study among the Ngoni. Economic recessions and the difficulty of finding jobs help to explain the frustrations of young males in South Africa who express themselves violently at times. It is not so easy to understand why this violence should be directed against the old, especially older women, and why its idioms should include the cursing of old people's genitalia and claims that they kill people by lightning or keep zombie workers in drums (p. 289). Perhaps the youths feel threatened by the sense that their elders have powerful knowledge, gained by experience in life, but are unwilling to hand it over; while the elders may feel that youths are impatient and unwilling to listen respectfully. In any case, it is curious, if in some ways predictable, that aggression should be turned inward against community members, rather than outward to the less easily targeted forces of government and company interests that presumably do influence the economic scene. Perhaps this point also tells us that the economic influence of capitalism is not the only or determining factor at work. A historical context suffused by successive waves of dislocation, exploitation, and struggle, combined with a pervasive and malleable emphasis on the importance of magical power akin to the Maka concept of *djambe* as discussed by Geschiere, would seem to contain within itself the multiple seeds of violence that we find portrayed in witch-killings.

In her comment on the Comaroffs' lecture, Sally Falk Moore remarks that it is the epidemic of violence associated with the occult rather than the occult itself that calls for explanation (1999: 306). "Millennial capitalism" and economic distress may provide a general context, she notes, but not a particular explanation, and she asks for another look at history in this regard (cf. Larner 1981 on explanations for witch-hunts in Scotland). In their response the Comaroffs acknowledge the importance of history but also pose the question of why there are so many similarities among "occult economies" today.

We offer two comments here. One we have already remarked on. Violence is often born out of violent traditions in history. If there are similarities in witch beliefs and cargo thinking between, for example, New Guinea and parts of Africa, but the violence of witch-killings is greater in some areas than in others, we must attribute this to the overall violence of historical experience in those areas. South Africa provides an obvious case. Furthermore, in South Africa, as in so many other cases around the world, the AIDS crisis does objectively threaten reproductive powers, and it is quite possible that anxieties over this problem become deflected onto the senior generation and women in particular, who are the guardians of fertility. Second, the similarity of ideas and phenomena is perhaps simply explained by the speed with which information is captured and transmitted (cf. Comaroff and Comaroff 1999: 297, note 24). The concept of the "global village" is oversimplified, but it points to the fact that cultural images are available for mimetic appropriation on an extraordinarily rapid basis. The media have magnified the powers of rumor and gossip to the n th degree. In this way rumor can become not just a quest for "truth" but a method of fabricating it. Rumor also, like witchcraft itself, thus enters into the multiple worlds of modernity not only as a factor "contiguous" with social changes but also as "constitutive of modernity" itself (Moore and Sanders 2001a: 12).

Conclusion

In Table 3 we summarize aspects of rumor that are highlighted in some of the main studies we have looked at in this chapter. These materials lend themselves to some further reflections on the historical conditions under which notions of witchcraft flourish. The first is the point stressed for Africa in particular by the Comaroffs: that "modernity," far from eclipsing witchcraft notions, itself becomes a vehicle for them, a source of new and potent forms of imaginative nightmares in which electricity, battery acid, and other industrial substances and processes become the very stuff out of which nightmares are built. As a further commentary here, it is important to note that these nightmares are by no means limited to Africa or the Third World. A whole genre of vampire films designed for viewing by people in Europe and America taps into the same concerns

TABLE 3. The Significance of Rumor in Contemporary Witchcraft Contexts

Author	Focus of Study	Significance of Rumor
M. Auslander	Intergenerational suspicions	Spreading of gossip can lead to individual suspicions and these into support for witch-finding movements.
P. Geschiere	The ambiguity of magical power; witchcraft of the house; ambivalence toward politicians	Rumor provides a flow of information on people's wealth and conflicts between them. In contexts of sickness or death, these translate into witchcraft accusations.
L. White	Vampire notions in parts of Africa; traffic in blood and organs for "medicine"	Rumor occupies an interstitial place between colonial outsiders and indigenous Africans. It blends together fact and fantasy.
N. Scheper-Hughes	The global traffic in body parts and the life experiences of poor people	In authoritarian regimes, rumor and gossip reflect terrorist actions against the poor, alerting them to perceived dangers.

as are exhibited in African contexts today. In general, these phenomena force us to recognize the final demise of the myth that modernity is based on the "triumph of rationality" in human affairs. Witchcraft ideas are themselves rational if we view them as logics of explanation. At the same time they draw their power from fantasies of guilt and desire that arise from sources that could be labeled as "irrational." The debate about rationality is not very helpful in this context, and is something of a red herring when we try to understand how people's ideas translate into moral practice (see Lambek 1997, commenting on Comaroff 1997; also studies in Kapferer 2002, and for a long-term folkloric set of studies, see Davidson and Chaudhri 2001.).

In her paper reviewing studies of the modern occult in Africa and elsewhere as a form of moral commentary on the world, Jean Comaroff identifies the figure of the witch as one who embodies the contradictions to be found at the intersection of the global and the local (Comaroff 1997). This is a reformulation of the earlier "modernity and its malcontents" argument. It is worthwhile to note here that the same argument can equally be applied to earlier phases of "modern" history in Europe. In these too persons were accused who were seen as threatening the moral order of society, and the order itself had been breached by forces of religious and political change.

Contradictions of one kind or another are also not confined to societies undergoing putative historical processes of "modernity." Modernity is simply a term for people's experiences of change in which the present comes to appear sharply different from the past. Ambivalent attitudes toward the power and privileges of leaders appear in many societies in which a generalized force or magical capacity is seen as belonging to leaders, who may use it either to benefit or to harm others. Morality is a dimension separate from power. Such notions are well dramatized in Elenore Smith Bowen's classic rendition of Tiv themes (Bowen 1964, e.g., pp. 190–1). Tiv elders exhibited a classic combination of beneficent and malevolent mystical powers. Such ambiguity of power helps to explain how, in changed circumstances, leaders may be perceived as dangerous or evil. The kinds of circumstances that may be involved are well outlined by Taussig (1980), who shows how ideas of the Devil, production, nature, and the landscape were all altered by the Spanish conquest and the development of tin mines in Bolivia. Taussig notes that "the landscape of symbols came to include the Indians' experience of Spanish greed, mastery, and violence" (p. 182). This experience was also encapsulated in a changing picture of gender relations in which "the male god is often seen as the embodiment of alien forces," whereas the female is seen as nourishing and protecting (p. 209).

Lucy Mair (1969: 161–79) makes some insightful remarks about situations of change in Africa and elsewhere. She notes that Africans themselves may claim that with modern changes witchcraft is increasing "because the government will not let us punish it" (p. 161). She cautions that this may be rhetoric rather than supported by quantitative evidence, recalling that "when in 1559 Bishop Jewel preached before Elizabeth I [of England] and urged her to introduce stricter laws against witchcraft, he too said the evil was increasing" (p. 161). Still, the fact that people *think* witchcraft is increasing has its own effects in the search for new shrines and talismans and the growth of witch-hunts and the activities of itinerant witch-finding prophets (p. 164). Mair further points to the incorporation of Christian symbolism into witch-finding rituals. She cites the case of the John Maranke Apostles movement in Rhodesia in 1938. Officials of this church acted like diviners in identifying witches and also in detecting unconfessed sins in general. Before an annual communion event, worshipers had to enter an enclosure through gates guarded by officials acting as "prophets" in this way, and all whom these prophets denounced were taken to a further tribunal held by church elders (p. 178). We see here the blending of indigenous and Christian ideas that appears to occur universally in such contexts, as people struggle to make sense out of their past and present. Mair's empirical examples point to this patchy process of acculturation, as we may call it, without appealing to the concept of globalization or the spread of capitalism. Generalizing her discussion, we may suggest that many elements may feed into people's attempts to restructure their lives and to exercise moral judgments over themselves and others. The same process occurred in the post-Reformation witch-hunts in Scotland, as Larner (1981) has persuasively argued.

Jean Comaroff broaches another comparison that is in line with our insistence that rumor and gossip provide a link between classic witchcraft scenarios and their transformations in contemporary affairs. She sees parallels between concerns over witchcraft and those over child abuse as a modern theme. The fear that evil things are being done to children is one such link, and the basic idea that social reproduction is threatened is the underlying form of this fear. Michael Lambek has further drawn out the implications of this parallel, noting that the theme of abuse has to do with ideas about "the moral collapse of the world" (Lambek

1997: 22) – as witchcraft may do, and increasingly does, in contemporary Africa. At a broader level again Lambek sees the abuse theme as linked to that of memory, in its guise of uncovering the secret, hidden source of ongoing misfortune in a person's life (Antze and Lambek 1996). We have only to think of the challenge to the Catholic Church caused by the allegations of abuse of children and young adults by priests that have emerged in recent years to understand the force of this point. Uncovering the source of evil is like exposing the witch, with the added point that evil, as sometimes happens, is identified at the heart of what is supposed to be sacred and good, thus threatening the very basis of order and requiring a thorough purgation of the perceived evil for the reestablishment of the cosmos.

Returning to our theme of rumor and gossip here, it is quite evident that accusations of Satanic abuse against child-minders reflect both people's anxieties about handing over their small children to others to look after them and their possible guilt about doing so, generated from their choice to pursue paid jobs outside the family setting rather than the job of child caring. It is also evident that this anxiety and guilt is mediated by participating in gossip networks and feeds on incoming rumors. Leaders in these networks may accuse others of abuse as a form of witchcraft, only to be exposed and driven out as witches if their accusations are proved baseless. Alternatively, the stigma of an accusation may persist even if an accused person is found innocent in law. The powerful need to externalize and attach blame is shown in all these examples. Rumor and gossip are the prime ways in which this is achieved.

FOUR

∽

India

From Crime to Insurgency

A switch from Africa to India brings us into a different world of colonialism, the British Raj in the nineteenth century, a world dominated by relations between landlords and peasants and marked by fears of peasant insurgents. In this regard it is a colonial world that bears direct comparison with Britain's presence in Ireland during the same period, marked by the same sorts of problems of excessive rent and evictions, followed by uprisings. Guha, in his classic study of peasant movements in India (1994 [1983]), points out that British colonial historiography at this time was much concerned with the phenomenon of insurgency and attempted to study it and subsume it under a kind of "science of colonialism." Guha is at pains to point out some of the deficiencies of that "science," noting that it tended to underestimate the forms of political and historical consciousness that these movements exhibited (cf. Bayly 1996: 97–141 and 315).

Common sufferings such as the increase in peasant indebtedness to landlords produced a common set of attitudes among the peasants and led them to seek ways to alleviate their situation. In addition, new landlords bought up impoverished estates at auctions and spread their influence as moneylenders to their own tenants, relying on the support of the colonial administration to enforce their coercive practices. Insurgency was the only possible remedy for any grievance, since the power of the state supported the landlords so directly, Guha argues (1994 [1983]: 8). However, the peasants, using their clan and caste-based councils, would hold extensive meetings, followed by deputations, petitions, and peaceful demonstrations, before entering into the dangerous business of insurrection (p. 9). When movements emerged, they were certainly not spontaneous but were the outcome of drawn-out historical processes in which the people's consciousness was painfully shaped. In some cases rebels adopted the nomenclature of the state apparatus for their own activities, designating themselves as an army with law-enforcing and civilian personnel. In this way they challenged the dominance of their rulers by threatening to overthrow them and set up their own state: another instance of what we have called mimetic appropriation. This peasant consciousness of resistance, Guha says, ran historically parallel with the colonial power's own consciousness of dominance (p. 11) and is mirrored within the reports by elite sources themselves.

The Raj also used the preexisting traditions of feudal dominance in India to pursue its own aims, encouraging attitudes of devotion to superiors based on the idea of self-identification with them. Negation of such a form of consciousness was therefore the first step of insurgency, marked by uprisings against selected members of the dominant class and subsequently by more general attacks on all entities and installations connected with the colonial power (p. 25). In a society well used to hierarchy, the idea of inverting hierarchy, of turning the world upside down, also easily caught on, going far beyond the ritually licensed temporary inversions built into hierarchical systems themselves (p. 30). Outside such controlled ritual inversion, breaking the codes of deference represented a significant mark of rebellion, including the rejection of respectful language (p. 49) and respectful postures encoded in the body (p. 56) and in clothing (p. 63).

In both the precolonial and the colonial regimes, attempts to flout the social order and to commit acts of violence against it were labeled as crimes and severely punished. Guha distinguishes here between crimes and insurgency, however, on grounds that they derive from "two very different codes of violence" (p. 79). Individual acts of defiance he calls "crime," public ones "insurgency." He recognizes that these can shade into each other. And he points out that colonial authorities, used to labeling oppositional actions as crime, tended to delude themselves into thinking that the spread of such actions was the result of secret conspiracies, missing the development of popular movements (p. 80). Hence "conspiracy theories figure prominently in the official response to many Indian peasant uprisings" (ibid.). The conspirators were also largely seen as local elites who were said to manipulate the "passive" masses. Waves of crime did precede uprisings, and must have both reflected and contributed to changes in people's attitudes to authority. Crimes were committed by gangs, called *dacoits* in the literature, made into outlaws through debt and inability to pay their creditors. Interestingly, in one example Guha gives, it was the expenses of funeral rituals that finally bankrupted a peasant and drove him to abandon his home. We receive a glimpse here into relations of articulation between the local kin-based social structures and the wider relations of dependency (see Carrier 1992).

Given these circumstances, the peasants would tend to see their rebellious actions not as "crime" at all but as justified resistance (p. 89), reversing the categorizations imposed by the authorities and conducing toward more general conflict. Class war recodes "crimes" as "political action" (just as, we may note, religious fundamentalist concepts may do in today's context of debates about "terrorism"). Robbers therefore turned into rebels (p. 95). Officials' failure to recognize this transformation quickly enough led them to underestimate the levels of popular support involved. Guha characterizes the shift from crime to insurgency as a shift from secretive, individualistic appropriation and partial modalities to public, collective, destructive, and total forms of action (p. 109). Analogous shifts can be seen in ways of dealing with putative witches in Africa, although the parallel is suggestive, not exact. Guha is attentive in this context to the symbolism of the actions of wrecking, burning, looting, and eating. They all signify the destruction of an order of society, not just a specific piece of property. The consumption of large quantities of plundered food, including slaughtered pigs, is not carried out simply to satisfy hunger, but as a kind of celebratory feasting and deliberate wasting of resources. Eating in this case is a political act (p. 148), just as, more obviously, killings are. Guha suggests that killings were not as frequent as they might have been, because of continuing attitudes of respect to the human body. (Curiously, he calls this feature a mark of a consciousness that was not liberated, p. 164.)

With the development of these movements, the desire to emulate the actions of others led to the emergence of new forms of solidarity, extending from one community to another (p. 167) and operating along lines of class, ethnicity, or religion. The ethic of solidarity was underpinned by the imperative to use force and to punish "traitors," including those who did not actively assist the cause (p. 201), but in particular those who actively collaborated with the colonial power (p. 215). "No sin to kill them" was the justification (ibid.). Guha sees these phenomena as part of the overall emergence of class consciousness. Perhaps it is also important to keep in mind their historical specificity and their connections with indigenous forms of morality, both of which Guha himself richly describes.

The Place of Rumor

Officials attempting to understand insurgency tended to label its spread as a form of "contagion" (p. 220), whereas from the peasants' own viewpoint, Guha says, it was seen as a collective enterprise, energized by emulation and solidarity. The same model of contagion was used in England itself to describe the rural laborers' riots of 1830. Social order was seen as health, its disruption as a disease almost passively caught by the hitherto loyal peasantry. The colonial authorities failed to understand how various grievances were all *encapsulated* into concerted movements (p. 224). The authorities referred to this process as one of "volcanic outbursts" or as "spreading like wild fire," and made the simultaneity of these events into "a convenient peg on which to hang a conspiracy theory" (p. 225). Such a theory individualizes a collective circumstance that arises simply out of the situation of colonial domination itself: out of common subjection, Guha argues (ibid.).

But not simply common subjection. Preliterate forms of transmission of views were important, and this is where rumor as "news" enters. British colonial authorities were also mystified by the transmission of "occult symbols" from village to village. Dances, songs, music, and decorations all played their part in mobilizing people. Guha picks out the drum, the flute, and the horn as instruments used to summon people to war. It should be pointed out here that the sound of instruments could probably carry further than the sound of human voices. Guha notes, too, that the translation of nonverbal sound to verbal meanings could be carried out only by the Indians themselves or those who understood this coding. This could increase the intimidating effect of hearing the instruments played. The British soldiers did seize the Indians' drums along with their weapons whenever they were able to do so (p. 233).

Insurgents used also the "messenger bough," a tree branch previously used to summon men to communal hunts (p. 234), and *telsindur*, a mixture of oil and vermilion traditionally employed to seek blessings from the gods, cups of which were sent round to summon people to join in the fighting.

Leaders of the insurgency movements might make general statements about the need to change the order of the world that were then transmitted widely by word of mouth and were often given a religious aura and were attributed to those who spoke them. Rumor, however, also carried important messages, but not ones attributed to any "author." Guha points here to the universal significance of rumor as a vehicle of insurgency in preliterate societies (p. 251). He mentions that Roman emperors employed *delatores* (informants) to collect and report rumors, and that centralized governments everywhere tend to employ spies who pick up news and pass it back to them. To support his view, Guha mentions Allport and Postman's statement that no riot happens without rumors to intensify it (p. 252, quoting Allport and Postman 1947: 159). He also notes the various effects of rumors: people fleeing from villages, people burying their wealth, even in areas not affected at all, owing to the panic caused by the news of insurrections and exaggerated stories about the violence that accompanied these events.

The Indian Mutiny

A prime case of the power of rumor is found in the Indian Mutiny of 1857, a movement that began with a revolt of Indian soldiers stationed at Meerut in Uttar Pradesh, north of Delhi. The revolt started on May 10, 1857. Its immediate cause was the issue of new cartridges for breech-loading Enfield rifles. These cartridges had to be bitten off before insertion and their manufacturers had supplied a fat of mixed beef and pork with which to grease them, which was offensive to both Hindus and Muslims among the Indian troops on religious grounds. Apparently, the error was corrected quickly enough, but this was not recognized. Up to this time the British had actually encouraged the recognition of caste-based rules regarding food consumption. The situation was apparently exacerbated by the behavior of the British colonial officer in charge at Meerut, who distributed the new cartridges to ninety men and ordered them to use them, at which all but five refused. The colonel then had the resisters placed in irons, after a semblance of trial by their peers. The next day the mutiny broke out and the mutineers marched on Delhi, catching the British by surprise. The mutiny turned into a much larger popular revolt that swept across northern India until it was put down by military action (Encylopaedia Britannica 1990 s.v. India p. 91; Kulke and Rothermund 1990: 254).

Around the original incident a number of rumors gathered. One was that not only were the new cartridges polluted, but soldiers were being issued wheat flour polluted by bone meal; another that the cartridges were part of a conspiracy to force the soldiers to convert to Christianity; another that a deliverer was about to come who would end British rule. All these stories touched on deeply emotive issues and merged into "one gigantic rumor" (Guha, p. 255). As a result the Indian troops merged with the peasants in a massive attempt to restore the rule of the old emperor or Mughal, who could potentially unite Muslims and Hindus. Meanwhile, the British army commander, Sir James Outram, thought that the mutiny was a Muslim plot, designed to foment Hindu grievances. Both sides, it seemed, adhered to conspiracy theories and relied on rumors to support their views.

Guha is interested in this process largely from the point of view of the peasants (just as Luise White discusses African vampire stories mostly from the perspective of the Africans). He writes: "It is precisely in this role of the trigger and mobilizer that rumour becomes a necessary instrument of rebel transmission" (p. 256). Word-of-mouth transmission stimulates people to continue the chain of communication, which is seen as privileged and immediate, outside the circuits of official communication. Rumor bonds people together around its message and helps to produce solidarity (p. 257). This in turn helps to explain the speed with which rumor can pass from place to place. Rumor also often begins in urban concourses such as markets and is then transmitted radially through surrounding villages, spreading out rapidly. The British colonial power would often speak of it as "the lies of the bazaar," misjudging its effectiveness and the sense of its authenticity generated out of its origins in economic exchanges between people. The authorities recognized the political significance of rumor but denigrated it as a corrupt form of news. Presumably, they thought that if it were exposed as "untrue," it would lose its dangerous quality. If so, they surely miscalculated, since rumor produces its own truth through repetition.

As we have seen in Chapter 2, Shibutani (1966) argues that rumor is a kind of improvised news in which people try to reach a consensus about information, and Jean-Noël Kapferer (1990) wrote of it as a search for the truth. These two perspectives highlight the tentative character of rumor that may hold in many circumstances. In the context of insurrections such as Guha discusses, this tentative element disappears. Instead, rumor is to be seen as political or military intelligence and as a tool of mobilization of the masses, not from any command center but diffusely, among themselves. Guha attempts to make a distinction between rumor and news, pointing out that news comes from an identified source that makes it possible to check on its veracity, whereas rumor belongs equally to all and at the same time to no one: the "Orly" characteristic, as we called it in Chapter 2, borrowing from the colonial context of Papua New Guinea. But printed news may itself be derived from rumor and is sometimes attributed to unnamed but "reliable" sources. At a deeper level of analysis Guha highlights *ambiguity* as essential to the power of rumor. People may not understand it well, but they give their own meanings to it. The sense of unease that it produces in turn inclines people to action. The mere fact of mental disturbances predisposes to political disturbance. In Papua New Guinea this kind of thinking occurred notably with millennial rumors around the year 2000. In the Mount Hagen area the vaguest form of rumor was, in the local language, *ukl ti etimba*, "an event will happen," where the word *ukl* has a variety of meanings that include the originary or creative actions that brought each major group into being according to mythology. In the Tok Pisin lingua franca this appeared as *wanpela senis bai ikamap*, "a change will occur." In the millennial context, people gave a Biblical coloring to these vague statements, which thus mobilized mass church services and intense confusion and anticipation (see Stewart and Strathern 2000a).

Rumor can therefore absorb and accommodate many meanings, because of its anonymity and transitivity from person to person. This also makes it a potent vehicle for political purposes, by broadening its appeal (p. 262). Guha refers again to the rumors of pollution that triggered the revolt of the sepoys (Indian soldiers in the British Army) in 1857. The various stories all amounted to a single allegation, that the British were deliberately polluting the bodies of the Indians. One version was that, on orders from the East India Company and the Queen, ground bones had been mixed with the flour and salt sold in the bazaars, thereby constituting a pollution of the very arena that the British themselves saw as the carrier of "polluting talk" but that the local people saw as their source of "truth." Another was that vegetable fat used for cookies had also been polluted with animal fat; that bones had been burnt with sugar; and that bone-dust flour and the flesh of cows and pigs had been thrown into wells. The rumor about the cartridges to be used by soldiers was only a part of the picture, which imagined a general defilement of the population, capped by the assertion that the great English lords had ordered that everyone would now be forced to eat English bread, which was seen as containing the polluting ingredients of flour, salt, sugar, fat, and water (p. 263).

The logic of this encompassing rumor might well appear to derive from some definite plan, constructed to give the appearance of a massive British conspiracy. The British did in fact interpret it as such. A rumor about a colonial conspiracy was seen as an anti-colonial conspiracy designed to unite the masses. Conspiracy theory clashed with conspiracy theory, centering on a model of society based on the idea of ritual purity and pollution. The British were hoisted on the petard of their own model of the caste-based society that they had used to extend their rule and establish themselves as like a new, superior caste in the society at large, while simultaneously using the model to construct the Indians as the Other. No actual planning was needed to produce the rumor cluster. It was a product of what Pierre Bourdieu called the "habitus," the "intentionless invention of regulated improvisation" (Bourdieu 1977: 265). As Bourdieu stressed, the body is a prime site for the inculcation and expression of habitus, an intimate center of culture. Hence a discourse about the integrity of the body and its vulnerability to outside pollution would have the power to appeal to many different people and to unite them. It could also emerge from the similarities in basic ideas of people, across the Muslim-Hindu divide. Guha's formulation of these points fits with Bourdieu's theory of the habitus, although he does not refer to Bourdieu's work.

Guha points out further how stories of the advent of a healer, prophet, or leader regarded as embodying divine qualities could provoke pilgrimages that issued in political action (p. 267). Political action was sacralized in this way, having been precipitated by rumors. The religious tinge of such rumors has to be seen as oppositional, directed against the encroachment of Christianity. Missionaries were an important part of the colonial project, and rumors arose from time to time that Christianity was about to be imposed as a state religion. These rumors recurred from one historical period to another. The pollution rumor gained currency at the time of a mutiny in Vellore in 1807, to be repeated in 1857, and it went with a statement that the government had ordered churches to be built in every town and village. In parts of the North-Western provinces (later Pakistan) in 1857 a rumor spread that all uncircumcised Muslim infants were to be baptized. In the resulting panic hundreds of children were rushed through the circumcision rite to save them from the religious power of the missionaries. The rumor was in the literal sense inaccurate, but its power lay in its quite accurate perception of the alliance between mission and government, leading to an indigenous form of conspiracy theory. The fear of losing one's freedom that lay behind these rumors was firmly grounded in the preexisting losses of freedom that had already taken place. Guha, following Marxist categories of interpretation, calls this "false consciousness"; yet he also, somewhat in contradiction with this position, recognizes its fundamental basis in historical facts and what Bourdieu would call their precipitation in "objective structures" of constraint.

Guha gives some further examples of what he calls chiliastic rumors and "sacerdotal mediation" of change by prophet figures and rumors of their miraculous birth and powers. In one such story a fort was magically created by rubbing grasses together and there a virgin gave birth to a son who grew up immediately and became a prophetic deliverer for his people (p. 269). The idea of the prophet was seized on here, as elsewhere, as a means of legitimizing insurgency by claiming it had the backing of higher powers (p. 271). In some versions rebels claimed that the British Crown itself supported their activities. Guha dubs this also false consciousness, yet we can see that it might be an effective way of rallying support. And confusion could have arisen because prior to 1857 the East India Company had ruled as proxy for the Crown, a position that was removed from the company after the mutiny. Statements attributed to the quasidivinized prophets of these movements were, unlike ordinary rumors, "textualized," that is, preserved in exact form and repeated as a form of revealed truth. Guha notes that such prophecies also circulated widely in premodern times in Europe, referring to the well-known work of Keith Thomas (1973), the same period of time in which witchcraft trials were prevalent, we may note. While Guha suggests again that adherence to prophets is a form of self-mystification or false consciousness, we may repeat the countersuggestion that all such adherences served to intensify the conscious will and determination of people.

Shahid Amin has provided a detailed study of rumors that developed in Eastern Uttar Pradesh in 1921–2 within Gorakhpur District and contributed to the emergence of Mahatma Gandhi as a charismatic, putatively miracle-working figure. Amin deals with a set of rumors that followed a visit Gandhi made to the area on February 8, 1921, and which were largely reported in the local press. These rumors attributed enormous powers to Gandhi, for example that he had been given an overriding mandate to address all grievances and that "the British would be cleared out of the District within a few months" (Amin 1984: 6). Gandhi was credited with "occult powers" (p. 25), including the ability to drive out the British and to produce miracles of nature such as a sudden abundance of sweets or a magical growth of crops (p. 27). These stories credited Gandhi with "thaumaturgic powers" resulting from his "signs of saintliness" (p. 29).

Clearly, such data align themselves well with Guha's observations on prophets as well as with cross-cultural studies of prophets in general.

Christopher Bayly (1996: 321) has provided some further observations on "the issue of the communication of dissent and anti-British ideas among the Indian population." He agrees that religious teachers actively spread the rebel cause and Muslim fighters further spread their messages. For example, Wahhabi Muslims "along with some older Sufi networks were used by rebels to try to coordinate different sectors of the resistance" (p. 321). But, Bayly argues, the British subsequently exaggerated the idea of a generalized conspiracy. Nevertheless, "the whole panoply of indigenous written communication . . . were employed to spread the message of revolt" (p. 323) and there were struggles to control the postal system and newspaper presses. Curiously, Bayly does not seem to make use of Guha's work here. Implicitly, his observations amount to a criticism of Guha, but his own preference for dealing with "modern" acts of resistance as opposed to "traditional" media of communication makes it difficult to assess the interplay between "rumors" and news passed in literate form. The distinction is moot in any case, since "news" may simply be a printed form of rumor, and rumors may be sparked by a particular reading of news (as Amin 1984 pointed out).

Comparisons

Throughout his text Guha intersperses with his discursive references to insurrections in colonial India a set of running comparisons with Europe and in particular England, often citing the laborers' uprising of 1830. His final excursion into the realm of chiliastic prophecy and his insistence on the mobilizing power of rumor tied to prophecy enables us to bring together a pair of parallels from New Guinea and Africa. The parallel with cargo movements and beliefs in New Guinea is quite plain, since prophets or charismatic leaders almost invariably played significant roles in these movements, and, equally, there were always inchoate rumors about impending events or signs of these that fed into the senses of excitement and anticipation that drew people into the movements. Such ideas, rather than taking away people's agency, returned it to them, at least in part. Interestingly, Guha himself quotes from one such study by Kenelm Burridge (1960) on the Tangu people of Madang Province in Papua New Guinea. His comparison is in a minor but significant key. He points out how Australian colonial patrol officers were suspicious of the beating of slit-gongs that tended to precede their arrival in villages, fearing that these instruments might be used to convey subversive messages (Guha, p. 231). The gongs or drums were taken to refer to a world of hidden or occult forces that might turn into a focus of resistance to colonial power. Indeed, a major fear that the Australian administration had in New Guinea was that movements they labeled as "cargo cults" might be vehicles of political opposition, a notion that would actually be reinforced by Peter Worsley's Marxist-inspired analysis of these movements as forerunners of nationalism with the potential to unite hitherto divided groups against the colonial power (Worsley 1957; see also Kaplan 1995 on Fiji). In these cargo movements rumor functioned in exactly the same way as Guha portrays for nineteenth-century peasant insurrections in India.

The parallel with witch-finding movements is clear. Anthropologists such as Sally Falk Moore, whom we have cited earlier, have wondered how it is that these movements can become lethal, resulting in the mass execution of suspected witches. The answer must surely depend on the kind of political mobilization that lies behind the movements, a mobilization that is often cut from the whole cloth of rumor itself and fitted as a kind of robe on the figure of a particular leader. Guha's account makes it clear how the act of sharing information itself constituted a mode of mobilization. With movements against witches also what begins as private gossip may swell into public rumor and political action over time. Guha's analysis of the functions of rumor in peasant insurrections therefore helps us to understand better the witch-finding movements we have discussed in Chapter 3.

The imputation of conspiracy is another telling theme for comparison making. We have seen how prone both the British and the Indians were to impute conspiracies to each other. Such claims are always a mark of fundamental distrust, and they make any achievement of trust harder. They also imply that everyone on the other side is actively against one's own and will try to hide the truth. This feature is found in many contexts where trust is minimal and factions have a vested interest in preventing its formation.

Brown and Theodossopoulos (2000) instance Greek conspiracy theories that emerged at the time of the struggle in Kosovo. Paradoxically, in these theories it was asserted that there was actually an alliance of sorts between the then Yugoslavian President Slobodan Milosevic and the Americans. Brown and Theodossopoulos explain carefully how the ambivalent and ambiguous position of the Greeks in relation to the conflict, which set their fellow-members of the European Union against their historical allies and friends the Serbians, on behalf of Albanians, seen as "ethnic others," led them to develop idiosyncratic and derogatory interpretations of the war, largely directed against the Americans and the British. In all of this the link between Greece and Serbia in terms of common adherence to Eastern Orthodox Christianity played a large part. The rumor of a possible collusion between Milosevic and the American government emerged only after the war had ended. At this point some people began to suggest that perhaps Milosevic was a secret agent of the Americans, helping them to destroy his country so that they could rebuild it. When asked further about this, they would say that it was hard to know about hidden motivations – which they had nevertheless freely speculated about. This is a typical characteristic of rumor as propagated from the sidelines of events.

Brown and Theodossopoulos see these indigenous Greek commentators or local pundits as stepping into the fray, not with weapons but with words, and employing cognitive bricolage to arrive at their analyses. They speak of how people combine "fragments of scurrilous rumor and speculation with economic and political analysis" (p. 6). They rightly go on to point out that although this Greek interpretation of the war might look implausible from an American or British viewpoint, people regularly make up their own explanatory stories of this kind, injecting their own agency into the affairs of the world, at least in narratives. Interpretations that impute conspiracy are common among "central powers" and "peripheral peoples" alike. "The notion that the relationship between events in the world and human agency is complex and not transparent seems to us rather more plausible than any alternative" (ibid.).

Greek guesswork is similar to how ethnographers interpret cultures, on the basis of fragmentary information, by importing certain interpretive assumptions into the discussion These narratives about leaders and their motives mixed their personal affairs with the politics of abstract interest and were rooted in "suspicion towards the role played by the Western Great Powers in modern Greek history" (p. 7). Anxiety, confusion, and uncertainty breed their own rumors and efforts to gain interpretive insight into events. And in Greece there are strong traditions of popular discussion of politics. David Sutton, in his study of Kalymnos, points out that "politics and politicians form a storehouse of references for conversations in the present" and that in making "often joking references to macro-politics, Kalymnians tie their local experience to national events" (1998: 123). In doing so, they make liberal use of analogies and metaphors, as people everywhere do.

People universally employ their own fixed interpretive frameworks when they improvise responses to events, and both the frameworks and the improvisations show in the rumors that are generated. The combination of framework plus creativity may often lead to ideas that appear intrinsically implausible or unlikely to others who operate on different assumptions. This disjunction of views reflects the measure of divergence of frameworks, often ones that carry political meanings and consequences. The point here can be applied to an "intrinsically unlikely" rumor that was among the many that emerged after the September 11, 2001, terrorist attack on and destruction of the World Trade Center in New York. This rumor declared that 4,000 Jewish people stayed away from work on that day, implying that the attack itself was caused not by an "Islamic" but by a "Jewish" conspiracy.

Like the Kosovo rumor, this one dramatically turns putative realities upside down in order to deflect blame and reallocate it. It also intransigently redraws the lines of hostility between Israelis and Palestinians. The rumor traveled to Afghanistan, where in the war against the Taliban and the Al-Qaeda movement that followed after the attribution of the September 11 attack to Osama bin Laden and his organization, American Special Forces, meeting potential allies there, were sharply told that "everyone knows that 4,000 Jews did not report for work that day." The sinuous and itinerant powers of rumor, tightly aligned with pathways of global hostilities, are demonstrated poignantly in this example.

Conclusion

This chapter has concentrated on delineating the complex and powerful ways in which rumors contributed to the rise of insurgency movements in colonial India. The materials surely illustrate well the picture of the power of rumor envisaged by the Roman poet Virgil as quoted in Chapter 2. Our purpose has been to link this power to its social context, defined by unequal power and a prevalent distrust and mutual fear between the colonizing British and the Indian population. The basic rumor behind the uprising in 1857 further centered on an idea of pollution, which here exactly corresponds to an imputation of sorcery, that is, that poisonous substances had been introduced into the supplies of food and water, threatening life itself. Such a rumor is able to generate strong reactions and to mobilize people swiftly. It thus functioned in the same way as rumors do in generating witch-hunts. We see in Guha's account of peasant insurgency important parallels with the mobilization of people in European and African witch-hunts.

Rumors and gossip feed into dramatic forms of political action or else into complex structures of legal institutions that transform them into instruments of power. Here is the relevance of our juxtaposition of the roles of rumor and gossip in witch-finding movements and in the history of insurgency in colonial India. The common analytical feature involved in both cases is the enormous potential power of rumor itself, an idea strikingly exemplified in Virgil's imagery.

FIVE

∽

New Guinea

The materials from Africa and India fit well, in somewhat different ways, into the historical contexts found in Papua New Guinea. One common feature, of course, is the encompassing influence of colonial powers, although the trajectories of colonialism differ considerably in different places, as many authors have shown (e.g., Thomas 1994). The imposition of new forms of hierarchy, the exploitative use of labor, the extraction of resources, and the creation of wide ranges of new desires without the capacity to realize them are all elements widely shared between colonial contexts, and these have fed into both the earlier patterns of insurgency dealt with by Guha and the latter-day forms of apocalypticism and witch-finding discussed by the Comaroffs. In all of these contexts the general conditions set out by Guha (1994 [1983]: 256–73; see Chapter 4) for the influence of rumor in social processes apply well: low levels of literacy and a dependence on oral transmission, the creation of solidarity through the motivated passing of information, the anonymous character of information passed by word of mouth, and the quality of ambiguity, uncertainty, and portentousness that emerges from these circumstances of its production.

The colonial contexts with which we are familiar from our Papua New Guinea fieldwork and which are replicated widely elsewhere include a number of characteristic event sequences in which rumors played a major role. These include, for instance, epidemics and rumors of epidemics, cargo cults and millennial rumors, and witchcraft suspicions and accusations.

Rumors of Cannibalism and Witchcraft in Papua New Guinea

In the Mount Hagen area (Western Highlands Province) of Papua New Guinea in 1977–8 cannibal witches (*kum koimb wamb*) were said to be spreading the desire to eat people by placing pieces of human flesh at the heads of streams. Those who drank the water and felt it to be "sweet" (*tingen*) would, it was said, become cannibals. At this point in time, shortly after the beginning of independence for the country, which took place in 1975, it was thought that both men and women were turning into cannibals, through the actions of these witches who were contaminating water sources. The fat (*kopong*) from the human flesh was thought to give a sweet taste to the drinking water, which then had the power to transform the drinker into someone who longed to taste human substance. People were enjoined to be very careful about drinking water in their own clan areas and never to drink water outside their own clan areas to avoid being turned into cannibals (Stewart and Strathern 1999a; Strathern 1982).

These fears were tied in with notions of greed and excessive consumption that were connected with the advent of a newly emerging cash economy based on the cultivation of coffee, along with other social changes (see Goldman 1999; Strathern 1982, 1988; Strathern and Stewart 2000a, 2000b). The connection between excessive consumption and cannibalism in the Hagen area had earlier, in the 1960s, been represented by ideas that persons who had greedily consumed pork at a feast and then went to slake their thirst at a stream gave an opportunity to little *kum* (witch) stones in the water to jump into their throats and lodge there. The personification of the agency of these stones was expressed in different ways; one image was of *namb* and *pilamb* ("let me eat, let me experience"). The stones were thought to possess the person thereafter by scraping at their host's throat and making them insatiable for pork.

The rumor about pieces of human flesh hidden at the headwaters of streams has its own etiological history. Ideas about *kum* have changed somewhat over time. *Kum* in its earlier set of meanings can be compared quite closely with the Maka concept of *djambe* from Cameroon, as discussed in Chapter 3. *Kum* is one category of magical or occult force, which in effect has the potential to be used beneficially or harmfully. Hermann Strauss, a missionary-ethnographer of the Hagen area who worked there from the earliest colonial times in the 1930s onward, spells the word as *kôm* and says that the *kôm* are pictured as bird-like beings who come to make their "nests" in people. He also describes them as "souls" that have desires within them (Strauss and Tischner 1962: 143; the term for "souls" here is *Seelen*). People as individuals have many desires, for food, sleep, possessions, land, sex, and reputation. If these *kôm* "break off" inside the person as a result of an unsatisfied desire, they may consume the life-force of their possessor, who may then die; as a result people try to satisfy one another's requests.

Strauss goes on to note that certain wild *kôm* (*kôm rakra*) exist that are stones which take the form of birds and have their abode in landslide areas and eroded riverbanks. They are thought to cause these movements of the earth by their presence. They fly out at night and try to enter people's bodies through their open mouths as they sleep, with the aim of consuming their life-force. *Kôm* that live inside people can also fly out in this way and attack others; they shoot out from the eyes of strangers, for example, or from acquaintances also, who see food or a valuable shell and desire it. In this case the *kôm* acts as an arrow and pierces someone. If it "breaks off" in that person, the person will again die. This concept reveals "the sorcery in the gift" in Melpa concepts of the obligation to give and shows the coercive side of the "gift-economy" celebrated in anthropological writings on New Guinea. Fear of *kôm* as sorcery/witchcraft/desire constrains people to meet the requests of others.

As with the Maka also, and in Africa generally, ritual experts are able to capture and tame these wild *kôm*, which are thought to live in the rugged Northern Melpa region known as Kopon. An expert among a Central Melpa group, living in the fertile and densely populated plains and valleys south of Kopon, described to Strauss how he had found two such *kôm*. He had been *kekedlip*, in a state of trance or disturbance of mind, and found himself away from his home, in a small hut in the forest in the Kopon area. He saw a flame burning by a river and went to investigate, finding the *kôm* stone on a bed it had made for itself. Picking it up, he promised to give it a good house to live in instead of the cold riverside, to give it pork to eat if it helped to cure people rather than attacking them, and so to make it famous. The stone was thus treated as a person.

The same expert declared he had another tame *kôm* that worked in tandem with the first. This was a stone wrapped in barkcloth to which pieces of fur, claws, and the jawbone of the *watsenga* marsupial (the quoll), signifying powers of biting and eating, were attached. This "quoll stone" had also been looking for victims to eat when the expert found it and tamed it, making both of the stones into his servants (*kentmants wamb*; Strauss and Tischner, p. 172).

Controlling the two *kôm* with the power of his magical words (*man-êk*), the expert used them now to drive out wild *kôm* from the bodies of patients and so to restore them to health. In return the patients slaughtered pigs as sacrifices so that the expert could feed the still voracious appetites of his stones, so he declared. To activate the tame *kôm* and send it out on its errand of ferreting out the wild *kôm*, the expert held it in front of him and blew on it with his breath (an emanation of his own soul, or *min*) and made an incantation quietly, graphically describing how the *kôm* can fly though the air from its home in Kopon and attack people (p. 173).

By the 1960s, in a part of the Kopon area among the Northern Melpa, this knowledge of how ritual experts themselves worked with *kôm* (or *kum*) stones was either muted or no longer maintained. Several men and women knew spells (*mön*) to cure sicknesses, but none were said, at least, to control *kum* stones in doing so. On the other hand, the witchcraft powers associated with such stones were known in their malevolent aspect and were said to be possessed by a few individuals (not ritual experts) in each clan, mostly women. The area had been greatly influenced since the 1950s by the teachings of the Lutheran mission (the same mission, from Neuendettelsau in Germany, for which Strauss himself worked), in which the use of pagan rituals and spells was discouraged, and the powers associated with indigenous ideas of occult force were seen as evil. In such a context, the aspect of the *kum*-complex, as we may call it, linked with healing would predictably be suppressed, and only the aggressive aspect would be preserved and perhaps highlighted. This kind of process has commonly occurred in New Guinea, Africa, and elsewhere, recapitulating the antecedent processes in early modern Europe itself as delineated by Margaret Murray (1970 [1931]), Carlo Ginzburg (1989 [1991]), and others. The resulting situation can be described as the genesis of a bifurcated epistemology, in which good and evil are entirely separate and opposed to each other (see LiPuma 2000: 9–10 on the relevance of epistemological ideas in contexts of change, and cf. Knauft 2002: 148 on the "bipolar" world of the Gebusi). In short, *kum* came to denote cannibalistic witchcraft, and the intricate specifics of how ritual experts could find and tame wild *kum* stones to use them in beneficial curing rituals dropped out of focus. *Kopon kum koimb* came to mean the destructive witchcraft powers that emanated southward from the Kopon area, and it became attached largely to women, in a gendering process that again paralleled the processes in European history. We cannot say, however, that this gendering process was also the product of mission teaching in any direct sense. It perhaps had more to do with the highlighting of the theme of female desire for pork consumption that existed as a motif in Melpa male discourse.

The 1977 story of a conspiracy, however, to seduce larger numbers of people into the world of cannibalism and witchcraft represents a further movement of ideas. This putative attempt to corrupt people at large was aimed at both women and men, so that both came under suspicion and both were afraid of contracting cannibalism like a disease. "Pacification" in the 1950s or earlier had brought with it an increased movement of people between clan areas along with an efflorescence of exchange links and events. Then in the 1970s enmities between large-scale groups set in again, during a difficult transition from colonial to postcolonial politics, and suspicions of sorcery and witchcraft also came to the fore. The idea that hidden enemies, operating transgressively between clans, might be perverting and corrupting the whole population with an epidemic of witchcraft arose out of the confusions of the times and carried within it an element from the old way of thinking described by Strauss.

It will be recalled that the rumor declared witches were placing human flesh at the headwaters of rivers. These were precisely the sites where the *kum* stones were traditionally thought to make their "nests," flying out from them at night to enter people's mouths and consume them from inside as internal mouths. In the old cosmology the *kum* stones flew as birds; in the new rumor, pieces of flesh were said to flow with rivers across clan boundaries. The rumor thus recaptured an essential element of perceived power from the traditional epistemological scheme, and no doubt gained greater force by this means. The figure or trope of the river as a bearer of pollution again represents the new bifurcated epistemology. In the earlier traditions of healing, experts would often call on the names of rivers and streams, telling them to carry away blood-borne infections and remove them entirely from the bodies of patients (Stewart and Strathern 2002b; Strathern and Stewart 1999a). In this image, river water carries destructive forces away but does so as a purifying, not a corrupting agency. In the old image, river water was seen as carrying sickness away from a patient down to its lower reaches, whereas in the new rumor, it was seen as bringing sickness to people from the "outside," or the remote headwaters. The rumor can thus be seen as an inversion of the earlier notions. The idea of danger coming from an outside area can plausibly be correlated with the processes of initial pacification followed by the resurgence of intergroup fighting that marked the 1970s in Hagen and with political uncertainties that followed national independence in 1975. Rumors subtly reflect such changes. But like the processes of change themselves, they are also highly volatile. This particular epidemiological rumor, which caused moral panic in the society for a while, vanished quickly and did not return in its exact form. Later phases of rumors regarding witchcraft in the mid-1990s were centered on anxieties regarding witches attacking graves of the newly dead and consuming their bodies. These resembled closely in form the fears Auslander discusses for the Ngoni (Chapter 3) and were also related to the consolidation of Christian modes of burial in communal cemeteries (Stewart and Strathern 1998a). The cemeteries, separated from people's residences, were seen as uncanny places subject to nocturnal invasion by witches who might appear as cows or dogs. Fires were lit and young men posted with weapons to repel witches who came to eat the dead (a dramatic image of destructive changes).

The basic idea surrounding concepts of witchcraft among the Melpa people of the Hagen area is greed, but nowadays it is also conceived of in terms of Satanic powers. In 1997 we found the Melpa to be experiencing a wave of millenarian notions concerning "world's end" ideas brought into the area by some of the Christian churches (Stewart and Strathern 1997, 2000b). In this light, witchcraft activity was seen to be on the rise because Satan had instilled this into his followers, thus increasing the powers of "evil" on the earth and heralding the "world's end." It was said that the domination within the world of greed and desire would consume everything and bring about retribution from the Christian God and Jesus (Stewart and Strathern 1998b, 2001a).

Epidemiologies of Change

In some ways descriptions of the spread of witchcraft within areas are also reminiscent of detailed accounts of how actual diseases such as typhoid spread through a population. Epidemics of dysentery entered the Hagen area in the 1940s and were followed in later years by other outbreaks of infectious diseases such as typhoid. Fears of water that can infect people with cannibalistic tendencies correlate in some respects with public health lectures given to the local people by colonial authorities on the need to avoid defecation in streams that were used for drinking water sources so as to reduce the spread of disease-causing organisms. Also, in some regards new infectious diseases were able to move through communities in ways that defied local reason. This sometimes led to people responding in unpredictable ways.

For example, among the Wiru speakers in the Pangia area (Southern Highlands Province) in 1960 shortly after Australian government patrols began coming into the area, there was a period of what the local people subsequently defined as collective "madness." This behavior reportedly manifested itself in ways that included gang rape and other forms of unprecedentedly brutal interactions (Strathern 1977). The "madness" was attributed to the coming of the colonialists and their activities, which dramatically altered the lives of the people who had been traditionally involved in classic patterns of warfare and exchange between local groups until the time of enforced "pacification" and the influx of Christian missions (Strathern 1984). The Pangia people experienced early colonial changes as rapid and disorienting. Colonially created villages were material concentrations of more dispersed forms of sociality that had existed previously. These villages were rapidly beset by internal factionalism. Pigs were no longer allowed to be kept in village houses and villagers were forced to labor on road work projects linking villages together that the government had begun. By the 1980s residents in the Pangia district were spreading rumors that sorcerers (called *māua* or *uro*) were increasing in their area and were especially attacking persons near the government station.

Here again we find an inversion or reversal of spatial values encoded in notions of the landscape (see also Knauft 1998). In 1967 ideas regarding *māua*, or assault sorcery, were concentrated on a tiny, peripheral settlement called Tangupane, situated far out on the southeastern forested fringes of the Pangia area, some eight hours' walk from the nearest other Wiru-speaking settlement. The whole of this area was called, in the new colonial context, Last Wiru, that is, the part farthest away from the newly established colonial center of power at the government station. In pre-colonial times, as people moved to the edges of Wiru settlement they feared encounters with assault sorcerers at the margins of their own cultural territory, and immediately beyond these margins, they thought, lived peoples who were cannibals. But the assault sorcerers and cannibals did not penetrate much into the bulk of the Wiru settlements. They were seen as dangerous only if one actually visited their areas. In Tangupane, visitors would take care to stand guard at night at doorways and entrances to latrines if one of their number had to go outside. And they would stuff up with leaves or rags any obvious holes in the house walls where they slept in case the *māua* sorcerers would look in at them sleeping. If the *māua* caught a person, it was thought they would disembowel them after opening an incision in their abdomen and stuffing their insides with rubbish, extracting one of their kidneys and putting it into the victim's mouth. The victim would go home dazed and roast his or her own kidney and eat it. Then their kin would know they were doomed to die. If the victim was a woman the *māua* men might first rape her, then disembowel her. Extreme danger was thus seen as located at the peripheries. However, with the new concentrations of people in villages, the construction of roads, the establishment of courts, a prison, and mission stations, and the availability of new consumer goods flown in by light planes to the government station, the remote periphery was now linked to a new center of power. The power of pacification was soon seen as challenged by the subversive power of the *māua*, threatening their better-off fellow Wiru-speakers near the station itself. Pacification brought, instead of a simple security, new fears. It also brought with it the regular experience of colonial violence in the shape of punitive actions by indigenous police recruited from other parts of Papua and New Guinea (cf. Stasch 2001 on Korowai, West Papua). The perceived passage of sorcerers across the landscape also went hand in hand in many areas, including Pangia itself, with the puzzling and frightening passage of new sicknesses, which in turn might be ascribed to sorcerers or witches. These passages were invariably heralded by rumors that spread fear beyond the frontiers of a particular episode of sickness. In the Wiru area mortality from a colonially introduced form of influenza was severe: in one village up to a quarter of the population died (Strathern 1984). Little wonder that rumors of sorcery increased. (For interesting parallels with the history of ideas about *kanaimà* assault sorcery in Guyana, see Whitehead 2002. Whitehead's rich ethnography and theorizing applies well to our New Guinea case studies.)

Colonial changes in New Guinea have frequently been accompanied by psychological changes of the sort described for the Pangia people, as well as epidemiological changes. Dan Sperber (1985) used the expression "the epidemiology of representations" in terms of the notion of the spread of ideas in "political space." We use the expression "representations of epidemiology" to refer to physiological events conceptualized by local people in cultural terms that are seen as invasions that intrude on and consume the people's lives and sometimes their minds and/or bodies in ways that are predictable from theories of the "social body" as propounded by Mary Douglas, Thomas Csordas, and others (Stewart and Strathern 2001b).

Inge Riebe (1987, 1991) describes the Karam people's narratives of witchcraft (*koyb*) that was said to have killed numbers of people during the nineteenth century and onward. The Karam live in a valley area just to the north of the Maring and Melpa people, and *koyb* is clearly the same term as the Melpa *koimb*, with a different orthography. *Koyb* ideas probably spread into the Melpa Kopon area from their northern periphery. The *koyb* was described as a small snakelike creature that was retained in the abdomen of the witch, enabling its human host to kill others. Further elaborations were added to these beliefs through contact with Ramu peoples from the north; *koyb* witches were said to have the ability to "change into animals, or other humans, become invisible, move at incredible speeds, or be in two places at once, kill without contact, and to sew together and temporarily resuscitate people killed with conventional weapons. Witches were also said to have a greed for human flesh" (Riebe 1987: 214). Witches were thought of as stingy and greedy people and "were thought only to kill when paid to do so by normal humans" (ibid.).

Koyb witchcraft was given as an initial explanation for sudden deaths. Riebe (1987) suggests that this correlates with the beginning of deaths from dysentery and malaria. Settlers from ethnically different northern valleys were more likely to be thought of as witches. They are in fact likely to have brought new diseases from their lowland areas into the highlands. At the psychological level, Riebe points out that proper social behavior depended on an ethic of generous giving, but "the underside of this world was the world of the witch – the world of greed, destructiveness and extortions under threat of witchcraft" (p. 221). She also adds that accusations of witchcraft took the place of revenge homicide, since "all deaths caused by human agency had to be revenged" and a large proportion of deaths of adults were now attributed to witches.

Riebe's analysis fits well with the historical situation in the Hagen area. The increased passage in colonial times of notions of witchcraft from the nearby Jimi Valley into central Hagen coincided with travel by Hageners on government patrols into the Jimi area in the 1950s and beyond. Epidemics of witchcraft fears in Hagen also correlate with historical perceptions of growing tension over the inequalities between people, marked by capitalist-style consumerism compounded by notions about Satanic forces brought into the area by Christian missions. As a means of "persuading" people to give up their traditional ritual and religious practices, which Christian missions often portray as competing for adherence to their imported religious practices, the traditional practices were said to be associated with Satan, who was said by these churches to be deluding the people.

Although the church narratives about Satan were often frightening and difficult for the local peoples to understand, the teachings of churches about "world's end" would often fit well with preexisting ideas held by New Guineans about the cyclicity of the ground and the necessity to conduct rituals to renew the fertility of the earth. In the Duna area (Southern Highlands Province) in which a wave of epidemics preceded the definitive arrival of the colonial administration in the early 1960s, rumors about, and the actual experience of, these epidemics of sickness were deeply woven in with notions that the arrival of the whites would herald in the end of the world. These early phases of rumor and experience have been paralleled much more recently, in the late 1990s, by the gradual realization that HIV infection and AIDS have entered into Papua New Guinea (Strathern and Stewart 1999a). Various new mythologies have developed around this frightening phenomenon. In the Hagen and Duna areas rumors have spread that persons in the city of Mount Hagen wait in stores with HIV-infected syringes that they use to stab unsuspecting shoppers with as a means of spreading the disease. These ideas are not unlike those previously held about assault sorcerers, who were held to pierce the organs of people with sharp instruments, for instance, sago-leaf spines among the Duna. Indeed, among the Duna one man declared that now the assault sorcerers were using hypodermic needles obtained from government medical aid posts, a rumor that parallels in its tone the vampire rumors detailed by White for parts of Africa (White 2000; see Chapter 4).

Assault sorcery is generally correlated with distance and hostility. The sorcerer is often conceived of as an outsider who penetrates a community or isolates victims when they are outside their home area. The attack, as we have noted, is said to leave the victims with their internal organs butchered or removed. The sorcerer is thought to sew together the victims so that they continue to live for some time afterward but will eventually die from their wounds. In some areas such as in Pangia, assault sorcery was greatly feared because there was said to be no counteraction that could be taken against these attacks. The internal invasiveness of these assaults was said, as we have noted, to extend to rape when the victim was female.

For the Duna people, assault sorcery and witchcraft are set into the same category. Both are referred to as *tsuwake*. Assault sorcery is called *tsuwake tene* and witchcraft is called *tsuwake kono*. In the early 1990s assault sorcerers were rumored to be moving into the Duna area in increased numbers. One of the local Duna men said that he had trained squads of youths to be assault sorcerers, and he repeated the point that nowadays instead of using the traditional sago-spine dart to pierce a victim's chest he was able to use syringes that he obtained from the local health aid post. In addition, new techniques were said to be employed in which women were persuaded to act as sexual decoys to lure victims into an area where an assault sorcerer could more easily attack them. The assault sorcerers were all said to be from the Oksapmin area west of the Strickland River, foreigners with cultural ways seen as distinct from those of the Duna. In precolonial times the Duna traded with the Oksapmin people and there was some degree of intermarriage with them, but Oksapmin women were often said also to be the carriers of witchcraft powers.

Witchcraft Fears and Sorcery Trials

Rumors of new forms of sorcery among the Duna were followed by heightened fears of witchcraft activity. These rumors passed between local groups and fed into internal gossip that eventually narrowed its focus to accusations against particular persons. Although the local Christian churches had forbidden the use of traditional methods of divination to seek out and punish witches thought to have killed and eaten victims, in 1996 this prohibition was relaxed after the death of two young Duna men who had taken part in a hunting expedition. The men had lit fires in grassy areas to drive wild pigs into the open for shooting, but the fire encircled and consumed them. A diviner was hired and four women were identified as being the responsible witches. These women were driven out of the community after they "confessed" to the killings.

In 1998 among the Duna a period of drought and food shortages was followed by the spread of an epidemic (of typhoid or perhaps pneumonia) that resulted in a number of deaths. Two of those who died were the children of a prominent community leader, including his only son and potential successor. He hired a diviner, and a number of women were identified as the witches who had caused the deaths in the community. All of the women were driven out with the exception of one, who was killed. The events leading up to the accusations of witchcraft and further actions against those said to be responsible were mired in clouds of rumors and gossip about the deaths. During the period of grieving, it seemed imperative to find some person or persons to blame for the deaths as a means of "making sense" of the event. Witchcraft and sorcery accusations are often linked to bereavement. Among the Mekeo people of coastal Papua New Guinea, the word for sorcerer (*ugauga*) translates into "a man of sorrow" (Stephen 1995, 1996, 1998). *Ugauga* are said to "bring sadness and grief to others."

Among the Hewa people, who live just north of the Duna in Papua New Guinea, the moment at which decisions were finally made to kill a person said to be a witch was at a funeral where the witch's supposed victim was being mourned (Steadman 1975, 1985; Steadman's fieldwork took place in 1966–9, at a time when the Hewa, were still largely "unpacified"). The Hewa witch (*pisai*) was said to cannibalize the viscera of the victim by opening the body, eating the organs, and closing the body again so that the attacked person died several weeks later. The accused person might be identified by a dying person or by divination. Among the Hewa, witchcraft accusations were "seen as threats not only to the witch but also to those associated with the alleged witch, and therefore represent a test of their power and courage" (p. 110). Steadman observed three ways of responding to witchcraft accusations: "1) they may challenge the accuser by fighting him; 2) they may move away from the accuser's area; or 3) they may ignore the accusation" (1985, pp. 110–11). Option 3 would leave the accused vulnerable of being killed. The killing was usually conducted by a band of eight to ten men who were bound by political, economic, and kin ties and who "invariably reflect grievances based on past hostilities" (p. 114).

Although Steadman does not focus on rumor as a significant part of his account, there are several hints in his exposition that point to its presence. For example, he notes that accusations of witchcraft were usually made at funerals, either as a result of the dying person naming the supposed witch or by expert divination. Significantly, the kin and close associates of the person accused never agreed with the charge; "they invariably and contemptuously dismissed it as a lie" (p. 110). Also, "prior accusations were almost always made months before the funeral or the killing, not necessarily by the group doing the killing" (p. 111). This means, in effect, that rumors and gossip generated suspicions against certain people well before a particular death. People were therefore already stigmatized and were made vulnerable to being scapegoats. Most of those accused and killed were women. When a party of males banded together to kill such a female, women might gather in opposition to them on the pathway and would shame "the killing party when they came along by lifting their skirts and exposing their genitals" (ibid.). This shows us that aggression was directed largely at females, in all likelihood ones married in from distant places without a strong support group nearby, who were therefore vulnerable to being killed if suspicion fell on them, but that females might also act to protect other females. Whether they were attacked or not would depend on the relative strength of the groups or networks of people who took sides for or against them. This in turn would depend at least partly on the character of rumors circulating about them and how these fed into local politics at the time. Steadman stresses the ambiguity of accusations and notes that the Hewa men themselves, if pressed, would always admit that identification of a witch was uncertain. No post hoc autopsies were held to "prove" whether a woman killed as a witch "in fact" was one by Hewa criteria, and no one would admit to having seen a witch eat someone's viscera as they were said to do, probably because only another witch would have the occasion to do so, according to Hewa ideas. Besides, one should add, we need to avoid any misplaced literalness here: in other places in Papua New Guinea witchcraft activities are cast in the realm of the soul or of spirits. It is the magical familiar of the witch that is said to eat the vital force or soul of the victim, and such acts are by definition invisible (see Stephen 1996 and her debate with Mark Mosko 1997 on this point). The realm of the invisible and the uncertain thus lends itself well to allowing rumor and gossip to be the judges of people's behavior. Witch-killings were essentially trials of strength between local sets of men, and the putative witches were the victims of rumor, as elsewhere. At no point does Steadman say that those killed merited their fate through their own actions of meanness or greed, so we are left with the idea that the role of rumor was particularly deadly in this context. Rumor in turn would be motivated by grudges and resentments that fed into gossip and could be seized on by others for their own purposes later. Females' gossip about other females might be appropriated by males and later used for their own political purposes. Steadman indicates that the reasons men gave for killing witches was that they were cannibals who were hungry for meat, and he relates this to possible jealousies over pork consumption. This would seem plausible. If so, as we have noted, the jealousies might first be expressed as grumbling between females, which would acquire their lethal potential only when taken up by men. This might in turn prompt women of the community to try to stop such a killing, as did happen.

When a person is finally killed after being accused of witchcraft, it is most often, then, after accusations against the person have circulated within the community for some time. In general, gossip is crucial in swiftly directing the foci of accusation and blame between people. In the broader contexts, rumors of sorcery forms or new varieties of witchcraft that putatively enter into areas from the outside reflect both alterations in relations of gender or of leadership and also the overall stress that results from the increased mobility of people in colonial or postcolonial contexts and the vicissitudes of spreading natural diseases (Anderson 2002).

Karen Brison's (1992) study of the Kwanga people in the Sepik area of Papua New Guinea shows very clearly how gossip acts as a political weapon in the context of fluctuating interpersonal struggles for influence. Equally, at the collective and historical level, it is an index of stress and change. Brison adds considerably to our overall understanding of how rumor and gossip work in small-scale communities that do not have hierarchical chiefship patterns and in which people compete for influence and prestige without ever gaining clear political control over one another. The Kwanga also live in small villages and people tend to marry within their own village. We gain a picture of different small groups tied together by kinship and marriage within the village but divided by many lines of factional cleavage created or exacerbated by the rivalries of individual men. These men, recognized in some regards as leaders in communal affairs, may either be suspected of being sorcerers or may drop hints in public meetings that they know about such things. In the past there was an institutional emphasis on male secret knowledge in the community, since males were initiated in the *tambaran* cult and the spirit of the *tambaran* was sometimes said secretly to authorize sorcerers to kill people who broke its taboos. People at the time of Brison's main fieldwork in 1984 had been variously converted to Christianity, but they still considered that deaths were mostly due to sorcery. Previously, such suspicions of sorcery might be followed up by challenges to engage in ceremonial exchanges of wealth or by threats of fighting. Christians avoided these activities as expensive or proscribed, and large-scale public meetings tended to develop instead, replacing the earlier modalities of conflict.

At these meetings leading men specialized in dropping innuendoes about matters to do with sorcery, incriminating others or making ambiguous claims about their own occult powers. Brison insightfully points out that this form of public rumormongering, effected through the use of indirect or elliptical speech, is one way in which men try to gain power without being fully accountable for their claims; but that this strategy can also backfire because of the transmutations that rumors undergo as they pass around the village over time. By an obscure hint a leader may be suggesting that a rival of his is a nefarious sorcerer, but his claim to knowledge may be interpreted in gossip and rumor networks as an admission or a sign of his own culpability. Leaders try to use rumor as a way of enhancing their influence, but in the end it may undermine their position.

Several formulations by Brison neatly sum up these points. For example, she points to "the power of stories," the title of Chapter 7 in her book, and in her preface she writes of "just so" stories that "could have an insidious effect on relationships and reputations" (Brison 1992: xvi). These stories were built out of gossip assiduously participated in by ambitious men. In public meetings long and fruitless efforts were devoted to trying to understand which of the current rumors were true and which false (ibid.). The meetings about sorcery rarely resulted in clear outcomes, but they were the venues at which "initiated men maintain their authority over fellow villagers" (p. 47), or attempted to do so. Almost all deaths were attributed to sorcery, so each death would lead to a series of such meetings.

The Kwanga attributed occult powers also to their leaders generally, considering that environmental disasters were a result of the malign use of their magic. Such a set of notions is quite common in many coastal areas of New Guinea. A corollary of it is that the powers of leaders are feared. The use of concealed speech intensifies these fears and makes people always look for hidden meanings and intentions. "In a society where everyone looks for the concealed meaning, rumors are quick to start and quick to distort the truth" (p. 154). Because of distrustful and rivalrous relations between kin groups, people tend "to think that alarmist rumors of slander and attack might be true" (ibid.). They try to avoid the ever-present possibility of open and violent conflict by resorting to metaphors, but these in themselves further create tension and the potentiality of conflict.

Brison notes that the Kalauna people studied by Michael Young (1971: 135) fear malicious gossip almost as much as sorcery itself (Brison, p. 216). Here, then, we find the interweaving of sorcery and gossip that we have taken as our own main theme for this book. Brison's study has advanced the understanding of gossip and politics considerably, and in particular enables us to understand both the intended and the unintended effects of initiating rumors. The sorcery debates she analyzes for the Kwanga parallel those that Edward LiPuma (2000: 182–4) describes as happening among the Maring people of Madang and Western Highlands Provinces in Papua New Guinea in 1979–80. LiPuma suggests that the Maring sorcery trials were moving to a more individual definition of responsibility for action than held previously, in line with Western legal definitions of the person. This may be so. Brison, however, speaks of "institutionalized duplicity in Melansian culture" (Brison, p. 154) and implies that notions about individual ambitions and proclivities are a feature of these cultures long predating the introduction of Western legal concepts. Melpa ideas of *kum* as "wild desires" appear to point in the same direction. Finally, Brison correlates many of her findings with the fact that the Kwanga live in "a social environment in which rumors have unusual power" (p. 238). She notes further that such a concern with gossip and rumor "is part of a more pervasive fear of the power of words" (p. 241) and that this may be widely true of Pacific societies. Talk does not only reflect or express social relations, "it plays a large role in creating them" (p. 245). As such, like witchcraft or sorcery, it can make or break people. No wonder, then, that talk about sorcery carried so powerful an interest for people such as the Kwanga.

Rumors, passing into oral history and legend, also contribute to another feature of Kwanga society that is found widely in the Pacific and elsewhere. Disputes and issues are rarely fully resolved, and are brought up again successively over time. The Mount Hagen people express this by saying *nit kel ti morom*, "there is a small *nit* there," where *nit* represents a mark, a cut, an indentation, an issue available for revisiting.

"Cargo Cults" and Rumor

Cargo cults and millenarian ideas are further contexts in which the place of rumor is very wide ranging and deep seated. Rumor fills the interstices between personal experiences in dreams and visions and social ideologies that result in specific cults or movements operating under specific leaders. Here we draw both on earlier literature on the Madang and Rai Coast areas in the writings of Peter Lawrence, Kenelm Burridge, and Peter Worsley, and on contemporary materials from the late 1990s that we have brought together in a coedited volume, *Millennial Countdown in New Guinea* (Stewart and Strathern 2000b). The materials in this volume amply demonstrate the pivotal place of rumor in defining the fluidity of contexts in which millennial ideas are operating.

As Worsley (1957) argued long ago, millennial and cargo movements can also be seen as forms of political protest and mobilization along the lines Guha speaks of as "peasant insurgency." It is important to bear in mind here the significance both of cultural ideas in themselves and the social contexts of uneven development and disparities of power in which these ideas operate. The ideas and their contexts conduce strongly toward the proliferation of rumor, and rumors in turn act as catalysts for social movements as such. Our discussion here focuses on the role of rumor in generating movements.

The term "cargo cult" refers to a variety of rituals and movements that have occurred historically in colonial and postcolonial times, notably in New Guinea. These focused variously on obtaining by magical or ritual means the wealth items brought into the area by Europeans. "Cargo" is a general word for such objects of wealth, which might vary from boxes of tinned meat and other foods to large supplies of money itself, depending on the historical stages of contact and the desires of the people. Political and moral concerns were invariably deeply woven into these desires. It was unclear to New Guineans at the time how colonial powers came to have so many supplies and goods, and when Christian missions moved into new areas of Papua New Guinea they brought a message of a religion that could offer well-being, wealth, and immortality. Rumors spread swiftly through regions about the wealth and power of colonial officers. Local people had to try to assimilate new ideologies brought by the colonial personnel and by the Christian missionaries who moved rapidly into regions after colonial administration stations were put in place. Often local people felt it was difficult to cope with the hurried changes brought upon them as well as the demands made by government officers.

Cargo cults were one way of making sense out of very confusing situations. They also can be seen in many respects as protests against the inequalities imposed by colonial rule, as new political organizations developed to resist colonial power, as searches for moral redemption through the establishment of equality between outsiders and indigenous people, and as a means of rectifying injustice seen as brought about by the trickery of the colonial intruders, sometimes linked with the idea that an indigenous ancestor had gone away to the lands of the "white people" and had intended to send back cargo to his kinsfolk, but the colonial powers had blocked this and taken the wealth for themselves.

Many significant studies have been made that indicate a "search for wealth" as basic to certain of these movements. Wealth in New Guinea is frequently seen by people as a means of attaining a sense of self-worth or equality with others. This is hardly surprising, since exactly the same can be said of some patterns of attitudes in Western, class-based societies. In New Guinea, as in many other places, wealth also has magico-religious significance. Wealth is seen by many peoples as a sign of cosmic well-being, of proper relationships with the spirit world, and therefore the lack of it is seen as the reverse, a sign of the cosmos and spirit-world being out of balance, requiring ritual and sacrifice to set it to rights. This is the basis for indigenous fertility practices. These practices are not unlike Christian prayers that are traditionally made for the well-being of the land and its crops, as are thanksgiving services held for harvest-time.

An example of a cargo cult is a Mount Hagen movement that centered on the magical acquisition of wealth that was known by the people as "wind work" (*köpkö kongon*) and described as "the red box money cult." This movement flourished between about 1968 and 1971 (Stewart and Strathern 2000a: 10–15; Strathern 1979–80; Strathern and Stewart 2000c: 163–5). Activities centered around a ritual for the acquisition of large quantities of money. The money was to be brought by spirits of the dead (who were said to prefer now to be known as "wind people") and placed into the kinds of red wooden boxes in which plantation laborers used to bring back their wages and goods from the coast when they returned home. Boxes filled with stones and metal were expected to be transformed into containers of money through the rituals performed. The cultists sacrificed pigs near to the boxes and decorated the area with flowers and shrubs to please the dead. The cult ended when the money did not materialize.

In contrast to the red box money cult, in some other areas, cargo ideas and movements have a much longer history, transforming themselves over time and developing complex organizational forms and aims. These tend to be areas with a long history of early colonial contact and mission influence and persistent problems of economic development. In these areas, movements that held within them magico-religious elements also have tended to have in-built ambitious projects of self-help and economic effort.

A classic early study by Peter Lawrence (1964) of cargo beliefs and movements on the Rai coast of the Madang area in Papua New Guinea begins with an account of the people's indigenous cosmic order. Lawrence traces a history of five different stages of activity, three from 1871 to 1933, the fourth from 1933 to 1945, and the fifth from 1948 to 1950, all interspersed with discussions of colonial society and the effects of administration activity. Lawrence also makes it clear how the indigenous appropriation of Christian teachings was an important component throughout these periods of time (e.g., p. 85). He quotes Tok Pisin versions of such teachings that he says were interpreted in cargoistic terms, such as "*Long Heven i nogat trobel, i nogat pen. Em i fulap long ol gutpela samting . . . Em i ples bilong peim ol gutpela man.*" Lawrence translates this as "Heaven is a place without trouble or pain. It is filled with every good thing. . . . It is a place where good men are rewarded" (loc. cit.). Here we must comment that it is the rich potential for ambiguity in Christian ideology itself, as much as anything else, that lends itself to varying historical interpretations, and the connection between Christianity and millennarian aspirations has also been shown much more recently in the years leading up to 2000 (see Robbins, Stewart, and Strathern 2001; Stewart and Strathern 2000b).

Millenarian ideas were globally experienced at the turn of the year 1999 into 2000. The Y2K computer problem was only one of the many fears that spread through rumors of apocalyptic computer crashes that could destroy data and potentially produce logistic, financial, and other forms of chaos. In Papua New Guinea "world's end" rumors associated with the year 1999/2000 were spread through various Christian churches. Some of the people in the Hagen area took any misfortune that they experienced as a sign that the "end" was soon to come to the earth. Some reported that God was preparing the earth for the year 2000 by sending the AIDS virus to Papua New Guinea. Others said that the increase in violent crime was a sign of heightened Satanic activity and that this signaled the onset of an apocalyptic battle of "good" and "evil." But many of the processes used to negotiate around the "world's end" visions surrounding the year 2000 were similar, and in some instances were the same as those seen in earlier movements that arose in response to a range of ideological, geographical, and temporal situations of change.

In all of these cultic contexts rumors played a major part. Cargo ideas in the Eastern Highlands of Papua New Guinea came not long after the early incursions by the Australians into the region in the 1930s, which themselves were preceded and followed by a medley of rumors as reports yodeled across the hills. Since the incomers were at first universally regarded as spirit beings, associated with the possibility of world's end

(Schieffelin and Crittenden 1991), and sometimes as cannibalistic sky be-ings, these earlier rumors already produced a sense of cosmic unease (Stewart and Strathern 2002a). Cargo rumors in the Eastern Highlands were said by the people to have come with a kind of wind that blew across their area, a wind that blew into their ears and changed their minds (Berndt 1952–3). In the Hagen red box cult, since the activities of the cultists were nominally secret, reports about them inevitably took the form of rumors or "leaks" from the cult sites. Some of these rumors cen-tered on the cemeteries that the Lutherans had established for the burial of Christians. Often these cemeteries were created at the back of cere-monial grounds used for exchange occasions, in sites that previously had been used for fertility cults or the individual resting places of deceased leaders. Lutheran mission rules were said to enjoin people to clean, weed, and broom the new cemeteries at set intervals, and these actions came to be associated with rumors of the discovery of coins on graves. The "cleaning" act was reinterpreted as a cargo ritual. This rumor was de-rived from similar and earlier rumors that originated in Lutheran areas in Madang, far away on the northern coast, as described by Lawrence (1964). Everything that happened in relation to the red box movement was subject to avid speculation and gossiping, always in a context of great uncertainty, tied in with people's desires. While apocalyptic visions of the sky opening and the "world bank" breaking out over the Hagen area reflected the optimistic and hyperbolic wing of these rumors, there was also much skepticism and doubt and concern that cult leaders were ly-ing or were embezzling actual funds contributed to the movement by its followers. As a result, when the movement ended, its demise had been predicted in advance just as much as its potential success. Rumor played a part, again, in making the movement and in breaking it.

Reputation is all in societies like that of Mount Hagen, and reputation is built largely on words, reports that appeal to images in people's minds, just as with the Kwanga. The power of the report is signified in a Hagen image of the "rumor beings," *rönang wamb*. According to Strauss, these spirit beings lived on high mountain tops at the *mugl-pagla*, "the fence of the sky." When a disaster happened, the people living down in the foothills of the mountains were said to hear the rumor spirits making a noise like moaning and beating on their shields as warriors did. This sound was taken as a portent of a death or war. If it was heard as a noise of jubilation, people took it that they would be successful in war and would go out to fight happily; if it was like a dirge, this meant they would be killed. The rumor spirits were thought to be clever, and they were praised when people were steaming pork as a sacrifice, so that they would be happy and bring good fortune. People praised them so that they would not pass on "bad news" too often (Strauss and Tischner 1962: 168–9). This set of images from Hagen graphically illustrates the kind of transcendent power people often accord rumor. For the Hageners, as for Hesiod, "talk, too, is a kind of deity."

Conclusion

Table 4 summarizes some of the trends and processes we have been considering in this chapter. Here we have drawn on some of our own field experiences as well as our reading of other cases from New Guinea in order to emphasise how gossip and rumor flourish in ambiguous situations of conflict, competition, and historical change. Such situations may issue in witchcraft fears and may also generate changes in the pattern of ideas themselves, as we have shown for the case of *kum* in Mount Hagen. They may also be expressed in terms of increased fears of assault sorcery. Or they may issue in millennial ideas of "world's end" or in phenomena that have been labeled as cargo cults. In all of these cases one element that is at stake is the moral status of desire. Inordinate desire is seen as greed and greed lies at the core of witchcraft. The idea of assault sorcery involves the notion of severe aggression against victims, not necessarily connected with the wish to consume human flesh, but expressing an analogous wish to annihilate or obliterate the victim's life force. Unlike the witch, who

TABLE 4. The Place of Rumor in Parallel Processes of Change in Papua New Guinea

Precipitating events	Rumors	Further results
Epidemics, individual sicknesses, deaths	Misfortunes are attributed to attacks by witches/sorcerers.	Witchcraft or sorcery trials, banishment, killings, community split-ups
Colonial change: prohibition of warfare, changes in political groupings	Deaths are attributed to increased sorcery activity of enemies and jealous people	Increase in public debates and trials for witchcraft or sorcery; agonistic exchanges and compensation ceremonies
Political and economic change upsets social balances in communities	Rumors develop on "supernatural" means to better people's lives.	"Cargo" movements
Christianity brings millennial ideas into the community	Rumors develop about world's end and the apocalypse; disasters and sicknesses are reinterpreted as Satan's work and signs of the end times.	Millennial trends and movements

is often seen as a threatening insider, the assault sorcerer is imaged as a hostile outsider. Identification of such a sorcerer tends, therefore, to lead not to accusation or punishment but to images of continual "supernatural war" between communities, built entirely on suspicions and gossip. In the case of witchcraft, efforts are made to buttress the suggestions of gossip by various uses of evidence or by extracting confessions.

The Hagen case has allowed us to sketch a history of Melpa ideas about *kum*, indicating the likely role played by Christian practices and ideology in altering people's notions. The possessors of ambivalent magical power perhaps became stigmatized more as sources of malevolent activity over time. New rhetoric brought in with Christianity would give people new resources in terms of which to express their antagonisms and fears. These recent processes in Hagen recapitulate much earlier processes in Europe, as the next chapter explores.

Brison's work on the Kwanga strongly supports our overall approach in this book. She stresses, as many peoples in New Guinea themselves do, the power of talk, in particular its power to do harm. New Guinea Highlands languages tend to have highly developed vocabularies of "talk about talk," and a good proportion of these terms has to do with talk that is negative, especially negative talk spoken behind people's backs. The Melpa term for this, *ik mburlung oronga*, literally translates as "talk at the back," emphasizing its secret and malicious character, but also its power.

SIX

∞

European and American Witchcraft

Much has been written on the topic of European and American witchcraft. A quick subject search on the Internet produces a result of thousands of books, articles, and web pages devoted to this specific topic. In this chapter we use some examples that we have selected from the literature that are illustrative of the themes running throughout this book.

Mary Douglas, in an early edited collection (*Witchcraft: Confessions and Accusations*, 1970), stressed the importance of the "accusation phase" in studying witchcraft. This phase is equivalent to the phase of rumor and gossip. Here we take cases from the European and American canon of materials and indicate how a prehistory of gossip and rumor invariably precedes an overt witch-hunt or witch trial and witch killings. These materials demonstrate how a sense of social hysteria can be induced, leading to persecution and violence against targeted groups. Our discussion of them in this chapter follows from materials already given in Chapter 1. First we give some general background.

The longer term background to ideas that became branded as witchcraft in Europe is contested. Margaret Murray (1970 [1931]) argued that witchcraft and its covens or sabbats represented an aspect of an old European pagan religious complex centering on fertility. Its prosecution by clerical authorities therefore represented the campaigns of the Christian church against the remnants of paganism. Murray's synthetic account of pre-Christian religion was not accepted in its details, and in particular the stress she laid on the existence or prevalence of covens was questioned. But it appears indisputable that all manner of pre-Christian ideas having to do with magic in general, whether for healing or harming others, were drawn into the arguments regarding witches.

Carlo Ginzburg (e.g., 1989 [1991]) similarly has argued that the mythology of witchcraft drew on an ancient cult of the goddess Diana or Herodias, in which its devotees were said to ride out at night on the backs of animals and to do the bidding of the goddess. Ginzburg relates this mythology further to old shamanic traditions emanating originally from Siberia, characterized by the production of an ecstatic state in which persons visualized themselves as making magical journeys through the air to secure powers of healing, to fight hostile witches, or themselves to harm others. The contested character of the *benandanti*, or "battlers against witches," in Friuli (northern Italy) fell into this shamanic category (Ginzburg 1989 [1991]: 9–10, 13–14; see also Ginzburg 2001). Ginzburg provides a composite map of the distribution of overlapping cult complexes in Europe. "Ecstatic journeys in search of predominantly female divinities" are mapped as characteristic of Scotland, France, and North-Central Italy (Ginzburg, pp. 98–9; cf. Henningsen 2001).

Hans-Peter Duerr (1985: 1–12) cites numerous records of witches allegedly rubbing their armpits and bodies with salves and ointments, which enabled them to turn into birds or otherwise to fly. One such concoction was supposed to have consisted of herbs thought to be cold and soporific, "such as hemlock, nightshade, henbane, and mandrake" (p. 3). Another salve was said to contain "cinquefoil, belladonna, waterparsnip, meadow salsify, wild celery, and aconite" (an inflammatory agent; p. 3). Some of these ingredients, Duerr notes, were hallucinogenic. Thus, they might induce sensations of flying or cause dreams in which nocturnal adventures in flight were experienced. Duerr's investigations tend to mesh with those of Ginzburg in this regard, since the shamanic image of flight is sometimes associated with the ingestion of hallucinogens.

Ann Barstow, writing about the women who were more often than men accused of witchcraft activities, reminds us that women who used herbs for healing, delivered babies or performed abortions, predicted the future, cursed others or removed curses, and could make peace between neighbors were vulnerable to witchcraft accusations (Barstow 1994: 109). Such women also carried out functions that "overlapped dangerously with the priest's job as well" (ibid.).

Lyndal Roper cites the case of serving-maid Anna Ebeler, who in January 1669 in Augsburg was accused of killing by witchcraft the young mother to whom she had served a bowl of soup made from malmesy and brandy. After drinking the soup the mother became delirious and accused her maid of killing her. When she died other women whose babies had died also accused Anna, and she became one of eighteen witches executed in Augsburg (Roper 1994: 199; cf. Willis 1995: 72). Folk remedies and nursing care could, then, lead to scapegoating by witchcraft accusations. In general, there is strong evidence that the development of trials and prosecutions for witchcraft placed a pejorative "signature" on many practices that stood outside or parallel to the male-dominated domains of church, government, and medicine. The association of certain women with "pagan" or "heathen" activities thus emerged. And in a further twist these activities were linked with the Devil.

The church in Medieval Europe played a strong role in associating witchcraft with the Devil. Thus, the acts of witches were labeled as both dangerous and sinful. The witch was depicted in church propaganda as the servant of Satan. "Scholastic philosophers, systematic theologians, and demonologists reached a gradual consensus on the nature and activities of witches. The witch, according to this consensus had succumbed of his or her own will to Satan's temptation and had entered into a contract or pact with the Devil, which usually was said to be sealed by an act of carnal intercourse with Satan or the demons" (Kors and Peters 1972: 9).

The association of witchcraft activities with sexuality and fears of female sexuality in particular were graphically illustrated in the fifteenth-century work on witchcraft, *De lamiis*. Its woodcuts depicted women cavorting with the Devil and conducting rituals with other women that would eventuate in disasters that would otherwise appear to be misfortunes of nature (Kors and Peters, pp. 18–19; cf. Bailey 2003: 48–53). Religious propaganda about witchcraft was widely distributed in a variety of forms (e.g., written works and pictorial representations). The *Malleus maleficarum* (Hammer of Witches) was pivotal in canonizing the church's affirmation that witches did exist and that they should be sought out and punished, "making disbelief, scepticism, or doubt concerning the very reality of witchcraft heretical in itself" (p. 12). Thus, those who did not believe in witches were themselves put in the position of being considered heretics.

The *Malleus maleficarum* was a manual to assist in "discovering" who was a witch. It sanctioned witch-hunts and provided guidelines and legal advice for inquisitors to take action against individuals accused of practicing witchcraft. It attempted to draw correlates between accidents or misfortunes of every sort with the involvement of Satanic influences as mediated by witchcraft. It is divided into three main sections: "The first part established that disbelief in witches is manifest heresy, offers a kind of census of the effects of witchcraft, and explains why it is that women are witches more frequently than men. The second part offers a typology of witchcraft as well as a typology for its investigation. The third part treats in infinite detail the nature of the legal proceedings against witches, and justifies all its deviations from orthodox civil and ecclesiastical legal procedures with careful citations of Scripture, the Church Fathers, and more recent theologians and ecclesiastical lawyers" (p. 106).

Its distribution and use was enhanced by the invention of the printing press. The book had fifteen editions between 1486 and 1520 and was reprinted at least nineteen times between 1574 and 1669 (Sidky 1997: 27). The use of the book was given further legitimization by the Bull of Pope Innocent VIII, *Summis desiderantes affectibus* of December 9, 1484, "in which the Pontiff, lamenting the power and prevalence of the witch organization, delegates Heinrich Kramer and James Sprenger as inquisitors . . . throughout Northern Germany" (Summers 1951: xiv). The work was influential in supporting and inspiring witch-hunts by both Catholics and subsequently Protestants (Sidky 1997: 27). It was also extremely misogynistic in its specific accusations against women in terms of their supposed associations with the Devil.

The *Malleus* is a highly organized treatise, dealing with its topics in a meticulous and plodding way, turning the extraordinary almost into the mundane by its methods of presentation. Part 1, question 6, takes up the issue of "Why it is that Women are chiefly addicted to Evil Superstitions." Women are described first as "the fragile, feminine sex." Sprenger and Kramer go on to say that the "tongue," "ecclesiastics," and women "know no moderation in goodness or vice." By the evils of the tongue they mean back-biting and slanderous speech; by the wrongs of ecclesiastics they refer to the corrupt behavior in some monasteries (which became a target in the Reformation); in the case of women, they quote a mélange of opinions from Ecclesiasticus, St. John Chrysostom, Cicero, and Seneca, including that "there is no wrath above the wrath of a woman" (where wrath means vengeful spite). Admitting that there are some good women, they generalize that women are on the whole more credulous than men, and therefore easier for the devil to corrupt; that they are more physically impressionable and so "more ready to receive the influence of a disembodied spirit"; and that they have slippery tongues and share their witchcraft secrets with other women.

Finally, they declare that "they are more carnal than men and therefore more quick to abjure their faith; and that they are liars and deceivers by nature, singing the song of the Sirens." They accuse witches of inclining men to inordinate passion, of making magic over men's penises so that they disappear, of changing men into beasts, of making other women infertile, of procuring abortions, and offering children to devils. (Sprenger and Kraemer 1951 (1486): 41–8). Midwives, who had knowledge not readily shared with men, therefore inevitably came under suspicion. (See Forbes

1966, who also refers to the salves witches used for flying as including baby fat, p. 119. Babies were supposedly slaughtered for this purpose.)

Stanislav Andreski (1989) suggested further that the witch-hunters were preoccupied with questions of sexual lust and disease, and argued that the Catholic, Calvinist, and Lutheran churches were more inclined to "demonise women" than the Anglican clergy in England (p. 50). A potent version of the sexually transmitted disease syphilis, Andreski suggested, was brought back to Europe by men who had traveled to America and engaged in sexual activities of various sorts with disease-carrying persons. Some of these men were sailors on Christopher Columbus's ship *Santa Maria* (pp. 6–7). Andreski thinks that fear of this disease, or the interpretation of it as God's punishment of sin, probably enhanced both the spread of Puritanism in general and in particular the clergy's rhetorical abhorrence of unrestrained sexual behavior. However, this would not explain the allocation of blame for the spread of the disease more on women than on men. Various writings at the time such as Kramer and Sprenger's work promoted misogynistic views. Much of this stemmed from the male-dominated clerical life at the time.

The imputation that witches engaged in carnal intercourse with demons became in some commentators' minds attached in particular to women and the imagined lusts that clerical males imputed to them. Andreski notes that the *Malleus* was at first not well received after its publication in 1486, but it became popular after 1500. His implication is that this popularity, which coincided with the growth of the Inquisition, was enhanced by the appearance of dire symptoms resulting from syphilis, although these may have been attributed to witchcraft (p. 59). People could explain their symptoms by attributing them to witchcraft, thus avoiding too great a sense of guilt. Court doctors who were unable to cure their important patients of the disease could similarly appeal to witchcraft, exhibiting what Andreski calls "an inextricable mixture of conceit, bluff, self-deception and superstition" (p. 61). In other words, witchcraft here, as in the classic formulation by Evans-Pritchard, played a renewed role as an explanation for misfortune that acted as an exculpatory device. Andreski further suggests that the general paralysis or dementia brought on by tertiary syphilis could have increased the likelihood of people who suffered in this way to accuse others of witchcraft. And he argues that the noted demonologist Jean Bodin, whose work *De la démonomanie des sorciers* was published in 1580, may himself have suffered from syphilis, although he offers no direct evidence for this. He declares that Bodin's insistence on the guilt of witches and his rejection of any refutation of this displayed a kind of neurotic obsession (p. 66). We may rather attribute it to the kind of political and legal infighting that surrounds any adversarial issue. Sidky (1997) makes many references to Bodin's work without mentioning Andreski's hypothesis. What does seem in general likely is that syphilis, like the plague, increased people's sense of malaise, led them to seek explanations for disease, and linked together sexuality, disease, and witchcraft (on the effects of syphilis in Venice, see Hatty and Hatty 1999).

Many complex factors, then, influenced the witch-hunts in Europe. A major force in the history of medieval Europe was the Black Death. Robert Gottfried's discussion of the impact of the Black Death states that in some areas of Europe, mortality rates of over 50 percent were experienced (1983: 46–9). The Black Death primarily consisted of the bubonic plague, which produced large subcutaneous blood-filled marks on the skin of those afflicted. These sores would be black in color. In some parts of Europe lepers were accused of spreading the disease, while in other places Jewish people were accused, by some Christians, of poisoning water sources in cities (p. 52). "In Basel and Fribourg thousands of Jews – men, women and children – were sealed in large wooden structures, made specially for the occasion, and set ablaze. . . . The hysteria over *pestis manufacta* (diabolically produced disease) and the brutal massacre of Jews and others blamed for the pestilence, bear many similarities to the subsequent witch hunts [in Europe]" (Sidky 1997: 88–9.) The plague continued to sporadically kill people over several centuries. During these times church inquisitors sought persons to blame for these deaths. In total as much as a third of Europe's population may have perished from the plague. Germany, Italy, England, and France were all dramatically affected by high numbers of deaths. Rumors spread that both the plague and witchcraft were works of the Devil aimed at destroying humanity (pp. 78–9).

At various times "deviant" categories of people were perceived as responsible for natural disasters and epidemics. Carlo Ginzburg reports that in 1321, the Pope ordered lepers to be imprisoned on grounds that they had prepared poisons to kill the population at large. Large numbers of lepers were sent to the stake and burned. A Dominican inquisitor declared that the lepers had spread poisonous powders in fountains, wells, and rivers so as to transmit leprosy to the healthy and enable themselves to take over (Ginzburg 1989 [1991]: 33). The form of the accusation here resembles the 1977 rumor regarding cannibals in Mount Hagen in Papua New Guinea (Chapter 5), but with the kind of dire results that are associated with centralized hierarchical kingdoms.

King Philip V of France had given an edict for the lepers to be exterminated. Those who confessed were to be burned. Others were to be tortured until they confessed and then burned. Those who refused to admit guilt were to be kept segregated from society. One chronicler declared that Jews were accomplices of the lepers (Ginzburg, p. 35). In some cases they were therefore burned along with the lepers. The Jews were said in some versions to have used the lepers as their front, paying them to scatter a dried mixture of human blood, urine, herbs, and consecrated Eucharist wafer in fountains and wells. In turn, the King of Granada in Spain was rumored to have approached the Jews to instigate all this as a plot to destroy the Christians, since he could not overcome them by force. The Jews had agreed to act covertly to this end and had then, with the help of the Devil, assembled the lepers and subverted them from their Christian faith to carry out this work of mass destruction. This was a conspiracy theory of similar magnitude to or greater than the recent Greek notion that Slobodan Milosevic and the Americans were in alliance over the war in Kosovo (Chapter 4).

Legends declared that among the ancestors of the Jews were a number of lepers driven out of Egypt (Ginzburg, p. 38). And both Jews and lepers had been pushed to the margins of society, requiring them to wear special identifying markers: for Jews a yellow, red, or green disk, for lepers a gray cloak, scarlet cap and hood, and wooden rattle (ibid.). Various further rumors both before and after 1321 also named sovereigns such as the Sultan of Bablyon or the King of Jerusalem as plotting to kill Christians by poison or to have Christian boys handed over in return for large sums of money. The casting of powder into the air was an imputed action of the conspirators that was said to be a sacrifice to the Devil (p. 51). When the plague was spread by rats from Genoan galley ships that had arrived from Constantinople and disembarked in Messina, Sicily, rumors again arose against the Jews, to effect that they were responsible for this actual epidemic (p. 63).

Questions were raised as to whether the sickness was spread by the scattering of powders. The "powder as poison" rumor can be seen here as a diving rumor which circulated in 1321 and surfaced again in the new context after 1347. Paupers and beggars were arrested in Narbonne, France, and made to confess that they had received the powders and had been given payments to scatter them. They were burned. In Toulon, a Jewish ghetto was invaded and forty people were massacred while sleeping (ibid.). Soon after, at the funeral of a plague victim in Barcelona, Catalonia, a number of Jews were also massacred. Rumors regarding the supposed or actual "confessions" of Jews were the means whereby such violence spread, along with the plague itself.

At a later stage again, these accusations against Jews became mixed with accusations against witches and heretics. A Papal Bull of 1409, issued during the conflict over the succession to the papacy itself, warned against the conglomerates of Jews and Christians who were practicing witchcraft and devilish arts that could corrupt "true Christians" (p. 69). One of these "devilish arts" appears to have been centered on the notion of lycanthropy, in which men and women were said to turn into wolves and devour infants, including their own children, and to use body parts as salves and potions, swearing first to renounce the Christian faith and trampling on the cross (p. 71; see also Sidky 1997: 215–54). An account of this alleged "new sect" appeared in the *Formicarius*, written by the German Dominican Johannes Nider in Basel, Switzerland, between 1435 and 1437 (Bailey 2003). In various other treatises further elements came together, such as the idea of the Devil appearing as a black ram or bear, the image of night flying, and drinking wine in cellars and defecating into the barrels. The stereotype was strengthened by trials and confessions, reports of which spread widely, and the composite picture of the witches' sabbat was formed. In turn, similar allegations were made against the sects of the Cathars and the Waldensians (p. 75). Inquisitors appointed by the Pope carried these themes with them wherever they conducted their trials (on the Cathars, see Cohn 1975: 128–30; and Strathern and Stewart 2001: 213–14).

An escalation in witchcraft fears occurred in post-Reformation times during the sixteenth and seventeenth centuries as waves of hysteria led to witch trials in England, Scotland, Switzerland, Germany, and France. During this time as many as 100,000 people may have been prosecuted as witches. Those afraid of being accused were eager to point a finger at others so as to divert accusing eyes from themselves. At least 75 percent of those accused of being witches were women who were either single or widowed and were propertyless. Those accused were vigorously interrogated and physically pressured so as to obtain confessions of witchcraft deeds (Duiker and Spielvogel 1998: 547–9).

Anti-witchcraft legislation was enacted in European countries that was used to accuse, arrest, torture, legally find guilty, and burn to death those said to be witches (Sidky 1997: 23). By the turn of the sixteenth century, "burning courts" were established in some cities (p. 27). Those accused of witchcraft were said to cause all kinds of misfortunes in addition to eating Christian children and the flesh of exhumed human corpses. Sidky, quoting from an anonymous Inquisitor's text, the *Errores gazariorum* (1450), states that witches were said to seal their contract of exchange with the Devil in their own blood. This marked the point of transfer of Satanic power (seen to be destructive to Christendom) to the witch and the enslavement of the witch to the Devil (pp. 37–9).

Witches were said to gather for meetings known as sabbats where the Devil appeared and was greeted by the devotees with a kiss to his posterior. This act was referred to by demonologists as *osculum infame* (the obscene kiss; p. 39). The sabbats were said to frequently end with the witches (both male and female) having sexual intercourse with the Devil (p. 42). Sidky quotes from the seventeenth-century treatise by Henri Boquet, *Discours des sorciers*, on the pact that witches were supposed to enter into with Satan: "At this point Satan forms a league with his followers against Heaven, and plots the ruin of the human race. He makes these wretched creatures repeat their renunciation of God, Chrism [anointing oil] and Baptism, and renew the solemn oath they have taken never to speak of God, the Virgin Mary, or the Saints except in the way of mockery and derision. . . . He then urges them to do all the harm that they can, to afflict their neighbours with illness, to kill their cattle, and to avenge themselves upon their enemies. . . . Also he makes them promise to waste and spoil the fruits of the earth . . ." (p. 39). After this pact the Devil is said to mark his followers with his talons to produce a *stigma diabolicum* (Devil's mark).

Confessions of witchcraft activities were in some countries extracted by various means of torture; devices such as thumb-screws, leg vises, whipping stocks, scalding liquid baths, and racks were sometimes used. The victims of these tortures might confess so as to ease their torment and be put to death. Also, a confession might assist in removing suspicion from relatives of the accused. Punishment of those found guilty was severe, often death by burning. Fire had been employed by the Inquisitors to put to death heretics and was seen as a means of "purifying" the environment. In addition to the actual physical persecution of those accused, an active campaign of terror was used to instill fear and subsequent conformity to religious and social pressures of the day. Sidky suggests that the European witch-hunts may have operated "as a form of government-sponsored, political terrorism involving the use of controlled violence" (p. 265).

Brian Levack (1987) has given an excellent historical and analytical overview of this whole period, pointing out chronological and geographical variations in the witch-hunts from country to country (pp. 170–211). He discusses the legal foundations of the hunts, pointing out that secular courts as well as ecclesiastical bodies were involved (pp. 63–92). He also looks at the impact of the Reformation, remarking that extensive witch-hunting took place in both Protestant and Catholic lands (p. 95), and that Catholic and Protestant reformers developed a similar desire to extirpate witchcraft (p. 96). He agrees that Martin Luther and Jean Calvin, two significant Protestant reformers, stressed the presence of the Devil in the world and the need to combat him doubtless in order to increase the force of these religious movements of renewal. Calvinism, in particular, brought with it deep senses of personal sin (p. 99), which might at times be projected outward onto witches. Protestant and Catholic religious conflicts did not on the whole underly witch prosecutions, but they did lead to a general sense of unease about Satan's power in the world, and the prosecution of witches was experienced as a counterattack against that power. ("Witches" here occupied a political and semantic space that has been occupied since September 11, 2001, by the concept of "terrorists"). Levack well recognizes the force of rumor in this context, citing the news of witch-hunts that spread from place to place and "could easily fan popular and elite fears. . . . It was because of such communications that many hunts spread from village to village" (p. 150). Accusers usually "had been nurturing suspicions of the accused for a long time" (p. 153).

Essex, England

Alan Macfarlane (1970a) has written a detailed account of how witchcraft accusations operated in the County of Essex in England during the Tudor and Stuart periods. He collected historical data from all the villages of the county, showing that cases of witchcraft were widely distributed and that witchcraft trials were second in frequency only to the trial of thieves at the Essex Assizes (1970a: 30). He found that informal reactions at the village level to witchcraft suspicions could be slow-moving, and court accusations did not always result from them. When a case came to court it was felt that only the death or complete confession of the suspect could solve the problem. In some instances, the healing of a putative victim was held to require the death of the witch (p. 109).

One of Macfarlane's more interesting findings is his evidence regarding village-level practitioners who were consulted to provide a recourse against witches (see also Davies 1997, Simpson 2001). He calls these practitioners "cunning folk." In the literature of medical anthropology they could be called "folk healers" or "ritual experts." Macfarlane writes: "Since witchcraft was such a mysterious force, a series of tests were employed to confirm that current gossip and suspicions were correct" (p. 109). For example, a piece of one of the belongings of the supposed witch would be burnt, to see whether the suspect came to investigate; "Ellen Smith, of Maldon in Essex, was among those caught in this manner" (p. 110).

Contemporary accounts showed how persons became increasingly disliked in the village, "the part played by gossip and rumor, and the pooling of opinions" (ibid.). Macfarlane refers to Richard Bernard's *A Guide to Grand Jury Men* (1627). After a person became identified as a witch in village consensus, people suspected their every word and deed, and in Bernard's view the Devil himself was actually involved in stirring up people to violence. The ripples of gossip reached the edges of village life and were then extended into court contexts. We see here a "rationalist" trend in discussions, which is also found notably in the work of Reginald Scot,

The Discoverie of Witchcraft. Scot, who lived between around 1538 and 1599, belonged to the County of Kent in southern England, and was a Justice of the Peace, published his *Discoverie* in 1584. He was skeptical about the doctrines and procedures of witch-finders and commentators such as Jean Bodin (Scot 1972: 51–8), and at the outset of his book declared that people have become unwilling to accept that their misfortunes are the result of God's correcting hand on their lives. Instead, "if any adversitie, greefe, sicknesse, losse of children, corne, cattell, or libertie happen unto them; by and by they exclaime upon witches" (Scot, p. 1). (To this tradition of skeptical writing belongs also the work of Charles Mackay 1841.)

In Essex, persons who wished so to "exclaim" were likely in the first instance, as we have seen, to seek out a village expert for confirmation of their suspicions. As Scot, and another witchcraft commentator, who had an Essex background and published books in 1587 and 1593, George Gifford, noted, such suspicions arose out of minor conflicts and altercations followed by misfortunes (Macfarlane, p. 111). Rumors grew until more and more misfortunes would be laid at a suspect's door. Macfarlane's records show that "cunning folk" were distributed all over Essex. He found sixty names of these practitioners in Essex records from 1560 to 1680. People might travel some miles to consult such an expert. Thomas Ward of Purleigh went to George Tailer, a "wysard" in Thaxted to ask about a theft of cattle he thought had been bewitched in 1599; Thomas Fuller of Layer Marney went to a man named Barnard in Danbury about some lost plate and other goods of his master (Macfarlane, pp. 275 and 284).

"Cunning folk" would be professionals in gathering information through gossip networks, and would put those who consulted them "in touch with suspicions circulating in their own village." Macfarlane neatly designates them as "entrepreneurs in the business of allocating blame and distributing antidotes" (p. 124). Sometimes they used "magic mirrors" in which the client was invited to see the face of a witch or of a thief who had stolen property. They employed oracles involving the manipulation of sieves and cutting shears (ibid.). Their consultants were likely to pay them for their services, but without set fees. They themselves are said by Gifford to claim that their power came from angels, while their opponents declared that it was from the Devil (p. 126). These experts were the exact equivalents of the diviners, ritualists, and "prophets" of contemporary Africa, Indonesia, and New Guinea frequently discussed in the anthropological literature (e.g., Strathern and Stewart 1999a). Professional witch-finders tied in with the clergy and the government tended to oppose them. One could comment that these "big" witch-finders were competitors of the "little" "cunning folk" and used their power to supplant and prosecute them. Among the ordinary people the "cunning folk" were popular and appreciated, even though the Anglican Church regarded them as evil (Macfarlane, p. 130).

The "big" witch-finders were also able to tap into village networks of suspicion. Macfarlane has a chapter examining details of the activities of Matthew Hopkins and John Stearne at the Essex Assizes held in Chelmsford in 1645 during the civil war between the Royalists and Cromwell's Puritans. At these assizes thirty-six women were imprisoned and tried for witchcraft, and nineteen of them were "almost certainly executed" (p. 135). Nearly all of them came from twelve small villages within fifteen miles of the village of Manningtree in the northeast corner of the county. Macfarlane's detailed reconstruction of who accused whom and who provided evidence shows clearly that complex networks of accusers were involved, some themselves suspected as witches. Counterfactions were formed to oppose the accusations. Self-professed female experts searched the bodies of the accused for the Devil's mark (lumps or scars). Hopkins himself used bodkins (needles) to probe parts of the flesh of suspects (see illustration in Scot 1972[1584]: 201, reproduced in Sidky 1997: 124). The witch-finders also seem to have imported into their allegations Continental motifs such as the witch's sexual interactions with the Devil. It was not uncommon for both women and men to be accused of having sexual relations with demonic spirits when prosecuted for witchcraft activities in Europe. The disruption of local government at the time of the civil war seems to have produced the anxiety and turbulence that led to a rise in these trials. Those involved in persecuting these people invariably received payments for the work (p. 140).

At the village level those who accused others were usually neighbors of those they accused, though not, it seems, necessarily their kin. In-laws were also sometimes involved (p. 169). Children sometimes gave evidence against their parents (p. 170), but often supported them against charges. Outward manifestations of either ill-will or excessive good-will could lead to suspicions. Most interestingly, Macfarlane found that in the records of the assizes of 1582 the alleged motives of witches invariably involved resentment at a denial of a minor request such as for food or a domestic animal (p. 173). The image of the witch as a neglected, slightly needy neighbor emerges from Macfarlane's tabulation, and led to his well-known hypothesis or explanation of his data that the materials reflect a period when people were breaking away from older communal practices of mutual help among villagers (p. 176). We find here a clear resonance with African materials in which people blame witchcraft on the rise of the monetary economy (Chapter 3).

Macfarlane also connects the rise in prosecutions in general with Puritanism, but not in any specific or detailed way, and in the Essex cases accusations were not made out of religious fervor or bias. Essex villagers were interested, rather, "in the link between anger and accident," that is, in establishing an explanation for misfortune rooted in the resentful feelings of others (p. 189). Interesting, here, is the point that the accusers were those who felt in some way guilty, and it is notable that those who held grudges do not seem to have had a legitimate way to get them resolved, for example, in village meetings. Perhaps such matters were resolved where the participants were kin. This seems to be an arena for further investigation. In any case the conceptual gap between "anger" and "accident" was always bridged by rumor and gossip. Macfarlane briefly suggests that Catholic ritual in the past "may have offered a solution to the misfortunes of daily life which did not involve the blame being centered on either the individual or his neighbours" (p. 195). This, too, would seem to be a topic for further investigation. In general, Macfarlane's materials bring us into a proximity of understanding these data from the 1500s and 1600s in Essex that is comparable to the detailed studies by Victor Turner (1996 [1957]) and Max Marwick (1965) on southern Africa in the 1950s.

In addition, Macfarlane's work, built partly on the studies by Keith Thomas (1973) and the viewpoints expressed by Hugh Trevor-Roper (1969), contributed to the formation of a new perspective on witchcraft in Europe, to effect that village-level ideas were centered on specific delicts and supposed offenses, that is, *maleficia*, while the church and legal authorities imported into this situation their own forms of theological demonology, specifically, the complex of ideas associated with the witches' sabbat. This view is generally reflected by the contributors to Ankarloo and Henningsen's coedited work on early modern European witchcraft (2001, first published in 1990). This volume, containing studies from Eastern Europe and Scandinavia, greatly increases the subtlety of comparisons that can be made *between* European countries. Here we make only one such comparison, between England and Scotland.

Scotland

Christina Larner's detailed work on witch-hunts in Scotland in the sixteenth and seventeenth centuries gives us an opportunity to compare her findings with Macfarlane's microsociology of witch trials in Essex, England. Larner notes (1981: 60) that witchcraft "was a statutory criminal offence punishable by death in Scotland from 1563 to 1735" and that there were peaks of intensive prosecution, the first stimulated by King James VI in 1590–1 and the second in 1597 when he published his *Daemonologie* book. Most of the cases came from the non-Gaelic-speaking areas with a concentration around East Lothian and fishing villages in Fife and Aberdeenshire (p. 82). Larner further points out that

while witches were often accused of causing disasters such as crop fail-
ures or shipwrecks, it is hard to correlate witch-hunts with general demographic disasters. Plague and famine occurred in 1600, 1607, 1624, and 1635,
when witch-hunts were at a low level (p. 82). She suggests that witchcraft
was rather used as an explanation for individual misfortunes. Perhaps the
background of disasters nevertheless conditioned people to feel anxious
and nervous. Larner herself remarks (p. 88) that "witch-hunting drew on
endemic fears and hostilities in the peasant population."

Witches "were predominantly poor, middle-aged, or elderly women"
(p. 89), often the wives or widows of tenant farmers; the quarrels that
led to accusations against them "were about the exchange of goods and
services in a tenant and sub-tenant economy" (ibid.). In England they
were usually even lower in the social scale, wives and widows of wage laborers or beggars (p. 90; see cases in Douglas 1978 on the Pendle witches
of Lancashire, also cited in Chapter 1). Not all of those accused of being witches were women. Larner computes for the period 1560–1709 in
Scotland that about one-fifth were men. In times of panic, however, the
hunts centered on women (p. 92). Larner relates the prejudice against
women to long-standing ideas in the Greek and Judeo-Christian traditions, as well as to fear of women's menstrual and reproductive powers in
general.

Prejudice fastened on women who were socially weak and who may
have claimed witchcraft powers to boost their status and may have been
attracted by the idea of the Devil promising them freedom from "want"
(p. 95) or by the notion that they could mystically harm others whom they
could not physically attack. Larner suggests that while men resorted to
physical violence in situations of stress, women used witchcraft. Finally,
she considers that witches were women with hot tempers. "The witch
had the Scottish quality of smeddum: spirit, a refusal to be put down,
quarrelsomeness. No cursing; no malefice; no witch" (p. 97). One witch
cursed a man with whom she quarrelled by saying to him, "[F]or work
what you can your teeth shall overgang your hands and ye shall never get

your Sunday meat to the fore" (p. 97). A capacity to insult or threaten others would mark someone out, as also would the fact of being related to someone already suspected (p. 99), especially being the daughter of a supposed witch.

Being thought a witch did not necessarily lead to being accused or put on trial. But the perceived egregious behavior of some women made them vulnerable to accusation, because they did not "fulfil the male view of how women ought to conduct themselves" (p. 100). The witch was seen as an independent adult woman, exercising free will but doing so in a way that challenged some men's sense of "correct" behavior. Nevertheless, witch-hunts were not primarily against women as such but against witches as "enemies of God."

Larner provides a diagram showing a network of accusations among a number of people in two witch-hunts from East Lothian in 1659 (p. 105), paralleling the complexities of similar materials given by Macfarlane. What is noteworthy in all of these cases is how a single individual might name many others, drawing them all into a net of suspicion, perhaps in an attempt to gain merit or a reprieve. But confessions of witchcraft were most likely to be obtained by torture, including sleep deprivation but also the "cashielaws" (leg crushing) and "pinniewinks" (thumb-screws; p. 108). Ordeals were used, for example, "bierricht," in which the accused had to lay hands on the corpse of a person they had supposedly killed, or pricking for the witch's mark to find the place where the witch allegedly did not feel pain (p. 111).

Some specific accounts of accusations and trials will help to facilitate comparisons. Larner cites one case from Loch Ken in Kirkcudbrigthshire, the Airds farm where Janet Macmurdoch was a tenant, married to James Hendrie. Janet was first accused in 1671 by John Moor, the rent collector for the laird of the estate that the farm was on. He had impounded her livestock for unpaid rent and she had "promised him an evil turn," after which a cow, a calf, and later a child of his all died, according to his testimony in court. Other landowners from nearby had also been in conflict with her over her stock that had eaten their grass, for example. All declared that she was "of evil reputation" (p. 121). Margaret Maclellan of Boghall accused Janet and her daughter of being witches after finding the daughter playing with dung when she had been sent to "muck out" (clean) the byre (cow shed). Margaret's husband fell sick and recovered only when Janet visited them and removed the curse. Within Janet's own fermtoun (farm settlement) she had much earlier asked for some meal and been refused by Robert Cairnes and Jean Sprot, who shared rigs (strips of land) with her (p. 122). The couple suffered sickness and loss of their livestock until Janet withdrew her malefice, and finally the husband died, "leaving his death" with Janet and enjoining his kin to exact retribution for it. It seems that Janet may have been a widow from a previous marriage, and although married to James Hendrie she ran the farm herself. She had economic difficulties and refused to be deferential to her better-off neighbors, on whom she needed to depend for help (pp. 122–4).

Accusations from neighbors that Janet, and others like her, were of evil repute clearly drew on a prehistory of gossip about these women. The jury persons who were called on to hear Janet's case were bonnet lairds (small landowners) and tenants from some ten miles around the town of Dumfries. "Reputations" spread among the scattered fermtouns of an estate. "The communications network was wide and so thus widespread the rumour of a person's character" (p. 131).

In the county of Angus there were famous witch trials in the 1660s, following a halt on them occasioned by the rule of Oliver Cromwell's Protectorate. Here also quarrels with neighbors and associates were central. Isobel Shyrie confessed to conspiring with the Devil to kill George Wood, a baillie, after he had taken from her a pan in lieu of payment of her cess (a local tax; Scharlau 1995: 15). She confessed to making a lethal powder containing "one piece dead mans flesh which the divill perfumed" (ibid.) that she slipped into Wood's drink, causing his death. (This act would be sorcery in some definitions of the term.)

One of the Forfar women convicted of witchcraft was Helen Guthrie. With her case we find the phenomenon of the accused implicating others in her confessions, leading to further arrests. Guthrie claimed to have been a witch for fourteen years, to have learned her arts from Janet Galloway of Kirriemuir and to be able to identify other witches by the use of pieces of paper with blood on them (Scharlau, p. 22).

All of the witches' confessions included accounts of meetings with the Devil and entering into a pact with him. Janet Howatt, who was about thirteen, declared the Devil had met her at the Forfar Loch and had kissed her and nipped her on the shoulder. Six weeks later he nipped her again and the pain from the first nip ceased. The confessions made by Helen Guthrie included accounts of ritual cannibalism and the smearing of a dead child's flesh on a broom to enable her to fly. She also accused local men as well as women of being witches and of being able to transform themselves into toads. Despite giving so much evidence against others, Helen was herself executed on November 14, 1662 (Scharlau, p. 48). In cases of this sort where a woman was imprisoned and tortured, her accusations against others would go well beyond the local gossip mills, even if taking off from them.

Scharlau's account of the Forfar witches follows leads given in Larner's work on the social status of witches, but it does not give an elaborate explanation for Helen Guthrie's actions. Occasionally, we are able to pick up on larger-scale local events, in addition to specific quarrels, that colored attitudes toward those accused of being witches. From the burgh of Pittenweem on the Fife coast, Larner notes (1981: 82) that the burgh "lost over 100 adult males at the battle of Kilsyth in 1649." (Magnusson (2000: 440) dates this battle to 1645. The Pittenweem villagers were fighting on the side of the Covenanters against Royalist forces.) Seventeen ships rotted on their moorings and the families of the men lost sank into poverty. At the same time accusations of witchcraft began to rise. This observation helps to make sense of the report that in one case from Pittenweem a woman, Janet Cornfoot, entered a blacksmith's shop and asked for some nails. The youth working there, Patrick Morton, refused her on grounds that he was busy making nails to be used in building a ship. When he later saw a "timber vessel with some water and a fire coal in it" at her door and fell ill, he accused this woman of bewitching him. Tensions surrounding nails as important items in rebuilding ships and hence the burgh's economy seem to lurk beneath the surface of this story (Cook in Conolly 1869: 215–19; see also Macdonald 2002 for a full-scale study of the "Witches of Fife").

Taken as a whole, these case materials from Larner closely parallel Macfarlane's picture from England. But Larner points out that in Scotland witch-hunts were especially vigorous and intense overall (1981: 31), though subject to considerable fluctuations (1984: 22–33). This feature is perhaps related to the attempts by both political authorities and church officials to extend their powers into rural contexts. Larner also attributes some significance to the activities of King James VI in seeking out witches after the storms that beset the ships of his Danish bride and himself in travel-ing from Denmark to Scotland (1984: 22). A high-level political element entered here, since one of the accused witches implicated the Fifth Earl of Bothwell as an instigator of the supposed attacks on James, and this imputation increased James's animosity. Bothwell was a powerful hered-itary official. He was also a nephew of the Fourth Earl of Bothwell, who was widely supposed to have assassinated James's father, Lord Darnley (Magnusson 2000: 353–63), and who had married Mary Queen of Scots, James's mother, after Darnley's death. King James therefore had reasons to be suspicious of the Fifth Earl, especially since the earl was also the leader of a strongly pro-Protestant faction among the Scottish nobles of the day and might be seen as a rival of James himself. A peculiar intertwining of personal and dynastic issues thus lay behind the witch trials that James instigated (see also Clark 1977). Rumors had played their part in whip-ping up the King's suspicions in the first place (Larner 1984: 11). With his book of 1597, James introduced Continental notions of the witches' sabbat and contributed to the "officialization" of witchcraft ideas in general. As

Larner points out, the doctrine of the witches' pact with the Devil, "far from being an experience of village life, . . . was evolved by churchmen and lawyers" (1984: 3).

Salem, 1692

Witchcraft fears had established themselves in the American colonies, and during the seventeenth century a number of trials were conducted and individuals put to death after having been found guilty of being witches. The events in the village of Salem, Massachusetts, in 1692 are a notable episode and were declared to have been initiated after two of the daughters of the village's minister were said to be possessed by a witch's spell. The symptoms of the girls included convulsive movements and malaise. Rumors quickly spread about the girl's conditions and soon other young girls claimed to be under the effects of bewitching spells. The girls were extensively questioned and the names of several persons were put forward as being the witches. One of those accused was an Indian slave girl of Arawak descent, Tituba, who confessed, saying that she had directly interacted with the Devil (confession could sometimes save a person's life). It was said that "[t]he witches frequented a secret society where the Devil appeared as a black man and baptized them in his name. They partook of an evil, black communion bread; they harboured demons in the forms of animals and suckled them with blood through their witches' teats, and they performed *maleficia* [harm] against their enemies, causing illness, moving objects supernaturally and, of course, tormenting the afflicted girls with fits and convulsions" (Russell 1980: 105). Hysteria spread from the gossiping of stories such as this, and by the end of the witch trials nineteen persons had been executed and more than a hundred jailed.

Local gossip had propagated the fears, and, interestingly, prayers and sermons in Salem Village were said not to be strong enough to stop the witchcraft deeds from occurring. (Fears of this kind underlay the search for judicial methods to deal with witchcraft and also the emergence of violent witch-hunts elsewhere.) The Reverend Cotton Mather was said to have been the most influential clergyman in the witch-hunt, claiming that "witches, having signed the Devil's book, were agents of the Devil in his plot to destroy the Church" (Robinson 1991: 13). Fortunately, much of the recorded legal documentation of this period in history has been preserved and published in three volumes of *The Salem Witchcraft Papers* (1977). Since witchcraft was a crime in 1692, a legal process was followed in hunting the accused and bringing them to trial. This involved the filing of a complaint against the accused, the issuance of an arrest warrant by the local magistrate, the preliminary examination of the accused by the magistrate, the collection of testimony from "witnesses" (some of whom provided written depositions), the imprisonment of the person if a formal trial was to be held, a grand jury decision on whether to indict, and, finally, trial by jury (p. 15).

The period leading up to the Salem witch trials was a particularly difficult time in New England. High taxation had produced resentments, pirate attacks on commercial vessels were reducing profits, a harsh winter in 1692 had affected crops, smallpox outbreaks were plaguing the region, and the French armies in conjunction with the local American Indians were presenting a lethal threat to New Englanders (p. 27). The Reverend Cotton Mather, who stirred the fears of people about witchcraft through his writings and sermons, had grown up during a time when New England had experienced numerous bloody battles with the local indigenous peoples who were being dispossessed by the Puritan settlers (p. 41; see Norton 2002).

As Mather developed as a preacher he employed a type of sermon known as a "jeremiad," being named after the "Old Testament Book of Jeremiah; a typical verse is 9:4, 'Take ye heed everyone of his neighbor, And trust ye not in any brother'" (p. 49). Preachers used the jeremiad to stimulate and retain the interest of parishioners in "battling evil" in the world around them. In pamphlets and sermons Mather warned that "the

Prince of Darkness was preparing to exterminate New England" (ibid.). During the winter of 1691–92 the villagers posted sentinels in the watch tower day and night who were on alert for American Indian raids. Cotton Mather's pamphlets told people to "tell mankind that here are Devils and Witches, and that New England has had examples of their existence and operation, and that not only the wigwams of Indians, where the pagan Powaws [medicine men] often raise their masters [devils], in the shapes of bears and snakes and fires, but the houses of Christians have undergone the annoyance of evil spirits" (pp. 131–2, Robinson's definitions in brackets). He went on to say, "*An Army of Devils* is horribly broke in upon our English settlements, and the houses of good people there are filled with the doleful shrieks of their children and servants, tormented by invisible hands, with tortures altogether preternatural" (p. 156, Robinson's emphasis). (It may be noted here that Klees (1950: 298–300) attributes "powwowing" as a folk medicine practice to the Pennsylvania Dutch in the nineteenth century.)

Salem Village had been established in a less than harmonious manner that left various families disturbed about issues over taxes, land use, religious hierarchy, and other matters. In 1679, before the witch-hunt hysteria, one Salem villager stated that "brother is against brother and neighbor against neighbors, all quarreling and smiting one another" (Boyer and Nissenbaum 1974: 45), and the Salem minister at the time said the community had "uncomfortable divisions and contentions" (ibid.). The Village was not an independent town and was held under the jurisdiction of Salem Town. The Town of Salem had been experiencing economic expansion by merchants and through trading endeavors. The farmers of Salem Village resented the political authority that Salem Town had over their affairs. Also, land disputes over property borders with neighboring hamlets were not uncommon (Robinson 1991: 60–1).

Struggles in the religious community of Salem had resulted in a number of ministers coming and leaving the Village prior to the witch-hunts.

Boyer and Nissenbaum suggest that when village factionalism is taken into consideration, often those accused fall into networks of relationships that involved either kinship ties or connections through real-estate transactions, executors in wills and estate settlements, and/or other sorts of links that might have motivated persons to accuse others (p. 183).

These materials from Salem also provide suggestive parallels with Macfarlane's data from Essex, although the economic relationships involved seem to have been different. John Demos's detailed and longitudinal study of Salem duplicates Macfarlane's methods of inquiry and his findings in many ways, showing that the events of 1692 in Essex County, Massachusetts, like those in Essex, England, in 1645, had a long prehistory and were a part of much wider patterns (Demos 1982). Demos makes numerous mentions of the significance of gossip and rumors that were unearthed at intervals in court testimonies (e.g., p. 138), and also of the potential confusion between being a witch and "a cunning woman" (ibid.), that is, a witch-finder and folk healer.

Boyer and Nissenbaum's very detailed study of the deep factionalism in Salem must surely also suggest to us that similar forms of division developed in the English and Scottish villages studied by Macfarlane and Larner. They also point out the shifting economic circumstances in Salem at the time. "All of these people were on the move, socially and economically. Yet to many New Englanders of the seventeenth century, the stability of the social order rested on the willingness of everyone to accept his given station in life" (Boyer and Nissenbaum 1974: 209). They go on to note that Cotton Mather preached against "rebellion," calling it "as the sin of witchcraft" (ibid.). Here they are arguing in parallel to the explanations of Macfarlane and others regarding witchcraft accusations in England. Enlarging their argument from the microsociological to the macrosociological level, and here anticipating the explanatory schemes of Taussig and the Comaroffs, they write that "the social order was being profoundly shaken by a superhuman force which had lured all too many into active complicity with it. We have chosen to construe this force as emergent mercantile capitalism. Mather, and Salem Village, called it witchcraft" (ibid.). Their final footnote traces this process through to the mid-eighteenth century and the "Great Awakening," in which efforts were made again to purge evils from the world and restore it to a desired form of unity (p. 216, n. 59). Surely in such circumstances, gossip would thrive, as it did among the Makah Indians cited by Gluckman, as a means of contesting about status. And surely also the turbulence here was every bit as great, if not on the same scale, as that which analysts today appeal to under the rubric of globalization and modernity in order to explain the idea of "occult economies."

Conclusion

The discussion of the witch-hunts in sixteenth- and seventeenth-century Europe, following the Reformation, contributes to our general theme by showing that, when we dig beneath the generalized narratives of devilish pacts and strange powers, we find neighbors quarreling over resources and the better-off people accusing their social inferiors who were quarrelsome and vindictive in their ways. It was precisely the pathway of local gossip that strengthened these accusations and its extension into wider rumors that influenced juries to convict people and have them executed. We also see that at the height of the witch-hunts witches were rarely acquitted and were liable to be executed. The dogmas of the church and the association of witches with the Devil may partially explain this severity. It is also evident from Larner's materials that those accused of being witches were often women who claimed powers of healing as well as harming. They were figures around whom adverse gossip could easily gather, especially if they were incomers. While such women may not regularly have been subjected to overt mob violence, this did happen to Janet Cornfoot, of the Pittenweem witches, a matter regarded with shame by later commentators (Cook 1869). As our next chapter shows, there is often a close connection between rumors and violence. Indeed state-mandated executions of witches may themselves be seen as just one step from such violence, since they were public and witnessed by those who otherwise might have "taken the law into their own hands" in order to purge their community of putative evil.

❧

SEVEN

Rumors and Violence

Rumors and gossip are often crucially involved in the genesis of overt violence in communal settings, sometimes taking the form of suggestions that covert violence is being practiced through witchcraft, sorcery, or other forms of ritual. Alternatively, rumors may take the form of protests against what is perceived as the imposition of violence by state authorities. These protests in turn can generate active and violent resistance movements. Rumors of atrocities often form a part of this overall process. Here we take the case of rumors of construction sacrifices in Indonesia to illustrate this point, setting these rumors into the overall regional literature on head-hunting (Stewart and Strathern 1998c). Violence against outsiders is easily generated by rumors also and these therefore invariably play a part in intergroup conflicts along ethnic and/or religious lines.

As we have seen in the materials presented from Africa (Chapter 3) and Papua New Guinea (Chapter 5), colonial and postcolonial conditions are important factors in establishing altered representations of relationships among people and among people and their environments. One example of this is the changed perceptions of headhunting in Eastern Indonesia where rumors spread that government officers were seeking to obtain human heads as forms of sacrifice. These rumors diffused widely and were in part stimulated by the increased state impact at the local level, which shifted preexisting power relations. In Borneo and Flores these rumors grew out of ideas surrounding what has been called "construction sacrifice."

Barnes has written about this among the people of eastern Flores, saying that they are "prone to suspect government officials or missionaries of capturing a child and placing its head in the foundation of new bridges and buildings" (Barnes 1993: 146). These rumors feature several elements: (1) kidnapping (or headhunting), (2) construction sacrifice, (3) state government perpetrators (formerly Dutch, now Indonesian), (4) feared strangers; and (5) victims. Drake (1989) suggests that these elements are combined in such a way as to form credible rumors owing to the cultural logic that has already existed. That is, headhunting was prevalent in Indonesia until its suppression by state governments in the late nineteenth century, and construction sacrifice (based originally on alleged human sacrifices during the construction of dwelling houses) was also a widespread religious practice. An important point that Drake makes in his argument is that the rumors of headhunting reflect the ideology of warfare in the villages where the victims are seen as falling prey to the needs of the state government. This situation emerges from the long-standing tensions between villagers and the state that arise from the villagers' distrust of the Indonesian government and its nation-building efforts.

Headhunting practices were a predominant factor in the political life of Borneo in precolonial times. They were a means of securing fertility for human beings and for the land. The colonial suppression of these renewal practices may have fueled the rumor mills, escalating fears of headhunting by those seen to be oppressors, that is, the government officials (Drake 1989: 277). Drake argues that headhunting was in the past one of the regular modes of interethnic relations, and its suppression bred resentment that was then transformed into a perception that the newly dominant colonial powers were themselves practicing the taking of heads for ritual purposes of their own.

This general argument is corroborated by Kenneth George's study in Sulawesi of relations between coastal political federations of the Mandar people and mountain peoples. These relations were founded on both trading and headhunting. The coastal dwellers were more prosperous and had external sea-based trading partnerships. The uplanders provided forest products and also slaves obtained in raids from other swidden cultivators around them. They saw themselves as less well off than coastals and thus sought to reverse the patterns of dominance by raiding them for heads that were then used in rituals of consecration in their houses to promote fertility and prosperity. At some point after intrusion by the Dutch into the area in 1906, surrogates in the form of a tuber or a coconut encased in a net bag began to be used instead of human heads, but the ritual practices and language continued with the same rhetorical formulations about violence as they had before. The uplanders also saw themselves as the "elder brothers" and the coastals as "junior brothers" from whom they took heads under cover of conducting trade: an imagery of siblingship that, like the headhunting theme itself, reversed the flow of dominance. George's complex account and analysis corroborates the point that headhunting was a part of interethnic relations and was itself a mode of sociality (George 1996: 73–100).

The ambush and killing of trading partners resembles the form of attack conducted by assault sorcerers (see the "Epidemiologies of Change" section in Chapter 5). Comparing the narratives of headhunting with those of assault sorcery and cannibalistic witchcraft in Papua New Guinea, we see that one common pattern is the breaching of the body in order to destroy the victim. Such an imagery is highly potent as a way of expressing general relations of power and domination.

Janet Hoskins, drawing on the contributions by the authors in her edited volume on headhunting in Southeast Asia (Hoskins 1996), has perceptively explored these themes in further detail. Bringing together her analysis with the insights of other writers on the topic, we can understand well Drake's point (1989: 269) that we are dealing with a "diving rumor" that has the power to produce social panic in local populations. A diving rumor is one that appears and disappears, then reappears at intervals of time. Its tendency to do this is a product of its close association with enduring cultural motifs, which become available for reuse in changed circumstances. As Allport and Postman (1947) pointed out, rumor may become sedimented into folklore or legend. Its themes are then preserved in oral traditions, and can be recovered from these and reappropriated as rumor later. This same phenomenon was pointed out by Guha in relation to the reasons given for riots in colonial India under the British (see Chapter 4).

The enduring and widespread motifs in this instance are: the fear of kidnapping and assault by strangers, the practice of headhunting and the values of fertility procured by violence that it signified, and the custom of construction sacrifice by which the heads or whole bodies of captured persons, especially babies, were supposedly taken and used as sacrifices to spirits in order to strengthen buildings and edifices such as large dams. These three motifs form an identifiable cluster of fears based on a proto-typical situation of a local group facing predatory outsiders.

The fear of kidnapping, assault, and bodily appropriation is common to this cluster of ideas and to notions regarding assault sorcery in New Guinea. In assault sorcery motifs, however, the bodies of victims are not necessarily thought of as consumed by the sorcerers, nor are their heads taken. Headhunting shares with construction sacrifice the idea of the reappropriation of a victim's vitality, and both themes overlap with the idea of taking organs and bodily parts and using them for magical or medicinal purposes. We have seen in Chapter 3 how such ideas have emerged or reemerged in the context of debates about organ transplants and organ "harvesting" that exactly parallel in their genesis rumors about construction sacrifices.

As all the commentators on this theme have pointed out, this genesis is to be found in the unequal and antagonistic relations between local populations and state authorities. The Dutch and, after them, the Indonesians condemned the former practices of headhunting and stigmatized local populations that followed these practices as "primitives" who therefore had to be pacified and brought into a "civilized" state. Cannibalism, and warfare generally, were used as comparable colonial tropes in places such as New Guinea and Africa. Colonial practices of confiscating heads and of exporting these to museums abroad, or even of lending them out again for use in rituals, unwittingly fed into a reversal of the trope over time. In construction sacrifice rumors it is the state itself that is portrayed as the headhunter, stealing local and indigenous forms of strength for its own enterprises, in a way that is compared to the rapacious ways of outsiders and strangers in the past.

Indeed, it is doubtful whether we should ascribe these images of fear simply to the Dutch and the Indonesian state. Local rajas or rulers seem to have acted either on their own account or in conjunction with Dutch practices to capture people for use in the slave trade, and slaves were customarily used as sacrifices at the funeral obsequies for their owners (Strathern and Stewart 2000b). The practice was widespread throughout Eastern Indonesia, including Irian Jaya (West Papua, the western half of the island of New Guinea). Given these traditions, the fear of kidnapping was certainly not based on fantasy. Other aspects of customary practices might well also have entered into the complexes of rumor and legend. As Hoskins remarks (1996: 32), people of the interior regions of Borneo often see the secret raiders who come to capture heads for construction projects as being Madurese or Buginese, "ethnic groups once heavily involved in the slave trade." The Dayaks of Borneo, for example, maintain these traditions, and they also have for long in the past been exploited by rajas, then the Dutch, and finally the Indonesian authorities, who conduct their projects under the rubric of nation building. The attribution of headhunting to these categories of people would thus fit with actual long-term historical experience. More recent episodes of violence against these same ethnic categories (Madurese and Buginese) on the part of the Dayaks undoubtedly stem from the same context of resentments held over time. Calling the state and its perceived agents "headhunters" neatly reverses the colonial ideology, claiming that it is the state that now terrorizes its own periphery. Drake observes also that peripheral peoples have often been drawn into projects of building roads and bridges as corvée labor, and these projects often result in the deaths of workers on the job (Drake 1989: 277). Actual experience therefore again feeds into the patterns of rumor.

The rumor seems therefore to be not only a "diving" one but also a "snowballing" one. It can take on numerous accretions and inputs over time and space. The idea of construction sacrifice, for example, may have taken a part of its impetus from the practice in some areas of burying people inside their own houses, as Forth (1991) suggested. In a quite different way, resistance struggles between the Indonesian state and local peoples have supplied images for the rumor as well. Hoskins states that "Fretilin, the resistance force fighting Indonesian government troops in East Timor, has published many photographs of human heads severed by government soldiers and displayed on bayonets to local people" (Hoskins 1996: 35).

Similar pictures entered the news in an opposite context when Dayaks in 2001 attacked ethnic outsiders resettled in their areas. Rumor flows across the troubled and diverse state of Indonesia can gather into themselves snippets of remembered custom, vivid experiences of actual brutalities, suspicions regarding the military, and the basic structures of enduring legendary or mythological themes. The more elements that come together, the greater the social and moral panic that can ensue. The same must hold for the riots and killings that have taken place during 2001 between Muslims and Christians in Maluku, including Ambon, in Eastern Indonesia, riots said in part to be fomented and carried out by bands of militant Islamic fighters who enter the region specifically to attack the Christian population.

Irian Jaya (West Papua, Papua) is a part of Eastern Indonesia near to Maluku. The Kabar Irian News web site published in Indonesia on December 5, 2001, reported that a rumor wave on Islamic militant activity had hit Biak, an island on the north coast. This rumor declared that an organization called the Laskar Jihad had been using local mosques to organize moves against Christians. The rumor was supposed to have been obtained from refugees coming from Maluku and also from government security authorities. One Christian leader declared there were 300 Laskar Jihad members present in Biak, citing an Air Force intelligence officer as his source. In response to the rumor, youths who were the children of retired members of the military and police in the Christian community formed a Christian unit to oppose the Laskar Jihad. The rumor therefore itself generated the replication of conditions conducive to violent confrontation, given people's knowledge of earlier events in Maluku itself (source: TAPOL, the Indonesia Human Rights Campaign). In the same way, rumors of construction sacrifice may not just be reactive responses to state power but proactive instruments of creating opposition to that power. The functions of rumor here are the same as those Guha identified for India (Chapter 4).

The conflation of modern and earlier elements in the construction sacrifice rumor is also comparable to the conglomerations of notions remarked on for Africa and elsewhere by the Comaroffs (1999; Chapter 3). R. H. Barnes (1993) collected a diverse set of observations together on this theme. The narratives he adduces testify to a prevailing state of suspicion, mistrust, and anxiety between Eastern Indonesian peoples and the colonial Dutch power and later the Indonesian state. Panic is the keynote of the examples he gives. An Indonesian politician who became the first Prime Minister of the Republic of Indonesia wrote in 1937, prior to Indonesian independence, that this was the time of kidnappers (*tjoelik* or *culik*), who came to villages to get heads for the government. He reported a rumor that the Dutch used to let out criminals by night who, accompanied by guards and traditional headhunters from Borneo, procured heads on the Moluccan (Maluku) island of Banda (Barnes 1993: 146–7). The account may be read as political rhetoric against the Dutch (camouflaged by a stance of irony on the Indonesian author's part, it seems). If so, it must have backfired over time, since this same rumor later attached itself to the officials of the Indonesian Republic itself.

Barnes reports how further notions become tied in. In one part of western Indonesia, the Lom people of Bangka "believe that electricity is made by tapping the energy of a pair of newborn babies placed in acid.... The energy lasts several decades, and the babies are kidnapped on commission by convicts serving life sentences" (Barnes 1993: 148, citing Smedal 1989: 77–9). The convicts are said to leave money as compensation for the babies, and they themselves are pardoned. In another rumor people declare that the government authorities order persons working in maternity wards to give newborn babies lethal injections, telling the mothers the babies could not be saved, or, to kidnap a pregnant woman near to term, cut her head off, open her abdomen and remove the fetus, since "the younger the baby, the greater its power" (Barnes, p. 148). And a third version is that the government uses "babysitters who steal the children in their care" or else tells people "to drive around in residential areas after school in cars without license plates in order to snatch children on the way home from school" (ibid.). With this version the Lom rumor comes into close alignment with those from parts of Africa extensively documented by White (Chapter 3) as "vampire rumors."

Other permutations of suspicions exist. Barnes gives us an anecdote from his field area, Lamalera, in Eastern Indonesia. The story dates from 1982, when Barnes was discussing with an acquaintance the steps taken many years earlier in the 1920s by a Catholic missionary Bernardus Bode to bury a set of ancestral skulls behind the church. In 1920 when Bode arrived he had found that certain clans kept ancestral skulls on a shelf at the rear of boat sheds, and made offerings to them when they went out fishing in the sea. Some families refused to give up their skulls to Bode. The missionary took a number of sacred stones and buried these behind the church, but later he took these and placed them "in the foundations of the new church" (Barnes, p. 149). Barnes rightly refers to this as "an act of overt appropriation of ritual capital of a familiar kind" (possibly one chosen by Catholic rather than Protestant missionaries; the latter perhaps more often chose destruction rather than reconsecration). With the memory of historical strategies of this kind, it is unsurprising to learn that Barnes's acquaintance pressed him to reveal "where Europeans get their heads to bury in the foundations of their large buildings" (p. 149). The missionary Bode wrote his own account of Lamalera, in which he reported that when people brought back an enemy as a prisoner, they would cut off his hands and feet and dry them in the sun. Prior to the next raid they would grind up these parts between stones and mix the powder in palm wine, which they drank to give them strong arms and swift feet in battle (p. 151). The idea of appropriating the magical force of outsiders was therefore apparently well established among these people. It would be only natural for them to extend this interpretation to the actions of Bode himself.

In his conclusions Barnes points out the many ways in which actual historical experiences fed into the rumors of government violence. Older experiences and cultural ideas were, we might say, constantly recycled and transformed when run through newer frameworks of experience. From the contemporary practices of the Indonesian military forces, we may conclude that local peoples would find plenty to correlate with their older stories that "the taking of heads was one of the forms of violence associated with holders of political and military power" (p. 155).

One element in the construction sacrifice syndrome seems to be largely taken for granted by the anthropological commentators, that is, the idea that these human lives were demanded as a sacrifice by spirit beings of the landscape or environment. While the rumors reflect fear and distrust of alien authorities, they also seem to depend on a logic of sacrifice intimately connected with the land itself. The spirit beings involved are also envisaged as potentially resenting or resisting interventions or interferences in their domains by causing buildings or bridges to collapse. The idea of the spirit beings thus also has the potential to hold within it an indigenous discourse of resistance. But, perhaps paradoxically, these local spirits demand that the sacrifice be made by the people of the land rather than by the intruders. Alternatively, perhaps the message is that the intruders seize on the indigenous strength of the people in order to withstand the assaults of their own indigenous spirits. Confused and inchoate representations of powers, loyalties, and their appropriations can be expected to be encapsulated within complex political rumors of the kind we have been exploring here. Indeed, the same is true for much of the material we have been examining in this book. What is clear is how important it is to pay attention to all the confluences, nuances, and even contradictions that characterize such complexes of rumor.

Rumors and Riots in India and Bangladesh

Anjan Kumar Ghosh (1998) has written an extended account and analysis of the role of rumor in the production and reproduction of communal violence between Hindu and Muslim populations over the turbulent period of the partition of India and Pakistan, India's independence from Britain, and subsequently through to 1992. Two of the major riots he discusses are the Great Calcutta Killing of August 1946 and the riots in both India and Bangladesh that followed the Hindu destruction of the mosque of Babri Masjid at Ayodhya in northern Uttar Pradesh, India, in 1992.

Ghosh's account gives full prominence to the historical factors that precipitated these and other riots. He traces the beginnings of problems between the Hindu and Muslim populations in what was formerly Bengal to the administrative division of the region made by Lord Curzon, the British viceroy, into Western Bengal (including Bihar and Orissa), and Eastern Bengal and Assam. Variants of a common language are spoken throughout the whole region, but in Eastern Bengal census counts of 1872 revealed that there was a majority of poor Muslims, while large tracts of land belonged to Hindus with ties to Western Bengal. Lord Curzon seems to have made this division partly to give support to the Muslims of Eastern

Bengal against the "unruly" Hindus to their west. The partition precipitated political reorganization on both sides, so that Hindu and Muslim political parties were ranged against each other after the two provinces (minus Bihar, Orissa, and Assam) were brought together again in 1912. Their struggles continued until 1946, when the Indian National Congress Party with Mahatma Gandhi as its leader refused to countenance the establishment of a separate state of Bengal as a whole, and Eastern Bengal became East Pakistan. After military struggles with West Pakistan, East Pakistan became Bangladesh in 1971, with assistance from India. Muslim-Hindu tensions, however, did not evaporate, since a movement for the creation of an Islamic state, backed by the ideology of *jihad,* or struggle for the Islamic way of life, took hold there. Calcutta, close to Bangladesh, remains a place where memories of these tensions prevail, going back to the events of 1946.

The idea of "Pakistan" as a political entity separate from India was what disturbed Hindus prior to the riots of 1946. The creation of Pakistan would make Hindus in Eastern Bengal subject to the majority Muslims, and some political commentators declared this would mean the destruction of Hindu culture there. When the Muslim League called for a general strike, the Congress Party opposed this, implying that participation in the strike would be treason to the cause of a united India (Ghosh 1998: 48). The Muslim League tried to assert control over Calcutta, although Muslims comprised only about a quarter of the city's population, and the Muslim-dominated state government allegedly imported "a large number of musclemen and *goonda* [rascal, terrorist] elements into the city" to assert its dominance there, transferring some Hindu police officers out of the city (p. 50). A rumor emerged that the League government had decided "to blow up Calcutta with dynamite before independence" (p. 51) – presumably if they could not keep control of it.

Rumors then circulated on both sides about the arming of their communities with spears, knives, and rods. Muslim butchers in Calcutta were declared to be sharpening their knives and choppers; others were said to be tearing metal railings from public parks. A large number of knives was said to have arrived from Bombay, the headquarters of the Muslim League. Rumors in local areas concentrated on points of territorial boundaries or convergence between Hindus and Muslims, and in particular "rumors of the molestation and killing of women were rife and incited the respective communities to greater vengeance" (p. 53). Hindus were agitated by reports that Hindu women had their breasts cut off prior to being disemboweled and killed (p. 54).

Stories of such atrocities on both sides were carried to different places and caused acts of putative retaliation. Muslim mullahs traveled between mosques with news of atrocities, and on both sides acts committed against women were taken as the greatest insults to communal identities. Muslim circulars invoked the idea of the *jihad*, linking it to the month of Ramzan in the Muslim calendar, when the Koran was first revealed, the same month in which the strike was planned to take place. General panic was increased by rumors that the city's water supply had been poisoned (p. 59). The rumors spread from working-class to middle-class neighborhoods, pulling the middle classes into the communal conflict. After four days of riots and killings in Calcutta itself the disturbances spread more widely, especially to areas subject to agrarian unrest where Muslim peasants cultivated lands of Hindu *zamindars*, or landowners. Thousands of Hindus fled from Muslim majority areas (p. 74), and more still after the actual partition took place. Such a massive displacement of people meant that reports and further rumors were spread over an even wider area, entering into local conflicts, memories, and senses of history, danger, and identity.

Ghosh's narrative of later riots indicates how both "stock" and "contingent" rumors contributed to events. "Stock" rumors are like "diving" ones: they recur over time because they appeal to cultural themes, such as the insulting of women's bodies or the poisoning of water supplies. "Contingent" rumors are narratives of particular events, detailing heroism or duplicity, with personal names attached. Both kinds of rumors are deeply inflected by ethnicity and nationalist political rhetoric. "Horror stories," or accounts of atrocities, may combine both stock and contingent rumor motifs, as Paul Brass shows in his detailed study of riots in Uttar Pradesh (Brass 1997: 129–203). The Babri Masjid riots resulted from an actual act of destruction of a sacred site, the enactment of a type of event that also regularly appears as a stock rumor, the rumor of desecration.

The mosque at Babri Masjid in Ayodhya was first built in 1528 by a noble in the court of the first Mughal emperor. As a part of their political agenda, designed to mobilize Hindus against Muslims, Hindu nationalists of the Bharatiya Janata Party (BJP) developed a story that this mosque had been built over the site of a temple commemorating the birthplace of Lord Ram, "a Hindu deity, an incarnation of Vishnu and widely revered in northern India" (Ghosh, p. 132). In 1986 the Indian government, led by Rajiv Gandhi, allowed the opening of the site of the mosque for Hindu worship, in an attempt by the Congress Party to take the theme of Hindu militancy away from the BJP. Disputes with Sikhs in Punjab and Muslims in Kashmir precipitated Gandhi's move in the direction of Hindu ethnonationalism (Brass 1997: 37). In 1990 the BJP renewed its earlier threat to "liberate" the site by pulling down the mosque and building a temple to Lord Ram (Ghosh, p. 133). The nationalists saw this as a work of revenge, treating the original building of the mosque as an act of disrespect to the Hindu deity. Conflict over their move to carry out this "liberation" led them to withdraw their support for the government, which then fell. We see here the political manipulation of cultural themes, in which conflict over a local sacred site becomes a lever to cause wider political disturbance.

In the first attack on the mosque on October 30, 1990, one of its three domes was damaged. In Bangladesh retaliatory attacks were made on Hindu temples. Ghosh suggests that President Ershad of Bangladesh, who had come to power in a military coup in 1982 and had declared Islam as the state religion to shore up his own control, may have influenced the tone of media reports of the attack in order to draw attention away from peasant unrest against his regime (Ghosh, p. 138). The press in Bangladesh announced that Muslims around the world must declare *jihad* in response to the desecration of the mosque, and street mobs proceeded to destroy Hindu temples and homes, beginning in Chittagong and spreading their activities to Dhaka (Dacca) on October 31. Ershad's government nevertheless later fell.

In Uttar Pradesh the BJP and other political groups had promised to build a new Ram temple as a part of their campaign to win the state government elections. Despite a court order to take no action until a legal decision had been made, on December 6, 1992, the mosque was this time fully destroyed, and in Ayodhya Muslim shops and houses were set on fire (Ghosh, p. 142). News reached Calcutta on December 7 and riots ensued there. Some rumors were replicative, declaring that further mosques or temples had been destroyed. Others were stock rumors reemerging in the chaos, for example, that women's breasts had been cut off. Contingent rumors about specific deaths and dead bodies multiplied, for example, that corpses were piled up in rural suburbs. Warning rumors flew around, for example, that Muslims armed with AK-47s and Kalashnikovs were about to attack a Hindu middle-class area (Ghosh, p. 146; we have supplied our own labeling of the rumors here). Some rumors were clearly exaggerated, for instance, that an entire Muslim neighborhood had been razed to the ground, or that thousands of people were gathered to attack a particular police station. As Ghosh points out, such exaggerations only bound people together more strongly in their fear, panic, and reactive aggression, linking the middle classes "with local hoodlums . . . now feted as community protectors" (Ghosh, p. 149).

The reverberations of aggression echoed far afield in Bangladesh. In Chittagong a new slogan emerged: "Hindu, if you want to live, leave Bangla and go to India" (Ghosh, p. 152). Local arenas became saturated with a national sense of history based on the violent expression of ethnic boundaries. Paul Brass reports that large riots also occurred at this time in Bombay and in Kanpur (Brass 1997: 214–59). Media broadcasts were the immediate occasion for these outbreaks. As Brass notes, Hindus and Muslims tend to give different accounts of the "cause" of riots of this kind, each blaming the other side for starting trouble. Popular hero figures emerged also in what we may reasonably call rumors. One such hero figure on the Hindu (BJP) side was called Kala Bachcha, who was rewarded with a nomination to contest a legislative seat open to a person of the Scheduled Castes. He was killed on February 9, 1994, after which BJP supporters gathered at his funeral and next day rioted against Muslims. Acts of provocation, rumors, riots, killings, further political events, more killings, rumors, and riots follow one another in these narratives in a ceaseless round.

In his general discussions of the literature on rumor and gossip, Ghosh catches well the sharp differences in tone of analysis that emerge when we shift from Max Gluckman's genial, almost joking proposition about gossip as defining the community or in-group and rumor in the harsher world of postcolonial societies. (We should remember, however, the experientially harsh world of colonial times also in Africa, revealed, for example, by Luise White's work.) In Ghosh's formulation, rumor also creates communities, but it does so in a hybrid world of violence, in which "history, memory, and rumor are entangled." Some of the classic formulations about rumor are confirmed by this study. Others are not. For example, rumor is not necessarily a force that operates in the absence of verifiable information. Rather, as Guha (1994 [1983]) stressed, and Homi Bhabha repeated (1995), it is itself a force of resistance and mobilization in these highly politicized contexts, where word of mouth communications bind people together against government forces or opposing groups. Rumor weaves together also the local, the national, and the global and can be seen as a creative way of relating to official news sources (as we saw also in the case of Greek commentaries on the war in Kosovo). Particular rumor cycles tend to belong to particular ethnic groups and are a part of their repertoires of political action. Ghosh quotes Veena Das's observation that rumor is performative and perlocutionary: it is speech that produces action (Das 1996; Ghosh, p. 20). Certain canonical events also tend to enter and reenter rumor through memory, for example, the events of the partition in India in 1946 that are recapitulated in later instances of intercommunal violence.

One of Ghosh's most interesting points is that the name of a new or envisaged political entity such as "Pakistan" may function as a kind of rumor (Ghosh, p. 35). In 1946 the idea of Pakistan was fluid and contradictory. It was a nation rumored to be in the making, around which contradictory imaginings gathered, which crystallized only over time. This seems a valuable observation, especially since it can be applied to the emergence of ethnic as well as nationalist discourse. In fact, Allport and Postman's account of the characteristics of rumor as involving the *leveling, sharpening,* and *assimilation* of accounts as they pass from person to person applies to the emergence of political concepts of ethnicity as well, since these too may begin as fluid and end as sharply defined, in accordance with the interests of those who propound them (see Chapter 2).

A similar observation can be made with regard to the shaping of ethnic ideas as these enter into the political realm. Brass, who is a political scientist, points out how violence may be used as a political tool and how politicians may use specialist rioters and provocateurs to execute it (see also Lessinger 2003). Violent acts are one of the ways in which the leveling and sharpening of identities is displayed, generating and feeding on the opposed identities it brings into focus. Jonathan Spencer, a social anthropologist with extensive experience in Sri Lanka, has considered the relationships between everyday action, nationalist ideology, and rioting, and finds the connections complex. Spencer's fieldwork was in the Sinhala village of Tenna in Sabaragamura Province in the southern part of Sri Lanka, far from the north and its separatist Tamil Tiger movements. Working in this area, he was not aware of any regular pattern of violence in people's interactions beyond the occasional scuffle (Spencer 1990b: 605), although he heard of murders and suicides, and in 1981 he observed that Tamil properties in nearby towns "were burnt in response to a Tiger attack in the north" (ibid.), in what was to prove "a dry run" for a greater episode of violence in 1983.

Spencer did note a kind of vicarious interest in violence, for example, in news and representations of it. He also observes that mythology often portrayed violence, but it was seen as emanating from kings and demons, beings who were considered to be the opposite of ordinary people. In everyday life Spencer saw a strong emphasis on restraint in the expression of conflict, tied in with local concepts of shame (1990b: 606) or modesty, fear of public humiliation. This shame, he tells us, is the private version of a public theme, "the creation of a shaky consensus by the aggressive use of the threat of humiliation" (p. 607). Such threats may be carried out in actual situations of violent conflict, but in ordinary life the emphasis is on quiet self-control, at least as an ideal. When self-control is lost, on the other hand, violence is expected, and Spencer suggests that data on homicides and suicides indicate that when violence comes it does appear suddenly and intensely (p. 609). An alternative to violence that is chosen by people who practice restraint in their overt interactions is sorcery, engaged in as a form of protest against perceived injustices, sometimes when the intended victim is otherwise "unassailable" (p. 615). Sorcery is therefore an alternative to direct physical violence (see Kapferer 1997) and is a marker of underlying aggression between people.

The overall point of Spencer's observations here is that social strains, tension, and aggression are present but are ordinarily handled without recourse to physical violence. Village-level conflicts require indirection. The argument about sorcery parallels similar explanations for witchcraft accusations elsewhere, such as in Africa (Marwick 1965; Turner 1996 [1957]). But to this Spencer adds a further, and crucial, point, "that party politics forms an invaluable cultural form for the expression of tensions and disputes which cannot be expressed in the pacific mode of 'normal' village relations" (p. 605), an argument that he explores in detail in his later book (Spencer 1990a). Party politics may become a vehicle in which other antagonisms can be expressed that may lead to violence. (The same process can be observed in contemporary politics in Papua New Guinea.) We should add that it probably also brings into the village context new focalizations and extensions of conflicts that operate on a wider communal basis such as those between Tamil and Sinhala political factions. In addition, specific events and the rumors about them characteristically play a crucial role in escalating and extending conflict. In this instance, Spencer is referring to events of July 23, 1983, when Tamil Tigers ambushed and killed thirteen Sinhala soldiers far north in the Jaffna peninsula. At the funeral in Colombo a large crowd massed and began attacks on Tamil suburbs. Subsequently, organized operators extended the destruction and violence to other towns, killing some 2,000 to 3,000 Tamils. Security forces did not appear to intervene, suggesting the complicity of a government party organization that had itself relied on intimidation (Spencer 1990b: 617) and now could not control the violence of its own supporters.

It was here that rumors played their part (p. 618). Tamils in general tended to be identified as "Tigers," in spite of the fact that "the Tigers had never operated within 100 miles of these southern towns" (p. 618). Even in remote villages people reported that Tigers had been seen (rather like assault sorcerers are from time to time rumored to be lurking near villages in Papua New Guinea). After a curfew and censorship of the news had been imposed, the rumors multiplied and began to include "stock" elements such as the poisoning of water supplies or claims that Tigers were disguising themselves as priests in order to infiltrate the countryside. Panics ensued, which in turn influenced people's attitudes to "retaliatory" violence. It is this syndrome that makes rumor such a potent factor in labile social situations: it redirects people's choices of action. In this regard Spencer recognized that Sinhala mythology of ancient struggles against the Tamils of the north, stressed by Kapferer (1988), came into play. Young men formed regiments with names reminiscent of these ancient battles and went to fight in the north. Unfortunately the Tamils won in these fights, and thereafter were stereotyped as cunning, demonic "terrorists" (Spencer 1990b: 620). New rumors then developed, drawing on this image of the demonic as a means of stiffening resolve against the Tamils, and the image duly washed off on all Tamils, no matter what their actions. In Spencer's view, the violence has to be seen as a *sequential process*, in which rumors played their part, not as a direct precipitate from *cultural ontology*. The invocation of the demonic realm at the culminating phases of this process both reflected and influenced the sense that people had that the world had lost its everyday feeling of security and had become a theater of danger. Aggressive nationalist politics flourished in the lurid light of this experience.

Witchcraft in Africa Revisited

The parallel here with witchcraft and witch-hunts is exact. A recent study examines communal violence during 1992–4 witch-hunts among the Gusii people of southwestern Kenya (Ogembo 1997), relating these events to national political turbulence stemming from economic hardships and their negative effects on health. In these witch-hunts mobs chased and caught people, bound them with ropes and threw gasoline over them, closed them in bags and then burned them to death in their own houses (Ogembo, p. 1). Ogembo notes that the violence involved here was a relatively new phenomenon, although accusations of witchcraft were not new, and legal proceedings within the patrilineage were a part of Gusii cultural practices. Gusii lineage members therefore had other ways of pursuing grievances against one another than through witchcraft accusations. Yet in 1992–94 they killed fifty-seven people in witch-hunts.

Three kinds of events gave rise to this violence. One was the illness and death of a special person, an orphan. The second was the putative "abduction" of a person by witches, after which the abducted person became mute but wrote down the names of the witches involved. The third was the discovery of notebooks that people believed were written by witches (Ogembo, p. 14). We move here from a kind of public event (a death), to which causes were imaginatively attributed; then to a putative event (an "abduction") and a personal act of writing down names, that is, an accusation; and, finally, to an apparently innocuous occurrence (the discovery of notebooks, a detail that invokes the context and history of literacy and the power of writing along with its power of universalization and diffusion), which was then also interpreted in terms of witchcraft. Gossip could develop about all three of these categories of happening, turning them in effect into signs of witchcraft. The notebooks were said to contain the names of witches who had met at night to plan killings. Those named in the books would become targets for mob lynchings.

In line with Auslander's findings from the Ngoni area in South Africa (see Chapter 3), the witch killers tended to be young men and their victims old women (p. 15). The young men were ones who were practiced in interethnic violence partly instigated by the government (compare the intrusion of national politics into community life in Sri Lanka detailed in the previous section of this chapter). Ogembo explains that in the precolonial past, Gusii youths were expected to be warriors in defense of their lineage against enemies. With colonialism, the enemies became poverty and disease, and education (literacy) was seen as a tool to fight them. The Bible defined both good and evil, and gave impetus to the Gusii attribution of evil to witches. Witch-hunters were seen as new warriors fighting this evil, and government and church officials commended them (p. 18).

One prominent meaning of evil for the Gusii is misfortune, or *emechendo* (p. 31), such as crop failure, loss of property, or illness. Mourning is also *emechendo*. Misfortunes can occur because of ancestral displeasure or the acts of witches, and people interpret natural events as signs of these supernatural causes. (We do not imply here that the Gusii make this natural/supernatural distinction.) Diviners carry out these interpretations. Witches are credited with an incorrigible desire to kill or harm others (like the Melpa *kum* concept; see Chapter 5), and they are usually said to be adult females (p. 33). Witches can spray herbs to make a fog around pursuers or they can turn themselves into animals. Special horns are used to "smell" them and destroy their "medicine" (p. 34), and the specialists who use these horns are always men. Male sorcerers are also hired to punish people for wrongdoing. This gendered pattern appears to go with the patrilineal structure of Gusii lineages and the Gusii notions of warriors.

The Christian churches have discouraged male sorcerers' use of herbal medicinal cures and the male practice of polygyny by which lineages expanded, thus producing various resentments, especially directed against women. The historical process intersected with community-wide events such as thefts or deaths of cattle and the discovery of "poison" in their bodies, the report of abductions of students, and the resurgence of illnesses such as malaria (p. 44). After the witch burnings began, rumors about them and about the activities of witches began to circulate widely, provoking more killings. Rich people hired mercenaries to kill their enemies and burn them, calling them witches (p. 45). Ministers cited the book of Exodus (22:18) as justification for witch killings (p. 50). People joined churches, such as that of the Seventh Day Adventists, in the hope of avoiding the stigma of witchcraft (a pattern found also among the Duna of Papua New Guinea, Chapter 5).

The killings of women were partially justified by the need to rid the local patrilineages of witches and to reestablish lineage unity threatened by change (p. 53). On one occasion a seventy-year-old man was killed because he was named as the "consultant" for the witches' network (p. 57). On another occasion an eighty-year-old woman was accused of bewitching her own grandchild (her son's child). The child's brothers seized her and bound her hand and foot, brought the thatched roof of her granary (identified with her personhood), covered her with it, and burned her to death (p. 64). The motivation of revenge often figured into these events. Those who were recruited into the mobs were often youths who had lost kin, supposedly at the hands of witches (p. 82). Animosities between people were exacerbated by a political "reform" in which secret balloting was in 1988 replaced with queue voting, revealing conflicts of opinion among kin (p. 98). Such intergenerational violence against older people in a community may usefully be compared with aggression exercised against senior members of academic departments as a way of forcing them into retirement and enabling the appointment of new junior members of faculty who will be clients of those holding power. In this context also gossip and rumor may crystallize into open hostility precisely over hiring issues.

Gusii ideas of evil are tied to the expectation of jealousy in the society, including among cowives (p. 101). Ogembo cites a myth, which appears to have a Christian theme, that people used to die and be buried but would rise again on the third day. One day a husband told one of his two wives to help the other when she was due to be resurrected in this way. Instead the wife struck her rival's grave with a stick, saying that the moon resurrects but humans die; since then her words have become true. Death is the prime *emechendo*, and it came about through jealousy, an emotion also attributed to witches. Cowives in the lineage are seen as the repositories of a form of primordial jealousy and therefore as prototypes of the witch figure.

These notions have since colonial times been recycled through the ideas of Protestant Christianity. Witchcraft ideas have been represented as forms of "devil worship," and first the colonial then the indigenous Kenyan government have endorsed this notion. A government-appointed commission was set up on March 1, 1995, to investigate the allegations (rumors) of devil worship, including "incantations in unintelligible languages [such as occur in "traditional" magic and in Pentecostal Christian worship], sexual abuse and rape of children and minors, black magic, use of narcotic drugs and holding snakes in reference" (Ogembo, p. 110, from the Pan African News Agency, September 20, 1996). A popular work, *Delivered from the Power of Darkness*, by a Nigerian author, Emmanuel Eni, was republished by the African Inland Church in Kenya in 1987 as a paperback and became a manual for dealing with witches (p. 114), a kind of latter-day *Malleus maleficarum*. The book offered the advice to have the name of Jesus always on one's lips and to rely on his saving blood to protect against witches. (These are idioms that are consistently practiced also in Pentecostal-style Christian movements in Papua New Guinea.)

Eni's book pinpoints a marital relationship with an affluent woman who practiced witchcraft as the author's entry into Satanism, from which he was later saved by being born again into Jesus. Satan is seen as the great envier, the source of jealousy and witchcraft in the world, and in this way the connection with local culture is made. Gusii ideas are thus linked to Christianity, with the addition that Jesus can provide deliverance from the powers of evil. This idea of deliverance is in turn linked to the theme of overcoming death, and Ogembo suggests that the perpetuation of the lineage signifies for the Gusii that theme, and that the killing of senior women represented for the youths who carried out these killings the destruction of their stepmothers.

Ogembo's analysis does not make great use of the concept of rumor and gossip, but it is clear from his examples that local gossip within the lineage defined who was accused as a witch. The "knowledge" brought in by Christianity and dramatized in popular literature seems to have provided the cosmological justification for the violence of the witch-finders' actions, and this "knowledge" can be compared to rumor in terms of its powers over the imagination. A study by Birgit Meyer (2001) on witchcraft among the Ewe people of Ghana shows how the ideas of early German Pietist missionaries, combined with a later popularity of Pentecostalism, worked there also to associate witchcraft with Satan and to provide a theology of protection against it. Meyer refers (2001: 121) to the same book, *Delivered from the Powers of Darkness*, which Ogembo cites as having become influential in Kenya, through the globalizing organization of the Assemblies of God. Pentecostalism in this context provides people with the excitement of an encounter with evil and the promise of victory over it. Where this struggle is located within the individual, the result is a battle within the soul; where it is externalized, as in the Gusii case study, it can issue in the killing of scapegoats.

Wolf Bleek, in his work with the Kwahu people, Akan speakers in Ghana, recognizes the significance of gossip in externalizing and focusing people's fears of "evil." Combining the approaches of Gluckman (1963) and Paine (1967) that we also discussed in Chapter 2 of this book, Bleek argues that such gossip both defined community solidarities and was utilized to further people's individual interests within small kin networks. In particular, he found that the young tended to accuse the old and more powerful (Bleek 1976: 538), and that women were the ones predominantly accused (p. 539). These patterns are the same as those found among the Gusii (this chapter) and more widely elsewhere (Chapter 3). However, the accusations did not lead to physical violence, although they were based on the same confluences of inchoate rumors (p. 532) that coalesce elsewhere to provide the occasion for violent action. What the Gusii case shares with Sri Lanka is the intense and embittering involvement of national politics, and reactions to politics, in local lives. Among the Gusii this involvement centered on the Kenyan President Daniel arap Moi and his autocratic rule. Changes in the terms of this rule led to great local disturbances and tensions, in the course of which the violence of witch-hunts emerged. Rumors then had their field day in promoting such violence. These examples indicate that neither indigenous nor introduced cosmologies of evil necessarily by themselves produce physical violence, but they are well adapted to do so given further tensions and justifications.

A further theme that runs through all these studies is the issue of economic change and the new inequalities it produces. Some analysts suggest that accusations of witchcraft against better-off members of a community represent an opposition to "modernity." This is doubtful. What they may represent is jealousy of those who are alleged to be successful and a wish to thwart them. It is clear, however, that discourses of witchcraft and sorcery are deeply constitutive of the conditions of "modernity" itself, as the contributors to Comaroff and Comaroff (1993) all argued.

Equally, these discourses may be said to call into question the concept of "modernity," since they bring together so many elements that carry the traces and images of other times and other places, in a kind of pastiche or bricolage that lends itself to the label of "postmodernity."

Harry West, in a study of people in the Mueda plateau in Mozambique carried out between 1993 and 1999, stresses the ambiguous and confusing effects of sorcery discourse in this area, which had also been greatly affected by the turbulence of civil war. Talk of sorcery could be used against others, but could rebound and harm the speakers themselves (West 2001: 139), a finding that parallels Brison's for the Kwanga of Papua New Guinea (Chapter 5). "Whether rich or poor, powerful or weak, Muedans of any group might also actually have terrorized themselves through talk of sorcery," West adds (ibid.). In a fluid and uncertain political world, power and talk tended to collapse on themselves. Muedans used rumors and innuendo to criticize the rich among them without condemning wealth in itself, expressing their frustration and hope in an uneasy juxtaposition with each other. It is especially in such awkward situations of suspense and limbo that rumors and ideas of sorcery or witchcraft tend most to flourish. It is not necessary, or even cogent, to suppose that these situations are unique to the late twentieth or early twenty-first century or to postmodernity. Fluid and awkward periods of time continuously recur in history, and rumors and gossip have always played a big part in both generating and mediating conflicts in such periods. The Reformation, for example, must have brought with it awkward changes, and witch-hunts in Scotland largely followed in its train, as Larner (1981) pointed out.

Conclusion

This chapter has been devoted to demonstrating connections between different kinds of rumors and the production of violence between opposed categories of people. Rumors are the very stuff of stereotypes about others. They generate and reflect fear and aggression between people.

They are powerful political tools. They can also outrun the intentions of their creators, producing more violence than is anticipated. Our examples of rumors about construction sacrifices in Indonesia have merged into accounts of interethnic disturbances and massacres. Rumors also have clearly fed into Sinhalese-Tamil conflicts in Sri Lanka and led to an escalation in killings, always within the general paradigm of revenge. Witch-hunts may also be seen as acts of revenge taken on people who putatively have destroyed others magically. A version of what Pierre Bourdieu would call "misrecognition" takes place. People attribute misfortune to witches and kill them in order to set matters right. In effect it is the supposed witch who is the victim, but in the world of rumor and gossip, perception is all, and perceptions justify retaliatory violence. Indeed, in European witch trials, people may have resorted to the courts as an enforced alternative to taking physical revenge on witches; Boyer and Nissenbaum comment on the same theme from Salem: "vengeance was a volatile obsession in late-seventeenth-century Salem village" (1974: 208).

EIGHT

❦

Conclusions: Conflict and Cohesion

As we explained in the Introduction to this book, our intention has been to bring together the discussion of rumors and gossip with materials on witchcraft and sorcery. At the most straightforward level, the aim has been to show that rumors and gossip play an important part in the overall processes that lead to witchcraft accusations. Starting from events that precipitate dislike between individual neighbors or kin, inchoate suspicions and suggestions may develop over time into judicial actions in which the particular dispute may come to be seen as a part of a struggle for social order, conceptualized in terms of good versus evil forces. In this phase the forces of evil may be seen as engaged in a conspiracy against the good. Violent actions in defense of "the good" then come to be seen as justifiable. The judicial executions and the mob killings that eventuate are seen by their perpetrators as ways of ridding the society of evil and of achieving a new balance in the cosmos, with tinges of millenarian desires and apocalyptic ideas entering people's consciousness. Political leaders and witch-finders may benefit from this process by increasing their power and/or their wealth. Individuals who feed accusations into a charged political or judicial context also may stand to gain in one way or another, most generally by ridding themselves of guilt and anxiety regarding the state of affairs in the world and their own actions within it. Accusations of witchcraft can thus sometimes be seen as psychological projections on others, particularly those who are thought to bear a

194

grudge or to resent the denial of a request. Rumors and gossip are used as crucial tools in the gathering of information against people and the development of a consensus about who is responsible for deaths, illnesses, misfortunes, thefts, "unnatural" weather, and the like. The processes involved are gradual and incremental until they reach a point of explosion through the catalyst of a particular event and the interpretations people make of it.

At the point where witchcraft accusations lead to violence we find a confluence with the question of the role of rumors and gossip in the production of violent political actions such as riots, in which specific matters to do with sorcery or witchcraft are not overtly involved. Circumstances of social malaise, disturbance, and anomie provide the universal background to all of the processes we have examined from Africa, India, Papua New Guinea, and Europe. All the theorists of rumor and gossip whose views we surveyed in Chapter 2 take it as axiomatic that rumor flourishes in situations of uncertainty, stress, and perceptions of danger. Either lack of information or difficulties in interpreting events or both may be involved. The circumstances are important, such as political threats to the collectivity and the aftermath of disasters (brought home again to people in America and elsewhere by the terrorist attacks of September 11, 2001, and the anthrax-laced letters sent to prominent government leaders and journalists). Rumors represent people's attempts to find or create a "truth" about events that helps them to make narratives about social values and judgments about the morals of others. They are "improvised news" and conversations "in search of the truth." When rumors pinpoint the blame for untoward events they help to precipitate retribution, violence, or uprisings against those felt to be responsible. The terrorist is the classic outsider who poses as an insider or the insider who betrays his own people, and therefore is seen to be something that needs to be expelled or controlled. In short, the terrorist stands in the same semantic space as the witch or sorcerer in the eyes of the person or people being terrorized.

In the case of the mid-nineteenth-century riots against the British Raj in colonial India, precipitated by widespread discontent over exorbitant rents and peasant debt, and in the example of the Indian Mutiny of 1857 prompted by fears that the British authorities had deliberately plotted to pollute the Indians' bodies, we find three important elements. First, rumors mobilized the population. Second, both the British and the Indians developed conspiracy theories about each other. And third, at stake from the Indians' viewpoint was a malevolent attempt on the part of the colonial power to corrupt them and force them to become Christians. The subversive action of polluting them was seen as comparable to an act of witchcraft or sorcery: a transgressive attack on their bodies. The colonial power was therefore seen not only as oppressive and malevolent but *corrupting* as well; just as in the ideas of European witchcraft the Devil was seen as corrupting his servants and turning them to his own imperial ends.

The parallel between the Indian Mutiny and other outbreaks of communal violence is therefore not incidental but integral with the processes by which witch-hunts come into being. Once the other side is defined as the embodiment or source of evil, violent resistance or punishment is bound to follow. This is particularly so where acts of pollution or transgression are involved, and rumors that play a part in generating violence stress actions of this kind, for example, rape, murder of babies, the destruction of sacred sites, cannibalism, sexual deviance, and abuse. Here again, rumors that are active in the context of political riots mesh with those that circulate during witch-hunts. While the examples we have deployed have tended to come from historical contexts associated with European, especially British, but also Dutch, French, and Australian colonialism, the processes we have been interested in, we argue, are universal and are rooted in the fundamental working of power, morality, and the emotions in human social life. They are therefore not peculiar to stages in European colonialism as such. The postcolonial contexts and contexts outside the immediacies of European colonialism that we have cited support this view.

In terms of power relations, we find the interesting topic of the ambivalence of power eloquently expounded by Peter Geschiere in his materials from modern Cameroon in Africa (Chapter 3). Holders of political office fear the sorcery and witchcraft of their constituents or the masses, because they assume that people are jealous of their wealth and influence and resent it. Reciprocally, the people themselves think their leaders must have succeeded as a result of their powerful magic, which makes them redoubtable and to be feared. In the postcolonial context of government this fear often translates into distrust of government programs such as vaccinations, which may be seen as carried out for the purpose of sterilizing people (Feldman-Savelsberg, Ndonko, and Schmidt-Ehry 2000). A mediating notion here is that power depends on the loyalty of kin. When a person's kin within the house open the way for witches to attack that person, a powerful person may be brought down. The "betrayal" involved arises out of their own moral failure to respect obligations to kin. The powerful are thus brought down by their own moral weaknesses or errors, as in the ancient Greek concept of the *hamartia* (mistake, wrongdoing) of tragic figures in dramas portraying their downfall.

Imputations of moral wrongdoing and treason can, on the other hand, be made against the politically weak and peripheral in society (e.g., in the examples we presented, lepers, Jews, male and female witches) who are, nevertheless, feared because of their supposed mystical powers or abilities, their wealth, or their ability to harm others by inflicting disease. The politically powerful may proceed to castigate, harass, and victimize these categories of people, on grounds that they have plotted to destroy the social order. By seeing themselves in relation to these peripheralized categories, the powerful realize their own vulnerability and therefore in a sense their weakness.

In all of these examples, then, conceptual reversals are at work. The powerful are also weak (i.e., vulnerable); the weak are also powerful (because they are seen as having special capacities). Each side therefore resents the other for their overt and covert power. In the case of colonial India, the colonial authorities saw the masses as weak because they had been dominated, but they correctly feared the power of insurrection. The peasants and their leaders, on the other hand, saw the authorities as holding great technical power but as morally corrupt because of their oppressive ways. When this was translated into a fear of pollution, moral panic ensued, succeeded by actual insurrection and an appropriation of limited amounts of power by violence.

In all of these contexts, again, it is the *interpretations* of situations and events that people make that most influences outcomes. Rumor and gossip are prime vehicles of interpretation. It is not at all that they simply pass on news. Rather, they give it its narrative shape and meaning, stimulating action. It is this, rather than the question of whether the rumor exactly reproduces "facts," that gives rumor and gossip their power. Rumors define and create worlds just as much as "facts" do (sometimes more so). They constitute realities *pro tempore*, until they are themselves superseded.

Severe circumstances and events invariably give rise first to gossip in a community, then to rumors that circulate more widely, and finally to legends ("diving rumors") that appear and disappear as they are caught up in or succeeded by events stimulating people's memories. The rumors of construction sacrifice in Indonesia (Chapter 7) are examples of diving rumors that tended to emerge in any context of suspicion between locals and the Indonesian state government and its militaristic ways of doing business.

Three illustrative examples not previously cited in our text but worthy of note here are (1) the rumors and subsequent legends that emerged out of the Great War (World War I, 1914–18). Fussell (1975: 114–54) deals with many examples. Two of them are the story of the Angels of Mons, who allegedly appeared in the sky to protect the British retreat in August 1914, and the story that the Germans were so short of fats that they took back battlefield corpses and rendered their fat to be used in nitroglycerine, candles, and lubricants, and boot dubbin (p. 116). The sanctification of the British side and the vilification of the Germans reveals here that the definition of the cosmos is at stake.

(2) In Britain in the 1880s great discontent was stirred up over poor conditions of housing in London's industrial slums, including fears that the poor were cohabiting indiscriminately and reproducing rapidly (Jones 1971: 223). Incest and juvenile prostitution were said to be rife. Politicians envisaged that a mass attack on landlords was imminent, and that the city might be incinerated. The English middle classes remembered the Paris revolutionary communes of earlier times and were afraid. Bread riots had taken place in 1860–1 in the East End of London and were still remembered (Jones, p. 240). Socialism had begun to emerge "as a challenge to traditional Liberal ideology" (p. 280), worsened by a trade recession and a severe winter in 1885–6. Rioters in the West End of London threw stones, broke windows, looted shops, and overturned carriages on February 8, 1886; social tensions were worsened by rumors conveyed in the newspaper in October 1887 that great numbers of outcasts and vagrants were gathering and sleeping out on the borders of the West End. A serious riot took place on "bloody Sunday," November 13, 1887. The reactions of the police and the public were heightened by the spread of rumors and the fears of a massive march by both rural and urban poor on the city. The poor were here also blamed for their moral weakness and depravity, but feared because of their potential power to commit violent acts (Jones, p. 296).

(3) Recurrent rumors in contemporary Britain and elsewhere relate to the concepts of child abuse and Satanism, sometimes linked together as in the old European notions about witches sacrificing babies. Ian Hacking (1999: 125–62) has pointed out that specific complexes of ideas (narratives, including rumors) about child abuse must be seen as socially constructed: while child abuse certainly takes place and has done so for a long time, stereotypes of it and ways of handling it in legal and bureaucratic

structures date from around 1961. Hacking contrasts child abuse with notions about Satanic ritual abuse, on which there was a wave of reported
cases in Britain around 1990 (Hacking, p. 126). Jean La Fontaine, a senior
British anthropologist commissioned to study these reports, concluded
that "none of the charges was substantiated by any evidence whatsoever"
(Hacking, pp. 126–7; La Fontaine 1998). Actual cases of child abuse had
been confused with ideas of Satanism. Bill Ellis (2000) traces this kind of
confusion to the creation of rumor panics that involve clusters of notions,
such as grave-robbing, vampirism, teen suicides, the Black Mass, "Hippie
Commune Witchcraft Blood Rites," and the like. The panics were associated with claims that a Satanic cult was about to unleash horror in a
particular venue (Ellis, p. 203).

Ellis links the creation of these rumor panics to teachings of Pentecostal Christianity, right-wing conspiracy theories, and the opportunis-
tic reportage of the media. We might comment here that the incidence
of actual horrors such as school shootings, violence in businesses and
supermarkets, and terrorist attacks by religious extremists of various per-
suasions must also surely feed into the situation overall. At any rate Ellis's
study reminds us again of the universality and contemporaneity of the
phenomena discussed in this book. The past continues to revisit and to re-
make the present. Violent events and rumors about their causes continue
to upset people's notions of cosmic balance, leading them to speculate,
panic, and seek scapegoats as well as genuinely to guard against and repair
the effects of hostile attacks.

An implication of these three examples, and of the many others we have
given, is that rumor and gossip form an important and central topic for
social research in general. We reviewed theories of rumor and gossip in
Chapter 2. We contrasted Max Gluckman's stress on the power of gossip
to define the boundaries of community with Robert Paine's argument
that gossipers seek to advance their personal interests. Both viewpoints
of course have some validity and they are not mutually incompatible.
But perhaps because they were dealing with in-group contexts and were

not, curiously enough, taking the literature on witchcraft and sorcery into their primary purview, both Gluckman and Paine seem to have downplayed the outright hostile intentions that can lie behind gossip and the violence that it may provoke.

Again, the definition of what the "community" is and how gossip or rumor relate to it can be moot. Networks in which people gossip do not in fact always constitute bounded communities. University departments are a case in point. They are a part of wider structures, they are small-scale, and gossiping takes place in them that relates to the hostilities, antipathies, desires, and patterns of opposition between their members. This does not make them bounded communities. And the gossip escapes into other circles and networks, turning into rumor and legend and causing misperceptions, misjudgments, and the skewed allocation of resources or jobs in a host of professional contexts. Those who do the gossiping may constitute an in-group, but they may also be hostile to each other as well as to outsiders. Clandestine circuits of information may be regarded as more valuable than written or otherwise public and accountable sources. Evaluations of persons, manuscripts, and projects may all be colored in this way. Academia therefore has its own versions of occult forces, assault sorcery, and witchcraft, as does the realm of politics generally.

At the collective level, we have seen rumor also as a powerful force, central to social movements from "cargo cults" to class conflicts, in precolonial, colonial, and postcolonial times. Rumors express the fluidity and ambiguity of information in situations of conflict and crisis. How people create and communicate them and what their effects are deserve to be central topics of social inquiry. They mediate significant social processes, as in Alan Macfarlane's formulation of what witchcraft in seventeenth-century Essex villages was about: making the links between anger and accidents. Indeed, we ourselves became increasingly convinced of the importance of rumor as we proceeded from case to case in different parts of the world.

We suggest finally here that a proportion of what is discussed under the heading of knowledge generally might also be considered under the rubric of rumor. This is especially so in the domains of witchcraft and sorcery (see, e.g., Lambek 1993). Diviners may manipulate the techniques of their trade, appealing to a background of sacred knowledge. But they also feed into their practices what they have heard from others about the background to cases of sickness or inquiries about the future that clients bring to them, just as "cunning folk" did in historical Essex and in New England. In Mount Hagen in Papua New Guinea a type of diviner was employed to determine the cause of a patient's sickness by pushing an arrow through a hole in a bark wall of the house and asking in turn which dead ghost among the patient's kin had caused the illness. When the right name was called out the spirit waiting outside was said to seize the arrow and hold it fast. Then the diviner called out the types of pig the ghost might want as a sacrifice to release the patient's "head," and again the ghost would make its choice in the same way. Operating such a system undoubtedly required local finesse, intelligence, and sources of information, all of which would come through conversations, including rumor and gossip. Rumor therefore entered into ritual, the reestablishment of moral order, and the rebalancing of the cosmos.

We see here two diagnostic poles of rumor. One is that which Max Gluckman put forward for gossip: the pole of integration, which may include rituals to solve conflicts and cure sickness. The other, however, is the pole of hostility and disruption in which people use rumor and gossip as a weapon against others and as a means of self-advancement. The two poles may be ideologically merged, as when witch-finders claim that they are cleansing the world, while at the same time earning a fee and facilitating the malice of accusers. Rumor and gossip both flourish in ambiguous social contexts and contribute further to such ambiguity, serving both selfish and collective interests. Through rumor, as through other forms of social communication, conflict and cohesion coexist, fueling the constant principle of struggle in life.

Conclusion

Our overall argument has been pursued through many different ethnographic venues, but our purpose has throughout been the same: to highlight the significance of rumor and gossip as constituent elements of social process, elements that are not trivial or epiphenomenal but central and fundamental. The source of their power is to be found in the networks of informal communication that always run parallel to more formal structures in society. These informal channels can be subversive of power, and they can be new sources of power. We have used the classic topic of witchcraft and sorcery to indicate specifically how informal and inchoate sectors of communication may feed into more formal ones, producing large-scale events or serious upheavals. We have been concerned therefore with a kind of universal substratum of social process, protean in its effects, starting from small things and leading to those that are greater and more salient. We have been concerned to expose this substratum and show how it is part of the foundations of larger scale processes that emerge into and out of history. Rumors and gossip thus cease to be a focus for specialized study and enter into the world of social and political analysis generally as important and challenging categories of human behavior.

References

Akin, David, and Joel Robbins, eds. 1999. *Money and Modernity: State and Local Currencies in Melanesia*. Pittsburgh: University of Pittsburgh Press.

Allport, Gordon W., and Leo Postman. 1947. *The Psychology of Rumor*. New York: Russell and Russell.

Amin, Shahid. 1984. Gandhi as Mahatma. In Ranajit Guha, ed., *Subaltern Studies III: Writings on South Asian History and Society*. Delhi: Oxford University Press.

Anderson, Jens A. 2002. Sorcery in the era of "Henry IV": Kinship, mobility and mortality in Buhera district, Zimbabwe. *Journal of the Royal Anthropological Institute* 8 (3): 425–50.

Andreski, Stanislav. 1989. *Syphilis, Puritanism and Witch Hunts*. New York: St. Martin's Press.

Ankarloo, Bengt, and Gustav Henningsen, eds. 2001. *Early Modern European Witchcraft: Centres and Peripheries*. Oxford: Clarendon Press (first published in 1990).

Antze, Paul, and Michael Lambek. 1996. *Tense Past: Cultural Essays in Trauma and Memory*. New York and London: Routledge.

Arens, William. 1979. *The Man-Eating Myth: Anthropology and Anthropophagy*. New York: Oxford University Press.

Auslander, Mark. 1993. "Open the wombs!" The symbolic politics of modern Ngoni witchfinding. In Jean Comaroff and John Comaroff, eds., *Modernity and Its Malcontents: Ritual and Power in Postcolonial Africa*, pp. 167–192. Chicago: University of Chicago Press.

Bailey, Michael D. 2003. *Battling Demons: Witchcraft, Heresy, and Reform in the Late Middle Ages*. University Park: Pennsylvania State University Press.

Barnes, R. H. 1993. Construction sacrifice, kidnapping and head-hunting rumors on Flores and elsewhere in Indonesia. *Oceania* 64: 146–158.

Barstow, Ann. 1994. *Witchcraze: A New History of the European Witch Hunts*. London: Pandora (Harper Collins).

References

Bastian, Misty L. 1993. "Bloodhounds who have no friends": Witchcraft and locality in the Nigerian popular press. In Jean Comaroff and John Comaroff, eds., *Modernity and Its Malcontents: Ritual and Power in Postcolonial Africa*, pp. 129–166. Chicago: University of Chicago Press.

Bayly, Christopher A. 1996. *Empire and Information: Intelligence Gathering and Social Communication in India, 1780–1870*. Cambridge: Cambridge University Press.

Berndt, Ronald M. 1952–3. A cargo movement in the East Central Highlands of New Guinea. *Oceania* 23 (1–3): 40ff., 137 ff.

Bhabha, Homi. 1995. In a spirit of calm violence. In Gyan Prakash, ed., *After Colonialism: Imperial Histories and Postcolonial Displacements*, pp. 326–343. Princeton, N.J.: Princeton University Press.

Bleek, Wolf. 1976. Witchcraft, gossip, and death: A social drama. *Man*, n.s., 11 (4): 526–541.

Boehm, Christopher. 1984. *Blood Revenge: The Enactment and Management of Conflict in Montenegro and Other Tribal Societies*. Philadelphia: University of Pennsylvania Press.

Bourdieu, Pierre. 1977. *Outline of a Theory of Practice*, trans. R. Nice. Cambridge: Cambridge University Press.

Bowen, Elenore Smith (Laura Bohannan). 1964. *Return to Laughter: An Anthropological Novel*. New York: Doubleday, published in cooperation with the American Museum of Natural History.

Boyer, Paul, and Stephen Nissenbaum. 1974. *Salem Possessed: The Social Origins of Witchcraft*. Cambridge, Mass.: Harvard University Press.

Brass, Paul. 1997. *Theft of an Idol: Text and Context in the Representation of Collective Violence*. Princeton, N.J.: Princeton University Press.

Brenneis, Donald, and Fred R. Myers, eds. 1984. *Dangerous Words: Language and Politics in the Pacific*. Prospect Heights, Ill.: Waveland Press.

Brison, Karen. 1992. *Just Talk: Gossip, Meetings, and Power in a Papua New Guinea Village*. Berkeley: University of California Press.

Brown, Keith, and D. Theodossopoulos. 2000. The performance of anxiety: Greek narratives of war in Kosovo. *Anthropology Today* 16 (1): 3–8.

Burridge, Kenelm O. 1960. *Mambu: A Melanesian Millennium*. London: Methuen.

Campbell, J. 1964. *Honour, Family and Patronage*. Oxford: Clarendon.

Carrier, James. 1992. Approaches to articulation. In J. Carrier, ed., *History and Tradition in Melanesian Anthropology*, pp. 116–143. Berkeley: University of California Press.

Carslaw, Rev. W. H. 1870. Editor's Preface. In John Howie, *The Scots Worthies*, pp. ix–xv. Edinburgh and London: Oliphant, Anderson and Ferrier (originally published in 1775).

Clark, Stuart. 1977. King James's *Daemonologie*: Witchcraft and kingship. In Sydney Anglo, ed., *The Damned Art*, pp. 156–181. London: Routledge and Kegan Paul.

Cohn, Norman. 1975. *Europe's Inner Demons: An Enquiry Inspired by the Great Witch-Hunt*. New York: Basic Books.

Colson, E. 1953. *The Makah Indians*. Manchester: Manchester University Press.

Comaroff, Jean. 1997. Consuming passions: Child abuse, fetishism, and "The New World Order." *Culture* 17 (1–2): 7–19.

Comaroff, Jean, and John Comaroff. 1999. Occult economies and the violence of abstraction: Notes from the South African postcolony. *American Ethnologist* 26 (2): 279–303.

Comaroff, Jean, and John Comaroff, eds. 1993. *Modernity and Its Malcontents: Ritual and Power in Postcolonial Africa*. Chicago: University of Chicago Press.

Conolly, M. F. 1869. *Fifiana: Memorials of the East of Fife*. Glasgow: John Tweed.

Cook, David. 1869. A sketch of the early history of Pittenweem. In M. F. Conolly, *Fifiana: Memorials of the East of Fife*. Glasgow: John Tweed.

Das, Veena. 1996. Rumor as performative: A contribution to the theory of perlocutionary speech. Sudhir Kumar Bose Memorial Lecture, Delhi: St. Stephens College (unpublished).

Davidson, Hilda Ellis, and Anna Chaudhri, eds. 2001. *Supernatural Enemies*. Durham, N.C.: Carolina Academic Press.

Davies, Norman. 1999. *The Isles: A History*. Oxford: Oxford University Press.

Davies, O. 1997. Cunning folk in England and Wales during the eighteenth and nineteenth centuries. *Rural History* 8 (1): 91–107.

Demos, John P. 1982. *Entertaining Satan. Witchcraft and the Culture of Early New England*. New York: Oxford University Press.

Douglas, Arthur. 1978. *The Fate of the Lancashire Witches*. Charley, U.K.: Countryside Publications.

Douglas, Mary. 1966. *Purity and Danger: An Analysis of the Concepts of Pollution and Taboo*. New York: Praeger.

Douglas, Mary, ed. 1970. Introduction: Thirty years after *Witchcraft, Oracles and Magic*. In M. Douglas, ed., *Witchcraft, Confessions and Accusations*, pp. xiii–xxxviii. London: Tavistock.

Drake, R. A. 1989. Construction sacrifice and kidnapping: Rumor panics in Borneo. *Oceania* 59: 269–279.

du Boulay, Juliet. 1974. *Portrait of a Green Mountain Village*. Oxford: Clarendon Press.

Duerr, Hans-Peter. 1985. *Dreamtime: Concerning the Boundary Between Wilderness and Civilization*, trans. Felicitas Goodman. Oxford: Basil Blackwell.

Duiker, William J., and Jackson J. Spielvogel. 1998. *World History*, vol. 2: *Since 1500*, 2nd ed. Belmont, Calif.: Wadsworth Publishing.

References

Ellen, Roy. 1993. Introduction. In C. W. Watson and R. Ellen, eds., *Understanding Witchcraft and Sorcery in Southeast Asia*, pp. 1–26. Honolulu: University of Hawai'i Press.

Ellis, Bill. 2000. *Raising the Devil: Satanism, New Religions, and the Media.* Lexington: University Press of Kentucky.

Encyclopaedia Britannica 1990. 15th ed. Chicago.

Evans-Pritchard, E. E. 1976 [1937]. *Witchcraft, Oracles and Magic among the Azande.* Oxford: Clarendon Press.

Favret-Saada, Jeanne. 1977. *Deadly Words: Witchcraft in the Bocage.* Cambridge: Cambridge University Press.

Feldman-Savelsberg, Pamela, Flavien J. Ndonko, and Bergis Schmidt-Ehry. 2000. Sterilizing vaccines or the politics of the womb: Retrospective study of a rumor in Cameroon. *Medical Anthropology Quarterly* 14 (2): 159–179.

Firth, Raymond. 1967. "Rumors in a primitive society." In R. Firth, *Tikopia Ritual and Belief*, pp. 141–161. Boston: Beacon Press.

Forbes, Thomas R. 1966. *The Midwife and the Witch.* New Haven: Yale University Press.

Forth, Gregory. 1991. Construction sacrifice and headhunting rumors in Central Flores (Eastern Indonesia): A comparative note. *Oceania* 61: 257–266.

Fussell, Paul. 1975. *The Great War and Modern Memory.* New York: Oxford University Press.

George, K. 1996. *Showing Signs of Violence.* Berkeley: University of California Press.

Geschiere, Peter. 1997. *The Modernity of Witchcraft: Politics and the Occult in Postcolonial Africa.* Charlottesville: University Press of Virginia.

Ghosh, Anjan Kumar. 1998. Partial truths: Rumor and communal violence in South Asia, 1946–1992. Ph.D. dissertation, University of Michigan.

Ginzburg, Carlo. 1966 [1983 translation]. *Nightbattles: Witchcraft and Agrarian Cults in the Sixteenth and Seventeenth Centuries*, trans. John and Anne Tedeschi. New York: Penguin Books.

Ginzburg, Carlo. 1989 [1991 translation]. *Ecstasies: Deciphering the Witches' Sabbath*, trans. Raymond Rosenthal. New York: Pantheon.

Ginzburg, Carlo. 2001. Deciphering the Sabbath. In Bengt Ankarloo and Gustav Henningsen, eds., *Early Modern European Witchcraft: Centres and Peripheries.* Oxford: Clarendon Press (first published in 1990).

Gluckman, Max. 1959. *Custom and Conflict in Africa.* Oxford: Basil Blackwell.

Gluckman, Max. 1963. Gossip and scandal. *Current Anthropology* 4 (3): 307–316.

Goldman, Laurence, ed. 1999. *The Anthropology of Cannibalism.* Westport, Conn., and London: Bergin and Garvey.

Gottfried, Robert S. 1983. *The Black Death: Natural and Human Disaster in Medieval Europe.* New York: Free Press.

Guha, Ranajit. 1994 [1983]. *Elementary Aspects of Peasant Insurgency in Colonial India.* Delhi: Oxford University Press.

Hacking, Ian. 1999. *The Social Construction of What?* Cambridge, Mass.: Harvard University Press.

Hatty, Suzanne E., and James Hatty. 1999. *The Disordered Body: Epidemic Disease and Cultural Transformation.* Albany: State University of New York Press.

Haviland, John B. 1977. *Gossip, Reputation, and Knowledge in Zinacantan.* Chicago and London: University of Chicago Press.

Henningsen, Gustav. 2001. "The Ladies from Outside": An archaic pattern of the witches' Sabbath. In B. Ankarloo and G. Henningsen, eds., *Early Modern European Witchcraft,* pp. 191–218. Oxford: Clarendon Press.

Hesiod. 1996. *Works and Days,* trans. David W. Tandy and Walter Neale. Berkeley: University of California Press.

Hoskins, Janet, ed. 1996. *Headhunting and the Social Imagination in Southeast Asia.* Stanford, Calif.: Stanford University Press.

Howie, John. 1870 [1775]. *The Scots Worthies,* ed. Rev. W. H. Carslaw, D. D. Edinburgh and London: Oliphant, Anderson and Ferrier.

Jones, G. Stedman. 1971. *Outcast London: A Study in the Relationship between Classes in Victorian Society.* Oxford: Clarendon Press.

Just, Roger. 2000. *A Greek Island Cosmos.* Oxford: James Currey, Santa Fe: School of American Research.

Kapferer, Bruce. 1988. *Legends of People, Myths of State.* Washington, D.C.: Smithsonian Institution Press.

Kapferer, Bruce. 1997. *The Feast of the Sorcerer.* Chicago: University of Chicago Press.

Kapferer, Bruce, ed. 2002. *Beyond Rationalism: Rethinking Magic, Witchcraft, and Sorcery.* New York: Berghahn Books.

Kapferer, Jean-Noël. 1990. *Rumors: Uses, Interpretations, and Images,* trans. Bruce Fink. New Brunswick, N.J.: Transaction.

Kaplan, Martha. 1995. *Neither Cargo nor Cult: Ritual Politics and the Colonial Imagination in Fiji.* Durham, N.C.: Duke University Press.

Klees, Fredric. 1950. *The Pennsylvania Dutch.* New York: Macmillan.

Knauft, Bruce M. 1998. *From Primitive to Postcolonial in Melanesia and Anthropology.* Ann Arbor: University of Michigan Press.

Knauft, Bruce M. 2002. *Exchanging the Past: A Rainforest World of Before and After.* Chicago: University of Chicago Press.

Kors, Alan, and Edward Peters. 1972. *Witchcraft in Europe 1100–1700: A Documentary History.* Philadelphia: University of Pennsylvania Press.

References

Kulke, Hermann, and Dietmar Rothermund. 1990. *A History of India*. London and New York: Routledge.

La Fontaine, Jean S. 1994. *The Extent and Nature of Organised and Ritual Abuse: Research Findings*. London: Her Majesty's Stationery Office.

La Fontaine, Jean. 1998. *Speak of the Devil: Allegations of Satanic Abuse in Britain*. Cambridge: Cambridge University Press.

Lambek, Michael. 1993. *Knowledge and Practice in Mayotte: Local Discourses of Islam, Sorcery, and Spirit Possession*. Toronto: University of Toronto Press.

Lambek, Michael. 1997. Monstrous desires and moral disquiet: Reflections on Jean Comaroff's "Consuming passions: Child abuse, fetishism, and 'The New World Order'" *Culture* 17 (1–2): 19–25.

Larner, Christina. 1981. *Enemies of God: The Witch-Hunt in Scotland*. Baltimore, Md.: Johns Hopkins University Press.

Larner, Christina. 1984. *Witchcraft and Religion: The Politics of Popular Belief*, ed. Alan Macfarlane. Oxford: Basil Blackwell.

Lawrence, Peter. 1964. *Road belong Cargo*. Manchester: Manchester University Press.

Lessinger, Johanna M. 2003. "Religious" violence in India: Ayodhya and the Hindu right. In R. Brian Ferguson, ed., *The State, Identity, and Violence: Political Disintegration in the Post-Cold War World*, pp. 149–76. London and New York: Routledge.

Levack, Brian P. 1987. *The Witch-Hunt in Early Modern Europe*. London: Longman.

Lienhardt, P. A. 1975. The interpretation of rumor. In J. H. M. Beattie and R. G. Lienhardt, eds., *Studies in Social Anthropology*, pp. 105–131. Oxford: Clarendon Press.

LiPuma, Edward. 2000. *Encompassing Others: The Magic of Modernity in Melanesia*. Ann Arbor: University of Michigan Press.

Macdonald, Stuart. 2002. *The Witches of Fife: Witch-Hunting in a Scottish Shire, 1560–1710*. East Linton: Tuckwell Press.

Macfarlane, Alan. 1970a. *Witchcraft in Tudor and Stuart England: A Regional and Comparative Study*. New York: Harper and Row.

Macfarlane, Alan. 1970b. Witchcraft in Tudor and Stuart Essex. In Mary Douglas, ed., *Witchcraft Confessions and Accusation*, pp. 81–102. London: Tavistock.

Mackay, Charles. 1841. *Memoirs of Extraordinary Popular Delusions*. London: Richard Bentley.

Magnusson, Magnus. 2000. *Scotland: The Story of a Nation*. New York: Atlantic Monthly Press.

Mair, Lucy. 1969. *Witchcraft*. London: World University Library.

Marwick, Max. 1965. *Sorcery in Its Social Setting: A Study of the Northern Rhodesian Cewa*. Manchester: Manchester University Press.

Mauss, Marcel. 1967 [1925]. *The Gift*. New York: W. W. Norton.

Mayer, Adrian C. 1963. The significance of quasi-groups in the study of complex societies. In M. Banton, ed., *The Social Anthropology of Complex Societies*. London: Tavistock Publications.

Meyer, Birgit. 2001. "You Devil, go away from me!" Pentecostal African Christianity and the powers of good and evil. In Paul Clough and Jon P. Mitchell, eds., *Powers of Good and Evil: Social Transformation and Popular Belief*, pp. 104–134. New York and Oxford: Berghahn Books.

Middleton, John, and E. H. Winter, eds. 1963. *Witchcraft and Sorcery in East Africa*. London: Routledge and Kegan Paul.

Moore, Henrietta L., and Todd Sanders 2001a. Magical interpretations, material realities: An introduction. In H. Moore and T. Sanders, eds., *Magical Interpretations, Material Realities*, pp. 1–27. London and New York: Routledge.

Moore, Henrietta L., and Todd Sanders, eds. 2001b. *Magical Interpretations, Material Realities: Modernity, Witchcraft, and the Occult in Postcolonial Africa*. London and New York: Routledge.

Moore, Sally Falk. 1999. Reflections on the Comaroff lecture. *American Ethnologist* 26 (2): 304–306.

Mosko, Mark. 1997. Cultural constructs versus psychoanalytic conjecture. *American Ethnologist* 24 (4): 934–938.

Murray, Margaret A. 1970 [1931]. *The God of the Witches*. Oxford: Oxford University Press.

Neubauer, Hans-Joachim. 1999. *The Rumour: A Cultural History*, trans. Christian Braun. New York: Free Association.

Niehaus, Isaac A. 1993. Witch-hunting and political legitimacy: Continuity and change in Green Valley, Lebowa, 1930–1991. *Africa* 63 (4): 498–529.

Niehaus, Isaac A., with Eliazaar Mohlala and Kally Shokane. 2001. *Witchcraft, Power, and Politics*. London: Pluto Press.

Norton, Mary Beth. 2002. *In the Devil's Snare: The Salem Witchcraft Crisis of 1692*. New York: Alfred A. Knopf.

Nutini, Hugo G., and John M. Roberts. 1993. *Blood-Sucking Witchcraft: An Epistemological Study of Anthropomorphic Supernaturalism in Rural Tlaxcala*. Tucson: University of Arizona Press.

Ogembo, Justus Mozart H'Achachi. 1997. The rise and decline of communal violence: An analysis of the 1992–4 witch-hunts in Gusii, Southwestern Kenya. Ph.D. dissertation, Harvard University.

O'Hanlon, Michael. 1989. *Reading the Skin: Adornment, Display, and Society among the Wahgi*. London: British Museum Publications.

Paine, Robert. 1967. What is gossip about? An alternative hypothesis. *Man*, n.s., 2 (2): 278–285.

References

Parry, Jonathan, and Maurice Bloch, eds. 1989. *Money and the Morality of Exchange.* New York: Cambridge University Press.

Rapport, Nigel. 1996. Gossip. In Alan Barnard and Jonathan Spencer, eds., *Encyclopedia of Social and Cultural Anthropology,* pp. 266–267. London and New York: Routledge.

Richards, Audrey. 1935. A modern movement of witchfinders. *Africa* 8 (4): 439–451.

Riebe, Inge. 1987. Kalam witchcraft: A historical perspective. In Michele Stephen, ed., *Sorcerer and Witch in Melanesia,* pp. 211–245. New Brunswick, N.J.: Rutgers University Press.

Riebe, Inge. 1991. Do we believe in witchcraft? In Andrew Pawley, ed., *Man and a Half: Essays in Pacific Anthropology and Ethnobiology in Honour of Ralph Bulmer,* pp. 317–326. Memoir No. 48. Auckland, New Zealand: Polynesian Society.

Risjord, Mark W. 2000. *Woodcutters and Witchcraft: Rationality and Interpretive Change in the Social Sciences.* Albany: State University of New York Press.

Robbins, Joel, Pamela J. Stewart, and Andrew Strathern, eds. 2001. Charismatic and Pentecostal Christianity in Oceania. *Special issue of Journal of Ritual Studies* 15 (2).

Robinson, Enders A. 1991. *The Devil Discovered: Salem Witchcraft 1692.* Prospect Heights: Waveland Press.

Roper, Lyndal. 1994. *Oedipus and the Devil: Witchcraft, Sexuality and Religion in Early Modern Europe.* London and New York: Routledge.

Rosnow, Ralph L. 1974. On rumor. *Journal of Communication* 24 (3): 26–38.

Rowlands, Michael, and Jean-Pierre Garnier. 1988. Sorcery, power and the modern state in Cameroon *Man,* n.s., 23: 118–132.

Russell, Jeffrey B. 1980. *A History of Witchcraft: Sorcerers, Heretics, and Pagans.* London: Thames and Hudson.

Sanders, Andrew. 1995. *A Deed Without a Name: The Witch in Society and History.* Oxford: Berg.

Scharlau, Fiona C. 1995. *The Story of the Forfar Witches.* Angus District Council: Libraries and Museums Service Publications.

Scheper-Hughes, Nancy. 1996. Theft of life: Organ stealing rumours. *Anthropology Today* 12 (3): 3–10.

Scheper-Hughes, Nancy. 2000. The global traffic in human organs. *Current Anthropology* 41 (2): 191–224.

Schieffelin, E. L., and R. Crittenden, eds. 1991. *Like People You See in a Dream: First Contact in Six Papuan Societies.* Stanford, Calif.: Stanford University Press.

Schmoll, Pamela. 1993. Black stomachs, beautiful stones: Soul-eating among Hausa in Niger. In Jean Comaroff and John Comaroff, eds., *Modernity and Its Malcontents,* pp. 193–220. Chicago: University of Chicago Press.

Scot, Reginald. 1972 [1584]. *The Discoverie of Witchcraft*, intro. by Rev. Montague Summers. New York: Dover.

Shibutani, Tamotsu. 1966. *Improvised News: A Sociological Study of Rumor*. Indianapolis: Bobbs-Merrill.

Sidky, H. 1997. *Witchcraft, Lycanthropy, Drugs, and Disease: An Anthropological Study of the European Witch-Hunts*. New York: Peter Lang.

Simpson, Jacqueline. 2001. Magical warfare: The cunning man versus the witch. In H. E. Davidson and A. Chaudhri, eds., *Supernatural Enemies*, pp. 135–46. Durham, N.C.: Carolina Academic Press.

Smedal, O. H. 1989. Order and difference: An ethnographic study of Orang Lom of Bangka, West Indonesia. (Oslo Occasional Papers in Social Anthropology, no. 19). Blindern, Norway: Department of Social Anthropology.

Spencer, Jonathan. 1990a. *A Sinhala Village in a Time of Trouble: Politics and Change in Rural Sri Lanka*. Delhi: Oxford University Press.

Spencer, Jonathan. 1990b. Collective violence and everyday practice in Sri Lanka. *Modern Asian Studies* 24 (3): 603–623.

Sperber, Dan. 1985. Anthropology and psychology: Towards an epidemiology of representations. *Man*, n.s., 20: 73–89.

Sprenger, Jacob, and Heinrich Kraemer. 1951 (1486). *Malleus maleficarum*, ed. M. Summers. London: Pushkin Press.

Stasch, Rupert. 2001. Giving up homicide: Korowai experience of witches and police (West Papua). *Oceania* 71 (1): 33–52.

Steadman, Lyle B. 1975. Cannibal witches among the Hewa. *Oceania* 46: 114–121.

Steadman, Lyle B. 1985. The killing of witches. *Oceania* 56 (2): 106–123.

Stephen, Michele. 1995. *A'aisa's Gifts: A Study of Magic and the Self*. Berkeley: University of California Press.

Stephen, Michele. 1996. The Mekeo "Man of Sorrow": Sorcery and the individuation of the self. *American Ethnologist* 23 (1): 83–101.

Stephen, Michele. 1998. A response to Mosko's comments. *American Ethnologist* 25 (4): 747–9.

Stewart, Charles. 1991. *Demons and the Devil: Moral Imagination in Modern Greek Culture*. Princeton, N.J.: Princeton University Press.

Stewart, Pamela J., and Andrew Strathern. 1998a. Invasions, dismemberments, consumptions. Okari Research Group Working Paper no 5. Pittsburgh, Pa.: Department of Anthropology, University of Pittsburgh.

Stewart, Pamela J., and Andrew Strathern. 1998b. Life at the end: Voices and visions from Mt. Hagen, Papua New Guinea. *Zeitschrift für Missionswissenschaft und Religionswissenschaft* 82 (4): 227–244.

Stewart, Pamela J., and Andrew Strathern. 1998c. Pathways of Power, rumours of fear: The imagination of space in Montane New Guinea. In Jelle Miedema, Cecilia

References

Odé, and Rien Dam eds., *Perspectives on the Bird's Head of Irian Jaya, Indonesia: Proceedings of the Conference, Leiden 13–17 October 1997*, pp. 313–320. Amsterdam: Rodopi.

Stewart, Pamela J., and Andrew Strathern. 1999a. "Feasting on my enemy": Images of violence and change in the New Guinea Highlands. *Ethnohistory* 46 (4): 645–669.

Stewart, Pamela J., and Andrew Strathern. 2000a. Introduction: Latencies and realizations in millennial practices. In Pamela J. Stewart and Andrew Strathern, eds., *Millennial Countdown in New Guinea*, pp. 3–27. Durham, N.C.: Duke University Press.

Stewart, Pamela J., and Andrew Strathern, 2001a. The great exchange: *Moka* with God. *Journal of Ritual Studies* 15 (2): 91–104.

Stewart, Pamela J., and Andrew Strathern. 2001b. *Humors and Substances: Ideas of the Body in New Guinea*. Westport, Conn., and London: Bergin and Garvey.

Stewart, Pamela J., and Andrew Strathern. 2002a. *Remaking the World: Myth, Mining and Ritual Change among the Duna of Papua New Guinea*. Washington, D.C.: Smithsonian Institution Press.

Stewart, Pamela J., and Andrew Strathern. 2002b. Water in place: The Hagen and Duna people of Papua New Guinea. *Journal of Ritual Studies* 16 (1): 108–119.

Stewart, Pamela J., and Andrew Strathern, eds. 1997. *Millennial Markers*. Townsville, Australia: Centre for Pacific Studies, James Cook University.

Stewart, Pamela J., and Andrew Strathern, eds. 2000b. *Millennial Countdown in New Guinea*. Durham: Duke University Press.

Strathern, Andrew. 1977. Souvenirs de folie chez les Wiru. *Journal de la Société des Océanistes* 33: 131–144.

Strathern, Andrew. 1979–80. The red box money-cult in Mount Hagen, 1968–71. *Oceania* 50: 88–102, 161–175.

Strathern, Andrew. 1982. Witchcraft, greed, cannibalism and death. In M. Bloch and J. Parry, eds., *Death and the Regeneration of Life*, pp. 111–133. Cambridge: Cambridge University Press.

Strathern, Andrew. 1984. *A Line of Power*. London: Tavistock.

Strathern, Andrew. 1988. Conclusions: Looking at the edge of the New Guinea Highlands from the centre. In J. Weiner, ed., *Mountain Papuans*, pp. 187–212. Ann Arbor: University of Michigan Press.

Strathern, Andrew, and Pamela J. Stewart. 1999a. *Curing and Healing: Medical Anthropology in Global Perspective*. Durham, N.C.: Carolina Academic Press.

Strathern, Andrew, and Pamela J. Stewart. 1999b. Outside and inside meanings: Nonverbal and verbal modalities of agonistic communication among the Wiru of Papua New Guinea. *Man and Culture in Oceania* 15: 1–22.

Strathern, Andrew, and Pamela J. Stewart. 2000a. *Arrow Talk: Transaction, Transition, and Contradiction in New Guinea Highlands History.* Kent, Ohio, and London: Kent State University Press.

Strathern, Andrew, and Pamela J. Stewart. 2000b. *The Python's Back: Pathways of Comparison Between Indonesia and Melanesia.* Westport, Conn.: and London: Bergin and Garvey.

Strathern, Andrew, and Pamela J. Stewart. 2000c. *Stories, Strength, and Self-Narration: Western Highlands, Papua New Guinea.* Bathurst, Australia: Crawford House Publishing.

Strathern, Andrew, and Pamela J. Stewart. 2001. *Minorities and Memories: Survivals and Extinctions in Scotland and Western Europe.* Durham, N.C.: Carolina Academic Press.

Strauss, Hermann, and Herbert Tischner. 1962. *Die Mi-Kultur der Hagenberg-Stämme.* Hamburg: Cram, de Gruyter.

Summers, Rev. Montague. 1951. Introduction. In Jacob Sprenger and Heinrich Kraemer (Institoris), *Malleus maleficarum,* 1486, trans. by Montague Summers. London: Pushkin Press.

Summers, Rev. Montague. 1972 [1930]. Introduction. In Reginald Scot, *The Discoverie of Witchcraft,* pp. xvii–xxxiii (reprint of 1930 translation of work originally published in 1584).

Sutton, David E. 1998. *Memories Cast in Stone: The Relevance of the Past in Everyday Life.* Oxford: Berg.

Taussig, Michael T. 1980. *The Devil and Commodity Fetishism in South America.* Chapel Hill: University of North Carolina Press.

Taylor, Christopher C. 1992. *Milk, Honey and Money: Changing Concepts in Rwandan Healing.* Washington, D.C.: Smithsonian Institution Press.

Taylor, Christopher C. 1999. *Sacrifice as Terror: The Rwandan Genocide of 1994.* Oxford: Berg.

Thomas, Keith. 1973. *Religion and the Decline of Magic.* London: Penguin Books.

Thomas, Nicholas. 1994. *Colonialism's Culture.* Princeton, N.J.: Princeton University Press.

Trevor-Roper, Hugh. 1969. *The European Witch-Craze in the 16th and 17th Centuries.* New York: Harper and Row.

Turner, Patricia. 1993. *I Heard It on the Grapevine: Rumor in African-American Culture.* Berkeley: University of California Press.

Turner, Victor. 1977. *The Ritual Process: Structure and Anti-Structure.* Ithaca, N.Y.: Cornell University Press.

Turner, Victor. 1996 [1957]. *Schism and Continuity in African Society.* Oxford: Berg (first published in 1957 by Manchester University Press, for the Rhodes-Livingstone Institute).

References

Virgil. 1990. *The Aeneid*, trans. by Robert Fitzgerald. New York: Vintage Classics, Random House.

Watson, C. W., and Roy Ellen, eds. 1993. *Understanding Witchcraft and Sorcery in Southeast Asia*. Honolulu: University of Hawai'i Press.

Weiner, Annette B. 1984. From words to objects to magic: "Hard words" and the boundaries of social interaction. In D. Brenneis and F. R. Myers, eds., *Dangerous Words: Language and Politics in the Pacific*, pp. 161–91. New York and London: New York University Press.

West, Harry. 2001. Sorcery of construction and socialist modernization: Ways of understanding power in postcolonial Mozambique. *American Ethnologist* 28 (1): 119–150.

White, Luise. 2000. *Speaking with Vampires: Rumor and History in Colonial Africa*. Berkeley: University of California Press.

Whitehead, Neil L. 2002. *Dark Shamans: Kanaimà and the Poetics of Violent Death*. Durham and London: Duke University Press.

Willis, Deborah. 1995. *Malevolent Nurture: Witch-Hunting and Maternal Power in Early Modern England*. Ithaca, N.Y.: Cornell University Press.

Worsley, Peter. 1957. *The Trumpet Shall Sound: A Study of "Cargo" Cults in Melanesia*. London: MacGibbon and Kee.

Young, Michael. 1971. *Fighting with Food: Leadership, Values, and Social Control in a Massim Society*. Cambridge: Cambridge University Press.

Index

Aberdeenshire, 156

academia, conflict in, 5, 32–3, 36, 37–8, 55–6, 189, 201

acculturation, 94

aconite, 141

adoption, international, 87

Aeneas, 53

Afghanistan, 111

Africa, xiii, 5, 8, 10, 11, 12–13; and vampire stories, 51; *see also names of specific peoples*

AIDS, 49, 69, 79, 91, 124–5, 135

Airds farm, 159

AK-47s, 181

Akan, 191

Akin, David, 73

Al-Qaeda, 111

Albigensians, 15

Allport, Gordon, 40–3, 101, 171, 183

Ambéli, 56–7

ambiguity, 30, 83, 93, 103

Ambon, 173

Amin, Shahid, 106–7

Anderson, Jens, 3, 79, 129

Andreski, Stanislav, 145–6

Angels of Mons, 198

Angus, 159–60

Ankarloo, Bengt, 156

anthrax scare, 24, 45, 48, 195

anthropological analysis, modes of, 3–4, 8, 9–10

Antze, Paul, 95

Arens, William, 51, 59

Assam, 177, 178

assault sorcery, 81, 170, 185; gossip, compared with, 83; in Pangia, 120–1, 124–5; among Duna, 124–5; and Oksapmin, 125; as appropriation of vitality, 171

Augsburg, 26

Auslander, Mark, 67–72, 92, 187

Ayodhya, 177, 180–1

Ayrshire, 15, 51

Azande, 2–3, 8, 65

Babha, Homi, 182

Babri Masjid mosque, 177, 180–1

Bailey, Michael, 16, 143

Banda, 174

Bangka, 175

Bangladesh, 178, 180, 181

Barnes, R. H., 169, 174–5

Basel, massacre of Jews in, 146

Bayly, Christopher, 107

Index

belladonna, 141

Bemba, 60–2

Bengal, 177, 178

Bernard, Richard, 152

betrayal, 44, 197

Bharatiya Janata Party, 180, 181, 182

Biak, 173–4

"bierricht," 158

bifurcated epistemology, 118

Bihar, 177, 178

bin Laden, Osama, 111

birds of paradise, 6

Black Death, 146, 147

Bleek, Wolf, 191

blood: in vampire stories, 81–6; and pollution, 118

blood feud, 40

Bocage, 57

Bode, Bernardus, 175

Bodin, Jean, 146, 153

bodkins, 154

body: social processes and, 73–76, 87, 88, 97, 99, 170; and pollution ideas, 104–5; and epidemiology, 122; and cannibal imagery, 170

body parts, theft of by witches, 68, 70; *see also* cannibal imagery

Bombay, 181

Boquet, Henri, 150

Borneo, 168, 172, 174

Bothwell, Fourth Earl of, 161

Bothwell, Fifth Earl of, 161

Bourdieu, Pierre, 104–5, 193

Bowen, Elenore Smith (Laura Bohannan), 93

Boyer, Paul, 164–7, 193

Brass, Paul, 180, 181, 182, 183

Brazil, 86–8

Brenneis, Donald, 54

Brison, Karen, 129–31, 192

Buginese, 172

Burridge, Kenelm, 108

Calcutta, 178, 181

Cameroon, 13

Campbell, John, 36

cannibal imagery, 6, 50–1, 73, 75; and *djambe*, 78; and ideas about Europeans, 81–6; in Mount Hagen, 114–19, 136, 147; among Hewa, 126; in European witchcraft, 150; in case of Forfar witches, 160; and colonial stereotypes, 172

capitalism, 75, 89–91, 94, 114, 123

"cargo" ideas, 77, 87–8, 132–7

Carrier, James, 98

Carslaw, W. H., 15

caste, 97, 101, 104

Cathars, 15, 149

cemeteries, 69–70, 136; *see also* funeral practices

Ceŵa, 10–11, 68, 79

charity, 22–3

Chaudhri, Anna, 92

Chelmsford, 154

child abuse, 87, 94–5, 189, 199–200

China, 88

Chittagong, 181

chisambe, 68

Christianity, 8–9, 10, 102; and theology of witchcraft, 14–15, 17, 142; and Catholic Church, 15, 19, 25, 85, 95, 142, 151, 155; and Calvinism, 15, 151; and Presbyterian Church, 15; and Anglican Church, 19, 154; and Lutheran Church, 25, 26, 117, 134–5, 151; among Makah Indians, 33; in New Guinea, 47, 125; in Africa, 65, 69,

71, 77; among Ngoni, 69; and burial
practices, 69–70, 175; and Zionist
Church, 71; and Baptist Church, 77;
and Watchtower movement, 85; and
John Maranke movement, 94; and
Eastern Orthodox Church, 109; and
world's end narratives, 119, 123–4, 135;
and divination, 125; among Kwanga,
129; and "cargo" movements, 132–7;
and paganism in Europe, 140–1; and
folk-healers, 142, 154; and Islam,
173–4; and Bible, in Gusii area, 187;
and Seventh Day Adventism, 188; and
Pentecostalism, 189, 190, 200; and
Assemblies of God, 190
Church's franchise, 48–9
cinquefoil, 141
civil war, in England, 154; in Scotland,
160
Clark, Stuart, 161
Cohn, Norman, 149
Colombo, 185
colonial change, 12–13, 62, 63–4, 71, 75,
196; and vampire stories, 81–6; in the
British Raj, 96–106; in Papua New
Guinea, 113–14, 120; in Pangia, 120–2;
in Duna, 124–5; and "cargo"
movements, 132–7; in Indonesia,
168–77; in India, 177–83; among Gusii,
186, 191
Colson, Elizabeth, 33–5
Columbus, Christopher, 145
Comaroff, Jean, 75–6, 91, 92–3, 94, 174,
191
Comaroff, John, 75–6, 91, 174, 191
community, definition of, 201
concealed meanings, 130
confessions, 52, 62, 125, 147, 150, 158,
159–60; see also torture

Conolly, M., 161
conspiracy theories, 104, 105, 109–10, 117,
147, 196; and Pentecostalism, 200
construction sacrifice, 168, 169, 173,
175–6
Cook, David, 161, 167
Cornfoot, Janet, 160–1, 166–7
cosmos, 95, 115, 133, 199, 200
Covenanters, 160
crime, 98–9
Crittenden, Robert, 136
Cromwell, Oliver, 154, 159
Csordas, Thomas, 122
"cunning folk," 152, 153, 154, 165, 202
cursing, 157–8
Curzon, Lord, 177–8

dacoits, 98
Daemonologie, 19, 156
Danbury, 153
Darnley, Lord, 161
Das, Veena, 182–3
Davidson, Hilda, 92
Davies, Norman, 15
Davies, O., 152
Dayaks, 172, 173
De lamiis, 143
death squads, 88
definitions, of witchcraft and sorcery,
1–2, 6
delatores, 100–1
Delhi, 101
Demos, John, 165
Denmark, 161
Device, Alizon, 18
Devil, the, 13, 16, 19, 20, 24; as El Tío, 4,
58, 93; and the plague, 24, 147; and
sexuality, 26, 150; and 9/11/2001, 46;
and Procter and Gamble, 46–7; and

Index

Devil (*cont.*)
  witchcraft, 59–60, 123–4, 142, 145–51, 156–62; in theme of occult economies, 89–91; and child abuse, 95; and world's end, 119, 123, 124, 135; and folk-healers, 142, 154; and the Black Death, 147; as instigator of violence, 152; in Salem witchcraft, 162, 164; as source of jealousy, 190; as corrupter, 196; and child abuse, 199
Diana, 141
Dido, 53
diviners, 11, 63, 125–6, 187, 202
djambe, 78–81, 115
Doctor Moses, 71–2
Doob, Leonard, 44
Douglas, Arthur, 157
Douglas, Mary, xi, 3, 50–1, 122–40
Drake, R. A., 169
du Boulay, Juliet, 56, 57
Duiker, William, 149
Dumfries, 159
Duna, 68, 75, 124–5, 188
Dutch colonialism, 170, 172, 174

East Lothian, 158–9
East Timor, 173
Eastern Europe, 156
ecstasy, 141
El Tío, 4, 58, 93
Elizabeth I, Queen of England, 20, 94
Ellen, Roy, 3
Ellis, Bill, 200
emechendo, 187
England, 99; *see also names of specific places*
Eni, Emmanuel, 189–90
epidemics, 7, 75; of cannibalism, 114–19; and witchcraft/sorcery, 119–23; of

madness, 120–1; of assault sorcery, 121–2; among Duna, 126
"epidemiology of representations," 127
Ershad, President, 180–1
Essex, England, xiii, 21–3, 152–6, 201, 202
Essex County, Massachusetts, 165
ethnicity, 47, 60, 68; and headhunting, 169, 170; and violence, 172, 173–4, 181–2; emergence of, 183
Europe, xi, xiii, 5, 8, 13–28, 117; *see also names of specific countries*
European Union, 109
Evans-Pritchard, Edward E., 2–3, 8, 65–6, 79
Ewe, 189
exploitation, 74, 75, 87, 113

Favret-Saada, Jeanne, 57
Feldman-Savelsberg, Pamela, 197
fertility, 64, 70, 133
Fife, 156, 160–1
firemen, 84
Firth, Raymond, 54
Flores, 168, 169–70
folk-healers (Europe), 142, 152–6, 166; (Africa), 188
Forbes, Thomas, 26, 145
Forfar, 159–60
Formicarius, the, 149
Forth, Gregory, 173
France, 43, 75, 85, 141; *see also names of specific places*
Fretilin, 173
Fribourg, 146
Friuli (N. Italy), 141
Fuller, Thomas, 153
funeral practices, 69–70, 79, 98, 173, 175–6
Fussell, Paul, 198–9

Gandhi, Mahatma, 106–7, 178
Gandhi, Rajiv, 180
Garnier, Jean-Pierre, 78
gender, witchcraft and, 22, 24–7, 68; and mourning, 70; and change, 93; among Duna, 126; among Hewa, 128; in Europe, 142–3, 144, 149, 154; in Essex, 154; in Scotland, 157–8; among Gusii, 186–91
George, Kenneth, 169–70
Germany, 25–6; and sexual fantasies, 25; and anal themes, 26; and Stasi files, 39; and spy story, 44; and story of rendering down battlefield corpses, 199; see also names of specific places
Geschiere, Peter, xiii, 13, 59, 76–81, 92
Ghana, 190, 191; see also Ewe
Ghosh, Anjan, 177–83
Gifford, George, 22, 153
gift-economy, 115, 123
Ginzburg, Carlo, 8, 117, 141, 147, 148
globalization, 60, 93, 94, 166; of the Assemblies of God, 190
Gluckman, Max, 9–10; theory of gossip of, 12, 30–5, 83, 182, 191, 200–1
Goldman, Laurence, 114
goonda, 178, 181
Granada, King of, 147
greed, 67, 68, 74, 75, 78–9, 114, 123
Greece, 56, 57, 109, 110; see also Ambéli
Guha, Ranajit, 96–106, 108, 171, 182
Gusii, 186–91
Guthrie, Helen, 160

habitus, 104
Hacking, Ian, 199–200
hallucinogens, 141
hamartia, 197
Hatfield Peverel, 22

Hatty, James, 146
Hatty, Suzanne, 146
Hausa, 73
Haviland, John, 5, 56
headhunting, 168, 169, 170, 172, 173, 174
hemlock, 141
henbane, 141
Henningsen, Gustav, 141, 156
Henry VIII, King of England, 19, 20
herbs, 141–2
heresy, witchcraft and, 16
Herodias, 141
Herskovits, Melville, 31–2
Hewa, 126–8
hierarchy, 97, 113
Hindus, 101–6
Hopkins, Matthew, 154
Hoskins, Janet, 170–1, 172, 173
Howie, John, 15

India, 96–106, 177–83; partition of, 177
Indian Mutiny, 101–6, 196
Indian National Congress Party, 178, 180
Indonesia, 168–76
Innocent VIII, Pope, 143–4
Inquisitions, 15, 23, 144, 147, 151
intergenerational conflict, 67–72, 187–91
Irian Jaya (West Papua), 172, 173–4
Islam, in Nigeria, 75; in Irian Jaya, 173–4; in India, 177–83; in Bangladesh, 180–1

Jaffna Peninsula, 185
James, VI and I, King of Scotland and England, 19, 20, 156
jealousy, 12, 66, 68, 73, 74, 75, 77, 81, 189, 191
Jews, 82, 110, 146, 147, 148
jihad, in Bangladesh, 178, 180–1; in Calcutta, 179

Index

Jimi Valley, 123
joking, 110
Jones, Gareth, 199

Kala Bachcha, 182
Kalashnikovs, 181
Kalauna, 131
Kalymnos, 110
kanaimà, 122
Kanpur, 181
Kapferer, Bruce, 92, 185
Kapferer, Jean-Noël, 44, 46–8, 75, 103
Kaplan, Martha, 108
Karam, 122–3
Kashmir, 180
Kenya, 186–91
Kilsyth, battle of, 160
kinship and marriage, 10–11, 18–20, 25, 69, 73; and witchcraft in Cameroon, 78–9, 80, 197; among Murambinda, 79; in India, 98; in Scotland, 157; in Salem Village, 165; among Gusii, 187–91
Kirkcudbrightshire, 158–9
Kirriemuir, 160
Klees, Fredric, 164
Knauft, Bruce, 117, 120
knowledge, as rumor, 202
Kopon, 116
kopong, 114
Korowai, 121
Kors, Alan, 142, 143
Kosovo, 109, 110, 182
Kraemer, Heinrich, 24, 143, 144–5
Ku Klux Klan, 48
Kulke, Hermann, 101
kum (kôm), 74, 114–19, 122, 131, 187
kum koimb, 114–19, 122

Kwahu, 191
Kwanga, 129–31, 192

La Fontaine, Jean, 200
Lamalera, 175–6
Lambek, Michael, 8, 92, 94–5, 202
Lancashire (Pendle), 18
Larner, Christina, 90, 94, 156–62, 165, 166, 192
Laskar Jihad, 174
Lawrence, Peter, 132, 134–5, 136
Layer Marney, 153
lepers, 146, 147, 148
Lessinger, Johanna, 183
Levack, Brian, 20–1, 23–4, 26, 151
LiPuma, Edward, 117
literacy, power of, 186–7
Loch Ken, 159
Lollards, 15
Lom, 175
London, 199
Lord Ram, 180
Lugbara (Uganda), 85

Macdonald, Stuart, 161
Macfarlane, Alan, xiii, 9, 20–3, 152–6, 165, 201
Mackay, Charles, 153
Macmurdoch, Janet, 158–60
Madang, 132, 134–5
Madurese, 172
magic, 14, 78; as appropriation of life-force, 175, 176; see also "cunning folk"; diviners; folk-healers; ritual experts
Magnusson, Magnus, 161
Mair, Lucy, 2, 10, 11, 93–4
Maka (Cameroon), 77–81, 115
Makah Indians, 33–5

malaria, 84
Maldon, 152
maleficium, 2, 14, 16, 156, 162
Malleus maleficarum, 24–6, 143–4, 190
Maluku, 173, 174
mandrake, 141
Manningtree, 154
Maring, 122, 131
mark of the Beast (666), 47
Marwick, Max, xi, 10–11, 59, 79, 156, 184
Marxist interpretation, 99, 105
Mary Queen of Scots, 161
Mather, Cotton, 163, 164, 165, 166
māua, 120–1
Mauss, Marcel, 18
meadow salsify, 141
medicalization, 87
"medicines," 61–2, 68, 70, 71
Mekeo, 126
Melpa, *see* Mount Hagen
Meyer, Birgit, 190
Middleton, John, 3, 85
midwives, 26, 142, 144
Milosevic, Slobodan, 109
mirrors, 61, 71, 152
misogyny, 145
missionaries, and conversion, 102, 105, 123
missions, *see* Christianity
modernity, as concept, 5, 75; and witchcraft, 76–81, 93, 191–2
Moi, Daniel arap, 191
monetization, 73, 82
Montenegro, 40
Moore, Henrietta, 73, 91
Moore, Sally Falk, 90, 108
moral imagination, 4, 62; and collapse of world, 94–5

moral panic, 119, 170, 173, 185, 200; as "rumor panics," 200
Mosko, Mark, 128
Mount Hagen, 74, 75, 103, 114–22, 131, 134, 139
Mozambique, 192
mucapi "medicine," 61, 62
Mueda plateau, 192
Mughal, 102, 180
mumiani, 81–2
mungoma, 63–4
Münsterberg, Hugo, 52
Murambinda, 79
Murray, Margaret, 117, 140–1
music, 100
Muslim League, 178, 179
Muslims, 101–6, 173–4
Myers, Fred, 54

Ndembu, 11–12
neighbors, accused of witchcraft, 23–4, 155, 158–9
Neuendettelsau, 117
New England, 162–7
New Guinea, *see* Papua New Guinea
New York Times, 86
nganga (*ng' anga*), 62, 69, 78
Ngoni, 72
Nider, Johannes, 149
Niehaus, Izak, 62–4, 65, 66
Nigeria, 93
nightshade, 141
Nissenbaum, Stephen, 164–7, 193
Nutini, Hugo, 7–8

occult economies, 75–6, 165
Ogembo, Justus, 186–91
O'Hanlon, Michael, 44
Oksapmin, 125

Index

oracles, 66, 153
ordeals, 158
organs, human, 68, 70; in vampire
    stories, 81–6; international trade in,
    86–9, 171; theft of, 86–9
Orissa, 177, 178
"Orly," 55, 103
osculum infame, 14, 150

"pacification," 118, 171–2
Paine, Robert, 35–7, 191, 200–1
Pakistan, 178, 183
Pangia: types of sorcery in, 6–7; and
    colonial change, 120–2
Papua New Guinea, xiii, 12, 18, 51, 68,
    80–1, 84, 185; Pangia area in, 6–7;
    Wahgi area in, 44; Highlands area in,
    55; Mount Hagen, 74, 75; "cargo"
    ideas in, 77, 88, 107–8; millennial
    rumors in, 103; *see also names of
    specific peoples and places*
patriarchy, 25
Pearl Harbor, 41, 44
peasant revolts, 96–106
Pendle witches, 18, 157
Pennsylvania Dutch, 164
Peters, Edward, 142, 143
Philip V, King of France, 147
pisai, 126
Pittenweem, 160
plague, in Europe, 23–4, 145–6
poison, 14, 26, 64, 69, 70, 146, 147, 148,
    179, 185
politicians, 75–81, 197
pollution fears, xi, xiii, 26, 72, 101–6,
    146–7, 196
polygyny, 10–11, 79–80, 188, 189
Postman, Leo, 40–3, 101, 171, 183
postmodernity, 191

pren-kros, 84
processual analysis, xi–xii, 27–8, 36–7
Procter and Gamble, 46–7
prophets, 61, 94, 105–6, 107–8, 154
prostitutes, 25, 82; *see also* sexuality
Protestant Reformation, 20, 25–6, 151,
    192; *see also* Christianity
Puritanism, 155
Purleigh, 153

quoll, 116

race relations, in vampire stories, 81–6
Radin, Paul, 31
Ramzan, month of, 179
Rapport, Nigel, 5
Reebok, 49–50
resistance, 4; and spirit beings, 176–7
revenge, 23, 40, 123, 188, 193
reversals, 198
Rhodesia, 9, 10, 11–12, 60–2
Richards, Audrey, 60–2, 65
Riebe, Inge, 122–3
riots, 101; between Muslims and
    Christians (Indonesia), 173; between
    Hindus and Muslims (India), 177–83;
    between Sinhalese and Tamils (Sri
    Lanka), 183–6; in nineteenth-century
    London, 199
ritual experts, 62, 115–17, 118, 152, 154, 202;
    see also "cunning folk"; diviners; folk-
    healers
rivers, 118
Robbins, Joel, 73
Roberts, Jack, 7
Robinson, Enders, 164
rönang wamb, 136–7
Roper, Lyndal, 25–6, 142
Rosnow, Ralph, 37

Rothermund, Dietmar, 101

Rowlands, Michael, 78

rumor and gossip, cases, ix–xiv, 27–8; in
Zinacantan, 5; among Ndembu, 11; in
Pendle, 20, 21; in Scotland, 21, 156–62;
in Essex, 23, 152–6; in Augsburg, 26; in
Trinidad, 31–2; among Makah, 34–5;
as urban legend, in U.S., 47–51; in
work of Hesiod, 52–3; in Virgil's
Aeneid, 53–4; in Tikopia, 54; in Papua
New Guinea, 55, 108, 114–19, 120; in
Ambéli, 56–7; among Bemba, 61; in
Transvaal, 64–5, 67; among Ngoni, 72;
in Cameroon, 77, 78, 80; in
Zimbabwe, 79; in East Africa, 82–3,
85; in Brazil, 86–8; and child abuse,
87, 95; in India, 99–101; in Indian
Mutiny, 101–6; and the millennium,
103; in Uttar Pradesh, 106; in "cargo"
contexts, 108; in Mount Hagen,
114–19, 136–7; in Pangia, 120; in Duna
area, 124–5, 126; among Hewa, 127–8;
among Kwanga, 129–31; in Kalauna,
131; in "cargo cults," 132–7; regarding
Jews and lepers, 148; regarding
poison, 148; on lycanthropy, 149; in
European witch-hunts, 151; in Salem
Village, 162–7; in Flores, 169;
throughout Indonesia, 173; in Irian
Jaya, 173–4; in Eastern Indonesia,
174–7; and theft of babies, 175; in
India, 177–83; in Calcutta riots, 181–2;
in Sri Lanka, 183–6; among Gusii,
190–1; among Kwahu, 191; in World
War I, 198–9; in London, 199; and
Satanic abuse, 200; in academia, 201

rumor and gossip, theories, 29–30;
functionalist (Gluckman), 30–5,
(Boehm), 40, (Campbell), 56;
transactionalist (Paine), 35–7; and gift
theory, 37; and scandal, 39; and
"truth," 39, 42, 44, 45–6, 52, 75, 102,
195; social-psychological (Allport and
Postman), 40–3, (Shibutani), 43–4,
(Kapferer), 44–7; and urban legend
(P. Turner), 47–51; historical survey of
(Neubauer), 52–4; and globalization,
60; as political tool, 78, 85; in
contemporary contexts, 92; as "news,"
99–101, 102–3, 107, 195; and conspiracy
theory, 104, 105, 109–10; and politics,
109–11; and epidemiology, 119, 122,
124; diving rumors, 170–1, 173; as
political instruments, 174, 193; stock,
contingent, etc., 179–80, 181, 185;
joining local and global, 182; in
sharpening ethnic identity, 183;
redirection of choices by, 185; and
fluidity, 192; generative of stereotypes,
192; conclusions regarding, 194–203;
and uncertainty, 195; in mobilization,
196; as vehicles of interpretation, 198;
rumor panics, 200; as universal
substratum of process, 203

Russell, Jeffrey, 162

Rwanda, 70

Sabaragamura Province, 183

sabbat, 14, 150, 161, 162

sacerdotal mediation, 105

sacrifice, 116, 136–7, 168, 172, 176–7; of
pigs, in Mount Hagen, 202; *see also*
construction sacrifice

Salem Village, 162–7; and battles with
indigenes, 163–4; economic
conditions in, 163, 165; and
"jeremiads," 163–4; conflict in, 164–7;
vengeance in, 193

Index

Sanders, Andrew, 10–13, 14–18
Sanders, Todd, 73, 91
Sarakatsani, 36–7, 56–7
Satan, *see* Devil
Sawny Bean, 51
Scandinavia, 156
Scharlau, Fiona, 159–60
Scheper-Hughes, Nancy, 86–9, 92
Schieffelin, Edward, 136
Schmoll, Pamela, 73–4, 75
Scot, Reginald, 152–3, 154
Scotland, 15, 19, 24, 90, 94, 141
September 11, 2001, 45–6, 110–11, 195
Serbia, 109
sexuality, witchcraft and, 24–7, 48–9, 69,
    75; and rape imagery, 124; and
    seduction, 125, 190; in medieval
    Europe, 142; according to *Malleus
    maleficarum*, 144–5; in sixteenth-
    century Europe, 150; in seventeenth-
    century Europe, 154
shamanic traditions, 141
shame, 184
Shibutani, Tamotsu, 43–4, 102–3
shipwreck, 160, 161
Shouters, 31
sickness and misfortune, 2, 6, 7, 8, 12, 22;
    and plague, 23–4, 146, 147, 157; and
    soul-eaters, 73–4; among Maka, 79;
    and theft of organs, 86, 87; and *kum*
    stones, 116; in Pangia, 122; and
    syphilis, 145–6; and lepers, 146–7; in
    Scotland, 157; among Gusii, 187–91;
    and divination, in Mount Hagen,
    202
Sidky, H., 143, 144, 146, 149, 151, 154
Sikhs, 180
Simpson, Jacqueline, 152
slavery, 66, 162, 172

smeddum, 157–8
social class, 60; and zombies, 66; among
    Ngoni, 67–8; among Hausa, 74; in
    Brazil, 87; in India, 99; in Papua New
    Guinea, 133
social dramas, 4, 5, 9, 12; as ritual, 16
socialism, 199
"sorcery in the gift," 115
soul-eating, 75
Spencer, Jonathan, 183–6
Sperber, Dan, 122
Spielvogel, Jackson, 149
spies, 44, 101
Spillius, James, 54
Sprenger, Jacob, 24, 143, 144–5
Sri Lanka, 183–6, 187
Stasch, Rupert, 121
Stasi, 39
Steadman, Lyle, 126–7
Stearne, John, 154
Stephen, Michele, 126, 128
Stewart, Pamela J., 47, 74, 81, 103, 114,
    118, 119, 122, 134, 135, 136, 149, 154,
    168
Strathern, Andrew, 47, 74, 81, 103, 114,
    118, 119, 120, 122, 134, 135, 136, 149, 154,
    168
Strauss, Hermann, 115–17, 136–7
Strickland River, 125
suicide, in Sri Lanka, 184
Sulawesi, 169–70
Summers, Montague, 19, 144
Sutton, David, 110
syphilis, 145, 146

Taliban, 111
tambaran, 129
Tamil Tigers, 183–4, 185
Tangu, 108

Tangupane, 120–1
Tanzania, 84
Taussig, Michael, 4, 93
Taylor, Christopher, 70–1
tenants, 96, 97, 157, 158–9
Tenna, 183
"terror," 24, 87, 98, 151, 171–2, 178, 192, 195
textualization, 106
thaumaturgic powers, 106
Thaxted, 153
Thomas, Keith, 13, 106, 156
Thomas, Nicholas, 113
Tikopia, 54
Tischner, Herbert, 115–17
Tituba, 162
Tiv, 93
tjoelik, 174
Tlaxcala, 6–7
tokolose, 63–4
torture, 149, 150, 158, 164
transnational themes, 81–6, 86–8; and occult economies, 89–91
Transvaal (South Africa), 62–4
Trevor-Roper, Hugh, 156
Trinidad, 31–2
tsuwake, 125
Turner, Patricia, 48–51, 60
Turner, Victor, 4, 9, 60, 156, 184; see also social dramas

ugauga, 126
uncertainty, 8, 110; see also ambiguity; moral panic
United States, 24, 46–51; see also Salem Village
urban legends, 42, 46, 47–51, 77, 89, 171; vampire narratives as, 81–6
Uttar Pradesh, 101–6, 107, 180, 181

vaccination programs, 197
vampire narratives, 13, 102; in East Africa, 81–6; in Malawi, 86; in Indonesia, 175;
Vellore mutiny, 105
violence, 90–1, 97–8, 99, 101, 166; the Devil as cause of, 152; and rumor, 168–93, 195; and Indonesian military, 176; Hindu-Muslim, 177–83; in Great Calcutta Killing, 177–80, 181–2; as political tool, 183; vicarious interest in, 184; party politics and, 184–5; and mythology, 185; as sequential process, 186; among Gusii, 186–91; conditions producing, 191; as result of psychological projections, 194
Virgil (Publius Vergilius Maro), 53–4, 111–12
Vishnu, 180

Waldensians, 15, 149
water parsnips, 141
Watson, W., 3
wazimamoto, 82, 83
wealth, 133
Weiner, Annette, 74
West, Harry, 192
White, Luise, 13, 81–6, 92, 124, 182
Whitehead, Neil, 122
wild celery, 141
Willis, Deborah, 142
Winter, E., 3
Wiru, 120–1; see also Pangia
witch-hunts, 5; in Scotland, 20–21, 156–62; in Europe, 26, 149, 151; among Bemba, 61–2; in Transvaal, 62–74; among Ngoni, 67–72; among Hewa, 126–7; in Essex, 152–6; in Salem, 162–6; among Gusii, 186–91

witch trials, xii, 5, 13–14, 18–20; and transition to secular courts, 20; at moots among Duna, 125–6; among Hewa, 126–7; among Maring, 131; in Europe, 149, 151; in Essex, 152–6; in Scotland, 156–62; in Salem, 162–7

witchcraft/sorcery, cases, ix–xiv; in Essex, England, xiii, 21–3, 25, 27, 152–6; among Azande, 2, 8, 65; in Pangia, 6–7; in Tlaxcala, 7–8; in Europe, 8–9, 13, 26, 151, 152–6; among Ceŵa, 10–11; among Ndembu, 11–12; in Lancashire, England, 18–20, 27; in Scotland, 21, 156–62; in Augsburg, 26, 142; in Trinidad, 31; in academia, 55–6, 189, 201; among Bemba, 60–2, 72, 189, 201; in Transvaal, 62–5; among Ngoni, 67–72, 187; among Hausa, 73; in Cameroon, 76–81; in vampire narratives, 81–6; in Mount Hagen, 114–19; in Karam, 122–3; among Duna, 125–6; in Oksapmin, 125; in Mekeo, 126; among Hewa, 126–8; among Kwanga, 129–31; among Maring, 131; and syphilis, 145; and accusations against Jews, 148; and lycanthropy, 149; in East Lothian, 158–9; in Forfar, 159–60; in Pittenweem, 160; in Loch Ken, 158; involving King James VI, 161; in Salem Village, 162–7; in Sri Lanka, 184; among Gusii, 186–91; among Kwahu, 191; in Mozambique, 192

witchcraft statutes, 20, 149–50, 156

World Trade Center, 46, 111; *see also* September 11, 2001

World War I, 198–9

World War II, 40–1, 43

Worsley, Peter, 108, 132

Wyclif, John, 15

Y2K, 135

Young, Michael, 131

Zambia, 9, 60, 67

zamindar, 179

Zanzibar, 82

Zimbabwe, 79

Zinacantan, 5

zombies, 62–3, 77